Movie Talk

Movie **Talk**

Who Said What About Whom in the Movies

DAVID SHIPMAN

BLOOMSBURY

First published 1988

Copyright © by David Shipman 1988
Bloomsbury Publishing Limited
2 Soho Square, London W1V 5DE

British Library Cataloguing in Publication Data

Movie talk: who said what about whom in the movies.
  1. Cinema films—Quotations—Anthologies
  I. Title
791.43

ISBN 0 7475 0181 5

Printed in Great Britain by
St Edmundsbury Press Limited
Bury St Edmunds, Suffolk

Contents

Introduction

Twenty years in the making! With a cast of thousands! Or something like that. These expressions, beloved of movie publicists in my youth, aren't entirely alien to this project.

In 1968, when the era of highly illustrated books was just beginning, I had the idea for a book of movie star portraits, to be captioned with flattering comments from colleagues and critics. As I began to collect them, I came to wonder about the whys and wherefores of the stars' careers, and the project evolved into the two volumes of *The Great Movie Stars*. In those books I used many of the quotations I had noted down, and they were not—in the end— always favourable.

In the Silent period, public interest in the doings of movie-people—especially the stars—was extraordinary, and their appetite was fed by a vast array of fan magazines. It would be difficult to say how many of the 'intimate' articles then published were written by people who had met their subjects. The publicity departments of the studios employed scribes to define the image on the screen. As the magazines (and the studios) became more sophisticated a number of independent journalists were allowed access to the stars. Interviews were strictly supervised by publicists, and with rare exceptions everyone loved everybody very much. There had always been publicity mileage in reports of the feuds raging between the famous, and it worked well for some of the Silent movie queens, but later it was difficult to know whether some feuds were in fact the notion of some publicity person. It was not, however, till the studio system began to break down in the 1950s that stars began to speak freely.

Even in the darkest days of the fan magazine you could—if you were a practised observer—learn by omission. The most experienced publicist could not always prevent their client from disclosing antipathy towards a colleague. In the period from the 1960s to the present, this has often become frank with a vengeance. Artists are no longer protected by the studio system, and interviewing in the cause of promoting a particular project is often written into the contract. Norma Shearer may have granted no more than six interviews in a year on the set. Today in city after city, day after day, Kathleen Turner may greet one journalist after another in her hotel suite. In researching this book, I have come across variations of the same interview, even a decade apart. But rereading the same tired anecdote it is difficult not to feel sorry for the artists, having to spread themselves so thin. Discretion does still prevail, because of the power game endemic to the industry.

Artists—directors, writers, players—in search of employment may well use euphemisms. 'I enjoyed working with him' may mean 'He wasn't the bastard he's been made out to be', while 'I loved working with him', being stronger, may well be true. A new vernacular is being evolved into show business and you will find it in the pages that follow.

I have tried for an overall picture and to be fair but it hasn't been easy. Some people, by virtue of great success or colourful personalities, have occasioned more comment than their fellows. Some workaday industry figures have been little discussed. By and large my criterion has been to include any remark which jumps off the page, because it is emphatically true, illuminating, outrageous, opinionated, self-revealing, witty or—well, *alive*. There are some, speakers and those spoken about, of whom I have my own opinions, either from watching them from my seat in the stalls, from having met them, or from having heard them discussed by colleagues. There are those of whom there is never a good word said. There are many who haven't earned the enmity of the press. There are others about whom some journalists refuse to be nice, just as there are likeable talents of whom few have said a word (or at least a memorable one), good or bad.

It worries me that some artists will emerge from these pages as 'difficult', while others, equally tough to work with, are lightly dealt with. There is one actor whom everyone agrees was a horror when he was a big star but who has been mighty sweet to everyone on his way down (not that it helped him to get up again). There is, for instance, an actress who never quite made it to the top because—two of her directors, both among Hollywood's greatest names, told me—she was too pretentious, a fact not evident from her performances, which were always warm, witty and wonderful.

From the above, you may well gather that there is little here of such comments of and by today's younger performers which I regret. I have not been entirely diligent in tracing comments on now-forgotten figures of the Silents, but it is with sorrow that I note the absence of many of the army of character players who have meant so much to so many movies. You will find that the quotations do not always apply to work for the cinema: it is unlikely that anyone discussing Olivier would not be aware of his career in the theatre, and that must go for many others. On the other hand I think it legitimate to include comment on the theatre work of people best known for their careers in movies.

I must acknowledge the sheer joy of reading and re-reading some of the best writers on film. It has been an amazing, extraordinary experience. In this respect, if I had my way, the manuscript would never have been delivered. I was still making fresh discoveries in this direction when my publisher called it in. My apologies to those I couldn't include, especially those whose work I much admire.

If the compilation which follows is first seen to be about talent, it will soon be perceived as also about ego and temperament. Some of the quotations are self-serving, others more eloquent on the speaker than the subject. Others say something on the matters of envy, of professional jealousy, on the question of fame—and what fame can do in elucidating fatuous statements from even the most fastidious of intellects. Fame itself may well provide the sub-text, if I may so call it: but what I hope the book is really about is professionalism. Nothing has given me more pleasure in putting together what follows than coming across admiration expressed by one artist about another. I find it agreeable when they like each other's talent but positively mind-boggling when they say they've enjoyed working together.

David Shipman
August 1988

BRIAN AHERNE (1902–1986)

- [In *Juarez*] he nearly acts Mr Muni off the set. With his forked and silky beard, the blonde whiskers and curls, the gentle worried inflexibility, he is every inch a Hapsburg, and the film is his from that first puzzled inquiry at Vera Cruz—'Why are the streets so empty'—to his long careful frock-coated stride up the rocky hill of the death-place.

  GRAHAM GREENE, 1939

ANOUK AIMÉE (born 1932)

- No actress either [like Bardot], but extraordinary–the way Gary Cooper was extraordinary.

  JEAN-LOUIS TRINTIGNANT

ALAN ALDA (born 1936)

- We're lucky that we don't have anybody there just trying to collect the money. There's plenty of money to be had and you can get the same amount by doing junk every week. By just showing up . . . But you also lose your soul. What's the pleasure in losing your self-esteem, your dignity?

  HIMSELF

ROBERT ALDRICH (1918–1983)

- Bob has a marvellous sardonic attitude towards films. It's the baroque thing again. Not realistic at all. He has a wonderful sense of irony. Sometimes he goes too far—but he knows that. I think he does it deliberately in order to say, as it were, to the public: 'Look. I've gone too far. How *about* that!' It's a big put-on about Hollywood.

  PETER FINCH, 1970

- A very good director. Beyond that, he has one fault: he is inflexible. He's horrified if you give him ideas; he only appreciates his own. He wants to use his own brain for everything. That's his greatest fault. If he wasn't so inflexible he would be very great. He refuses to give in. Well, it's impossible for one man to know everything.

  CHARLES BRONSON, 1977

- I think I am a much more humorous and funny fellow, and I would like to do a comedy or a musical, and I think I could easily adapt to that because of my knowledge of music. But it has nothing to do with what you think of yourself, but only what others think of you.

  HIMSELF

- I loved Aldrich. Very saddened by his passing. Richard Jaeckel was a good friend of his. He went to see him on his last stretch in hospital. He was in a coma much of the time. And Jaeckel asks if there is anything he can get him. And Aldrich says, 'Yeah, a good script'.

  LEE MARVIN

FRED ALLEN (1894–1956)

- An urban comedian, Allen was usually the centre of the wildest surrealistic occurrences. What he did wasn't particularly funny—only what was going on around him. A magnificent figure of beaten dignity, Allen faced the calamities of modern life with a weary resilience. Plunging into the most hair-raising situations, surrounded by the weirdest

1

collection of crackpots, Allen trundled on unperturbed except for the occasional savage verbal rebuke.

PETER BARNES

WOODY ALLEN (born 1935)

■ Most stars like to be thought of as being private people, being shy. We even grant those attributes to Woody Allen, this in spite of the fact that he must be the most visible celebrity in New York.

WILLIAM GOLDMAN

■ Woody is at two with nature.

DICK CAVETT

■ He seems to strive for some kind of excellence for himself in what he does that keeps him from anything that might smell of smugness.

TONY ROBERTS

■ At the end of *Manhattan*, making a list of the things and people that make life worth living, Allen compiles a list of just such glories: Groucho Marx, the second movement of Mozart's *Jupiter* Symphony, Louis Armstrong's recording of *Potato Head Blues*, Flaubert's *A Sentimental Education*, Cézanne's still lives of apples and pears, among others. As it happens, he leaves out one important name. That name, of course, is Woody Allen.

RICHARD SCHICKEL

■ The Woody we have come to know is nothing more eccentric than a chap of yearningly normal desires and high accomplishment who can't get things together because together isn't where things are heading now ... In some strange way, Woody's own operation as a performer is Kafkaesque—he accepts the gross dangers of the world with a terrified innocence disguised as comic equanimity.

JACK KROLL

■ I have never been a fan of Woody Allen's. I'm sorry. Somebody closed the door on me there. God knows, many people say he's the funniest in the world, but I've never been able to appreciate his humour. I find him neurotic.

GEORGE C. SCOTT

■ Woody Allen is a genius. His films are wonderful.

MEL BROOKS

■ Woody plays racquetball and dines at the Russian Tea Room; Kermit prefers bicycling and the El Sleazo Cafe. Woody loves Bergman, Kermit loves Rainbows. They are both soul-searching for happiness. Kermit ... could never be called pretentious. Woody easily could. Yet the praise never ends .. Woody makes many Important Observations, yes, but the neuroses and the ennui of his fellow *Manhattan*–ites becom● just tedious to watch. This 'I Love New York .. But Hate Myself' commercial is beautifully filmed ...

RICHARD ROTHENSTEIN, 1979

■ *Manhattan*, a picture in which, toward the end, the Woody Allen character makes a list of reasons to stay alive. . . . This list is modishly eclectic, a trace wry, definitely okay with real linen; and notable, as *raisons d'être* go, in that every experience it evokes is essentially passive. This list of Woody Allen's is the ultimate consumer report ... it suggests a subworld rigid with apprehension that they will die wearing the wrong sneaker . . . preferring *Madame Bovary*.

JOAN DIDION, 1979

■ I really didn't like Woody Allen at all; . . . suddenly, he turned around and got better and better, and I think his three latest films have been great. I recognise that he's really learned a lot and come a long way, but what really blows my mind is that I've recently seen some of his old ones, and now I think they really *weren't* so bad.

JULIE ANDREWS, 1982

NESTOR ALMENDROS (born 1930)

■ I use him because he is the best of all. I will speak against the French, although I'm very chauvinistic, because in France I don't think we have any good directors of photography.

ERIC ROHMER, 1973

ROBERT ALTMAN (born 1925)

■ I understand the allegiance people feel for Altman. He's very smart in knowing what can be said in dialogue and what has to be shown. He knows more about narrative films than anyone else, but he chooses to make more oblique films because he wants to try something new.

ROBERT BENTON

DON AMECHE (born 1908)

■ He's really a wonderful person, and I was thrilled for him and his big success in *Cocoon*. He's such a very nice man.

ALICE FAYE, 1987

JUDITH ANDERSON (born 1898)

■ Claire Trevor once went back to see Judith Anderson after a performance of *Medea*. She had been truly bowled over and she said, 'I simply can't find the words to tell you how superb you were'. Judith Anderson just said, 'Try'.

ROCK HUDSON

LINDSAY ANDERSON (born 1923)

■ Anderson is as a-visual as Richardson and, like him, tries to conceal the fact by using cinematic 'effects' where they are not needed or are positively destructive.

DWIGHT MACDONALD

■ I think he's a very talented man, but I think he's a difficult man to work with. He really prefers theatre and not film, and that's a little depressing, I must say.

BETTE DAVIS, 1987

URSULA ANDRESS (born 1936)

■ I've had luck with my leading ladies. The real shocker was Ursula Andress, with whom I made *What's New Pussycat?* She's a bloody sex symbol and all that, and yet she's one of the nicest people you'll ever meet. A real mother hen, looking after everybody.

PETER O'TOOLE

JULIE ANDREWS (born 1935)

■ The last of the really great dames.

PAUL NEWMAN

■ She has that wonderful British strength that makes you wonder why they lost India.

MOSS HART

3

■ The girl's got everything. She's young and she's pretty. She can dance and sing. What more do you want?

BEATRICE LILLIE

■ How's she got to the top? It cannot be all just talent. A lot of talented people don't begin to make it the way she has made it. There is a genuineness about her; an unphoniness. She goes right through the camera, on to the film and out to the audience. Julie seems to have been born with the magic gene that comes through on the screen.

ROBERT WISE

■ I suppose what I like most about working with Julie is that one has the feeling that the other half of the scene is well taken care of. You can relax and do your own role because you know she's doing hers.

ROBERT PRESTON

■ I admire Julie tremendously. She's never hit a bad note in her life.

HENRY MANCINI

■ It's marvellous to direct her. She's enormously professional and understands that in the final analysis the last word is mine, . . . Actually, working with Julie on a film is a whole lot easier than working with many people that I'm not married to!

BLAKE EDWARDS

■ Working with her is like being hit over the head with a Valentine's card.

CHRISTOPHER PLUMMER

■ A gutsy lady.

GEORGE ROY HILL

■ It takes a star to convey the magic vibrations of another star, and the miracle of Julie's performance is that she has located the essence of Gertrude Lawrence's individual aura . . . She once again proves that she is an actress of considerable range and stature. Her presence on this occasion is breathtaking.

CLIVE HIRSCHHORN

■ I mean, you in Britain have some of the best comediennes. Julie Andrews is a comedienne—oh yes she is!

LUCILLE BALL

■ Julie Andrews is the best of the crop. She's got so much talent that it's just not to be believed! I'd rather work with her than almost anybody I know. She doesn't seem to *me* to have that 'everybody's nanny' effect. *I* think she is *very* sexy.

JOHN GREEN

■ It's the film [*Torn Curtain*] in which the official Andrews image merges with mine. She's not lacking in sex appeal. But in her chemistry sex is somehow welded to duty—which makes it both ambiguous and publicly acceptable. For once, Hitchcock has it all wrong. Julie Andrews is vulnerable, but she is no victim. For her, ardour is all—provided it's in a good cause.

PHILIP OAKES, 1976

■ Julie Andrews [in *Star*] was talented, charming, efficient and very pretty but *not* very like Gertie.

NOËL COWARD

■ Take Julie Andrews . . . one of the last of the great English music-hallmarks. She can sing effortlessly, make a mug or *moue*, throw away a line and reel it back in with the best—when she is given half a chance. Her latest, *Darling Lili*, is only a quarter of a chance.

STEFAN KANFER

4

■ Julie was like Mary Poppins in that she was practically perfect in every way! I never saw her get at all impatient, or lose her composure, and she always looked just as fresh at 7 in the evening as she did at 7 in the morning . . . If I have anything against Julie it is that the rest of us got older and she looks just the same today as she did in *Mary Poppins*.

DICK VAN DYKE, 1987

ANN-MARGRET (born 1941)

■ She is the most uninhibited, sweet actress that I have ever met. She is quite unspoiled by success. Whenever she sees me she says, 'Oliver, you're so funny.' She's the only person who's ever said that to me in my life. I'll sit there spilling my beer and she'll say, 'You're so funny'.

OLIVER REED

LAURA ANTONELLI (born 1941)

■ Laura Antonelli [in *Till Marriage Do Us Part*] is like your first glimpse of Venice, your first bite of Fettucine Alfredo . . . She is the best thing to come out of Italy since Chianti! She has the most impressively designed Italian body since Ferrari . . . What differentiates Antonelli from such magnificent predecessors as Sophia Loren, Gina Lollobrigida and Silvana Mangano is her aristocratic style.

JAMES BRADY

■ [She] is so richly suggestive that she promises things no mere flesh-and-blood creature could deliver. *Till Marriage Do Us Part* is designed primarily as a vehicle for her, and a funny, relatively classy vehicle at that.

JANET MASLIN

■ . . . don't underestimate Laura Antonelli. She's burning to do well. And then she has an extraordinary face, even without make-up. It's not with her that I'd discuss literature. I speak only of the film [*L'Innocente*], and what she does she does well.

LUCHINO VISCONTI

MICHELANGELO ANTONIONI (born 1912)

■ Antonioni . . . even in *Blow-Up* is a pathfinder and a master.

JOHN SIMON, 1967

■ I like some of Antonioni's work, not all of it. I particularly like *The Red Desert*, and I hate *Zabriskie Point* . But I'll qualify that. I like all of his pictures in colour because he uses colour so immensely well . . . . *The Red Desert* I liked for its visual concepts. *Blow-Up*—excluding myself as an actor—was I think a more interesting picture simply because it did bridge the gap between the public and the film-maker.

DAVID HEMMINGS

■ One of my unfavourite directors, if I may say so, is Antonioni, because he tells the same story all the time in the same style. To me he is like a fly that tries to go out of a window and doesn't realise there is glass, and keeps banging against it, and never reaches the sky.

FRANCO ZEFFIRELLI

■ An Antonioni movie . . . forces us to see again our preconceptions of the way things are. No other artist deals with the hang-ups and delusions and possibilities of love, which is to say life, in our time as profoundly and truthfully as Antonioni.

JONATHAN BAUMBACH, 1967

5

- Antonioni says he just tries to make something beautiful because truth is beautiful and beauty is truth.

  JACK NICHOLSON, 1974

- It seems that boredom is one of the great discoveries of our time. If so, there's no question but that he must be considered a pioneer.

  LUCHINO VISCONTI

ALAN ARKIN (born 1934)

- Alan's a rare combination, a profound actor and a terrific comedian. I remember one picture he made—I won't name the title—where I had read the script and it was *lousy*. But when Alan played it on the screen, it was terrific, which had to be all Arkin, because it sure as hell wasn't there on paper.

  PETER FALK

ARLETTY (born 1898)

- *Les Enfants du Paradis* ! Maybe the best movie ever made. You know that's the only time I ever fell in love with an actress. I was mad about Arletty . . . My first trip to Paris, the thing I did right away, I asked to meet Arletty . . . was that a mistake! What a disillusionment! She was a tough article.

  MARLON BRANDO

JEAN ARTHUR (born 1905)

- One of the greatest comediennes the screen has ever seen. When she works she gives everything that's in her, and she studies her roles more than most of the actresses I've known.

  GEORGE STEVENS

- She'd stand in her dressing room and practically vomit every time she had to do a scene. And she'd drum up all kinds of excuses for not being ready . . . . out in the lights, turn the camera on and she'd blossom out into something wonderful. And when the scene was over, she'd go back into that dressing room and cry. She's quite a study.

  FRANK CAPRA

- She has the sexiest voice in the history of the talkies.

  DEREK OWEN, 1972

- Jean Arthur was a man's star. She was no raving beauty, but men liked her directness and her good-pal personality, often revealed in her roles as a working girl in a masculine environment.

  LARRY SWINDELL

- A difficult person out in the street, so they say—I never knew her—but everyone who went to the movies *liked* her, and that's unusual. Every movie star is disliked by some people—Gable, Crawford, Dietrich certainly, even Garbo, Ronald Colman—but everyone liked Jean Arthur.

  JOHN CROMWELL

DOROTHY ARZNER (1900–1979)

- Isn't it wonderful you've had such a great career when you had no right to have a career at all?

  KATHARINE HEPBURN

PEGGY ASHCROFT (born 1907)

- I'm absolutely devoted to her. People can't behave badly when she's around. She has such integrity.

  JOHN GIELGUD

6

ANTHONY ASQUITH (1902–1968)

■ A hell of a good director.

DAVID LEAN

FRED ASTAIRE (1899–1987)

■ He's the greatest dancer who ever lived—greater than Nijinsky.

NOEL COWARD

■ Except for the times Fred worked with real professional dancers like Cyd Charisse, it was a twenty–five–year war.

HERMES PAN

■ But when you're in a picture with Astaire, you've got rocks in your head if you do much dancing. He's so quick-footed and so light that it's impossible not to look like a hay-digger compared with him.

BING CROSBY

■ Poor old Ginger never stood a chance. Even when they share the screen equally, the eye is ineluctably drawn to Fred. I'm not suggesting that there was a witting competition between the two. How could there be, when one partner is the best there is and, to judge from this assembly of dancing clips [*That's Dancing*], the best there is ever likely to be?

IAIN JOHNSTONE

■ When you talk about Fred Astaire, you talk about heaven! What more can I say?

JOHN GREEN

■ Fred Astaire is the best singer of songs the movie world ever knew. His phrasing has individual sophistication that is utterly charming. Presumably the runner-up would be Bing Crosby, a wonderful fellow, though he doesn't have the unstressed elegance of Astaire.

OSCAR LEVANT

■ Six years of mutual aggression. From 1933 to 1939 they did nine pictures for me. Overnight, they became one of the hottest box office attractions in the industry. But I've never known two people who wanted to be further apart. It was a constant struggle. I'll never forget how horrified Fred was when I notified him that Ginger was going to play the part of a titled English lady in *The Gay Divorcee* . . .

PANDRO S. BERMAN

■ Astaire is the motherless man-about-town, all sophistication quite debonair, yet with a lope in his walk rather than a swagger, for—despite his receding hair—he is essentially boyish, youthful, innocent.

KAREL REISZ

■ I work bigger. Fred's style is intimate. I'm very jealous of that when I see him on the small screen. Fred looks so great on TV. I'd love to put on white tie and tails and look as thin as him and glide as smoothly. But I'm built like a blocking tackle.

GENE KELLY

■ I can watch Astaire anytime. I don't think he ever made a wrong move. He was a perfectionist. He would work on a few bars for hours until it was just the way he wanted it. Gene was the same way. They both wanted perfection, even though they were completely different personalities.

CYD CHARISSE, 1987

■ Fred knew the value of a song, and his heart was in it before his feet took over.

IRVING BERLIN

■ The difference is that there have been a lot of imitators of Gene Kelly, but no one has been able to imitate Fred Astaire. I wish I did know what it was with Astaire. If I knew I'd add it to my own bag of tricks.

GENE KELLY

■ What do dancers think of Fred Astaire? It's no secret. We hate him. He gives us a complex because he's too perfect. His perfection is an absurdity. It's too hard to face.

MIKHAIL BARYSHNIKOV

■ The greatest dancer in the world . . . You see a little bit of Astaire in everybody's dancing—a pause here, a move there. It was all Astaire originally.

GEORGE BALANCHINE

■ He is a truly complex fellow, not unlike the Michelangelos and da Vincis of the Renaissance period. He's a supreme artist but he is constantly filled with doubts and self-anger about his work—and that is what makes him so good. He is a perfectionist who is never sure he is attaining perfection.

ROUBEN MAMOULIAN

RICHARD ATTENBOROUGH (born 1923)

■ He has always been something of a Brutus of the British Establishment: loyal and loving, but not averse to sticking the knife in when it takes a step too far in the direction of authoritarianism.

NEIL SINYARD

■ One cannot escape the suspicion that Dickie is acting out all his roles as mediator, peace-maker, director, chairman, businessman, yet he is redeemed by a true goodness of heart,

which drives him to pursue the common good. He has reached out to me just at the moment I needed it, alone and embattled. This is his genius.

JOHN BOORMAN

■ By far the finest, most decent human being I've ever met in the picture business.

WILLIAM GOLDMAN, 1983

CLAUDE AUTANT-LARA (born 1903)

■ He was a very nervous man . . . but charming. I liked him very much. You should have seen him at the camera when he was directing. He was just playing every part, his hands in front of the camera, and we had to say 'Please, Claude!'.

DANIELLE DARRIEUX

DAN AYKROYD (born 1952)

■ Robotic the way he handles people: 'Ah, yes, good to meet you.' Very straightforward, very clean-cut, very polite, real nice guy.

EDDIE MURPHY

LAUREN BACALL (born 1924)

■ 'Betty' Bacall was the perfect mate for Bogey . . . beautiful, fair, warm, talented and highly intelligent. She gave as good as she got in the strong personality department. Women and men love her with equal devotion.

DAVID NIVEN

■ We discovered Bacall was a little girl who, when she becomes insolent, becomes rather attractive. That was the only way you noticed her, because she could do it with a grin. So I said to Bogey, 'We are going to try an interesting thing. You are about the most insolent man on the screen and I'm going to make this girl a little more insolent than you are'...

HOWARD HAWKS

■ She has a javelin-like vitality, a born dancer's eloquence in movement, a fierce female shrewdness and a special sweet sourness. With these faculties, plus a stone-crushing self-confidence and a trombone voice, she manages to get across the toughest girl a piously regenerate Hollywood had dreamed of in a long, long while.

JAMES AGEE

■ First honours in spreading mirth go to Miss Bacall. She takes complete control of every scene with her acid delivery of viciously witty lines. At times she has wavered badly in her dramatic career, but she stamps herself here [in *How to Marry a Millionaire*] as a champion at rowdy comedy.

ALTON COOK

■ I loved her. She's one of the most straight-ahead ladies I've ever known in my whole life. A very honest woman.

ROSEMARY CLOONEY, 1978

■ A warmer version of Dietrich. Dietrich knew it the moment she saw the picture. She said 'that's me, isn't it?' and I said 'yeah'.

HOWARD HAWKS

LUCILLE BALL (born 1911)

■ You were taken in charge and trained... They have none of that today *any place*

... I regret the passing of the studio system. I was very appreciative of it because I had no talent. Believe me. What could I do? I couldn't dance. I couldn't sing. I could *talk*. I could barely walk. I had no flair. I wasn't a beauty, that's for sure.

HERSELF

ANNE BANCROFT (born 1931)

■ The greatest actress of her generation, who begins in performance, where we poor mortals, who call ourselves actors, end.

RICHARD ATTENBOROUGH

■ The only reason I'm not still doing *Daughter of Gorilla at Large* is that my personal life had become a shambles. ... every picture I did was worse than the last one, and every man I was in love with was worse than the last one. I was terribly immature. I was going steadily downhill in terms of self-respect and dignity.

HERSELF, 1984

■ I'm married to a beautiful and talented woman who can lift your spirits just by looking at you.

MEL BROOKS

TALLULAH BANKHEAD (1903–1968)

■ The greatest performance I have ever seen was given by Tallulah Bankhead in the test she made to play Amanda Wingfield in *The Glass Menagerie*. Karl Freund photographed the test. He cried. She *was* that woman! She had promised not to drink: she could not keep her promise. Jack Warner said, 'Errol Flynn

9

is enough'. It cost a fortune to do an Errol Flynn picture because he was always drunk. And thanks to Errol Flynn, Tallulah lost the part.

IRVING RAPPER

■ Watching Tallulah Bankhead on the stage is like watching somebody skating over very thin ice—and the English want to be there when she falls through.

MRS PATRICK CAMPBELL

■ [In *Lifeboat*] There were complaints that she was climbing in and out of the bright lights with nothing under her skirt. . . . the production manager [had to] do something about it . . . 'Well somebody has to tell her', he said. 'Whose department is it anyhow?', I thought about that for a moment and then I said, 'It's either the make-up man's department or the hairdresser's'.

ALFRED HITCHCOCK, 1972

THEDA BARA (1890–1955)

■ She is pretty bad, but not bad enough to be remembered always.

ALEXANDER WOOLLCOTT

■ To understand those days you must consider that people believed what they saw on the screen. Nobody had destroyed the grand illusion. Audiences thought the stars were the way they saw them. Why, women kicked my photographs as they went into the theatres where my pictures were playing, and once on the streets of New York a woman called the police because her child spoke to me.

HERSELF

■ She was one of the best informed women that I have ever known. She knew who she was.

ADELA WHITELY FLETCHER, 1974

JUAN ANTONIO BARDEM (born 1922)

■ The film career of Juan Antonio Bardem spans the whole history of the modern Spanish cinema. No major Spanish director suffered more at the hands of the Francoist regime. Few film careers better suggest the trials, achievements and limitations of trying to make a political cinema under a dictatorship.

JOHN HOPEWELL, 1986

BRIGITTE BARDOT (born 1934)

■ She needed physical love as flowers need sunshine.

ALLAN CARR

■ She glows in the dark like an open stove.

ALAN BRIEN

■ You are very beautiful. I can imagine that God thought of you when he created women.

CURD JURGENS

■ She eats when she is hungry and she makes love in the same matter-of-fact manner.

SIMONE DE BEAUVOIR

■ All I can say is that when I'm trying to play serious love scenes with her, she's positioning her bottom for the best angle shots.

STEPHEN BOYD

■ Brigitte Bardot reminds me of a shapely, tasty concoction of all sorts of exquisite flavours and ingredients. Unorthodox to

10

a degree, conventional in some ways, she either buries her head in the sand or soars to great heights.

WILLI FRISCHAUER

■ Just the kind of girl to take home to mother if you want to give her a heart attack.

TONY CRAWLEY

■ Her attitude toward sex (both in films and out) was said to be symptomatic and symbolic of the times. Marilyn Monroe was merely a tease, it was suggested, while Brigitte Bardot was the real thing. *She* frankly enjoyed sex, and no double standard for her either.

HOLLIS ALPERT

■ In France today, we have too many Bardots. We have big Bardots and small Bardots, fat Bardots and thin Bardots— and they all pout. But still there is only one Bardot. She has something of her own. She was born Bardot.

FRANÇOISE ROSAY

■ I have always felt that Brigitte Bardot has something of the quality of Alice in Wonderland. If we talk about 'professional' players and 'instinctive' ones, I definitely put her with the instinctives. Although the shooting of *Vie Privée* is not a good souvenir, I did get interested in Brigitte from that first time I worked with her, because she had the quality that I'd put in the same category with the very young people I've directed.

LOUIS MALLE

■ With Brigitte the relations were very courteous but no more than that. She did not want to make an effort to understand.

MICHEL PICCOLI

■ Brigitte bowled me over with a sort of insolent grace and her extraordinary ease. She was very young when I met her for the first time. She seemed to be dancing through life, dancing through her films. I think that she didn't really like it so much to be an actress. Celebrity weighed heavy on her.

EDWIGE FEUILLÈRE, 1987

LIONEL BARRYMORE (1878–1954)

■ He told me one day that he ascribed his brother John's sad finish to the fact that John once brought back a totem pole from an Alaskan holiday and put it up in his garden. Up to that point John could do no wrong. But after that his luck turned. Lionel attributed this entirely to the totem pole. John had handled this holy object casually and thereby angered some Eskimo god.

JOHN HUSTON, 1980

RICHARD BARTHELMESS (1895–1963)

■ The most beautiful face of any man who went before the camera.

LILLIAN GISH

KIM BASINGER (born 1955)

■ She has this quality—absolutely indispensible for an actress, specifically for a *beautiful* actress—which is not to *know* that she's beautiful.

ROGER VADIM, 1985

■ She's a positive, positive delight . . . I think we have the makings of a star. First of all, she has the most sensual lips in the business.

VIDAL SASSOON

11

- She is abstract femininity . . . the prototype of a galactic New Woman.
  FEDERICO FELLINI

- Having rehearsed with Kim, filmed with her and seen the early results, I can say she's terrific, the kind of totally professional actress I enjoy working with.
  SEAN CONNERY

ALAN BATES (born 1934)

- He's got amazing colours as an actor . . . When I found the script for the picture [*Impossible Object*], I realised that I needed an actor with every nuance—comedy, pathos, the chaos of everyday life—and no self-pity whatever. I saw all these things in Bates' *Butley*, and I realised that only he could play it.
  JOHN FRANKENHEIMER

- For most actors it is enough that they manage one mood with competence, Bates reflects three or four moods at the same time.
  MICHAEL CACOYANNIS

ANNE BAXTER (1923–1984)

- We never had a cross word . . . However, I did not find her enormously warming and there was no great personal stirring between us as friends.
  CHARLTON HESTON

WARREN BEATTY (born 1937)

- Anyone who has come close to Warren has shed quite a few feathers. He tends to maul you.
  LESLIE CARON

- Warren is a teddy bear, though I used to become annoyed when the teddy bear hugs turned to bottom pinches.
  SUSANNAH YORK

- The difference between us is sex. I can take it or leave it. But my kid brother . . . well, now, he enjoys his reputation. Sex is the most important thing in his life. It's his hobby, you could say.
  SHIRLEY MACLAINE

- He doesn't drink, he doesn't smoke, he plays the piano beautifully, he's extremely intelligent, learned, knowledgeable. You look for something to get him on and you can't. They say he's obsessed with women, but he isn't, he's obsessed with power. He likes to dominate men as well as women.
  GABRIEL BYRNE, 1988

JACQUES BECKER (1906–1960)

- Of Jacques Becker, what can I say? He was—everyone said it—a most exceptional man, a man with constant ideas whose presence alone was enriching. Perhaps it's sufficient to say that I married him.
  FRANÇOISE FABIAN

- It has become a commonplace to say that *Casque d'Or* was a formidable moment in my career. However, I remember that the film opened in Brussels four days before Paris and the Belgian critics had pronounced it 'very feeble'—which had already influenced the punters.
  SIMONE SIGNORET

JEAN-PAUL BELMONDO (born 1933)

- One of the three best actors in the world.
  HENRY FONDA

■ He is the most accomplished actor of his generation . . . He can play any given scene in twenty different ways, and all of them will be right.

JEAN-PIERRE MELVILLE

■ Alain Delon moves through [*Borsalino*] like a still-warm stiff en route to a comfortable slab in the morgue, but Belmondo, mugging furiously and retaining just the right air of detachment, compensates by providing enough energy for this and at least three other movies.

JAY COCKS

■ He's no longer a great actor. He makes money. He amuses audiences who don't expect too much. It's a pity. He could do better.

CLAUDE AUTANT-LARA

■ Despite everything, I think it's a pity for him making popular films because he could enjoy his metier so much more. He has extraordinary comic gifts. I remember at the Conservatoire he did astonishing things. Alas, now he's become a sort of stunt man de luxe.

CLAUDE BRASSEUR, 1981

WALLACE BEERY (1885–1949)

■ Here was a lovable boy whose father deserted him, and here was a lonely actor who always wanted a son. What a perfect combination! The truth, however, was not that touching. Beery was a sad man . . . he was a lonely, mean old man. He didn't like people. And according to those who knew him, he was selfish and stingy to the point of making Scrooge look like a philanthropist.

JACKIE COOPER

JOAN BENNETT (born 1910)

■ With a career that spans forty years, from a charming young girl to the nicest grandmother in the world, it's hard to decide which Joan Bennett you like best.

DEREK OWEN, 1973

JACK BENNY (1894–1974)

■ Jack was the sweetest sonofabitch in the world. he never said a mean word about anybody—but I suspect he did a lot of *thinking*.

IRIS ADRIAN, 1987

CANDICE BERGEN (born 1946)

■ Bergen has the sort of beauty that thinks about itself and leaves no fingerprints. Like a Chinese vase in T. S. Eliot, she moves around in her own stillness.

JOHN LEONARD

INGMAR BERGMAN (born 1918)

■ I don't begin to share his way of seeing things any more than his obsessions. All the same I find him interesting. And his universe is much stranger yet than any Japanese film-maker.

LUCHINO VISCONTI

■ He's a large, powerful man—ever stood next to him? He's nice and kind and sweet and humble, but his power is *immense*. On set, he works totally as if he has everybody on strings like puppets. He's very kind about it and everything, but everybody does exactly what he wants at all times. Must say, he never told me a wrong move.

DAVID CARRADINE

13

■ I think he's very close to being some sort of genius. I like *The Silence* and *Wild Strawberries* and a number of other pictures, but on the whole I dislike what he says, and it's extremely foreign to me, although he's Swedish. It's very Lutheran and very agonised and very personal and sometimes very evil. He's fighting it himself, but he's a wicked man. I know him.

MAI ZETTERLING

■ Although Ingmar Bergman's talent was obvious from the beginning, it has developed by way of so many detours and cul-de-sacs that now and then one has felt tempted to give up. And it is greatly to the credit of Carl Anders Dymling, of Svensk Filmindustri, that he did not give him up.

ERIK ULRICHSEN, 1956

■ I just don't know what the hell he's after.

FRANK CAPRA, 1972

■ Ingmar uses you in the right way—after your own personality, your ability as an actor . . . So much has been written about Ingmar as a sort of demon. It's not true. He has lots of fantasies, experiences and imagination. For us it feels like a collaboration.

ERLAND JOSEPHSON

■ When he puts his arm around you, watch out.

HARRIET ANDERSON

■ It isn't just that he likes women—he is interested in learning more about them.

GUNNEL LINDBLOM

■ The test of a film for me is if I go into the cinema to see it, and while I'm there I'm completely unaware of time: then it has succeeded for me. And I find that quality more consistently with Ingmar Bergman than with any other director: I can sit there and be absolutely timeless.

SEAN CONNERY, 1973

■ My all-time favourite because he embodies passion, emotion and has warmth.

FRANCIS FORD COPPOLA, 1974

■ Living with Ingmar Bergman is not like living with Bob Hope. Other couples meet for breakfast and have coffee and English muffins and cuddle. Do you know what Ingmar Bergman did at breakfast? He told his nightmares and then told me I had to act in them! I got another script [probably *Fanny and Alexander*] from Ingmar in the mail and I returned it to him unopened and wrote 'Do your own nightmares!'

LIV ULLMAN

■ Working with him is so interesting; he's such a kind and understanding man, full of ideas and invention. You feel you're in good hands. And he listens to his actors; he's big enough to listen to your ideas and if he likes them then he'll use them. He's very flexible and open, allowing his actors to feel they are creating too, and not just marionettes in his hands.

INGRID BERGMAN, 1978

■ I have many things to talk about— because of my fascination with the human being, the human face—which fascinates me more and more—all the dimensions of reality, and the conditions of human life, of the human being . . . The problem is that I'm sixty–two years old. I have been in this business forty

14

years, and more and more I feel it physically. I get tired. Making a picture is a very tough job.

HIMSELF, 1980

INGRID BERGMAN (1915-1982)

■ She's an angel . . . Brother, she is bullet-proof. There has never been another figure like her before the camera; you can shoot her any angle, any position. It doesn't make any difference; you don't have to protect her. You can bother about the other actors on the set. But Ingrid's like a Notre Dame quarterback. An onlooker can't take his eyes off her.

VICTOR FLEMING

■ She's so honest that she will always prefer a scandal to a lie . . . For years I had been wanting to make something gay with her. I wanted to see her laughing and smiling on the screen, to enjoy—and let the audience enjoy—the sort of uncomplicated sensuality which is one of her characteristics.

JEAN RENOIR

■ When she walks on screen and says 'Hello' people ask 'Who wrote that wonderful line of dialogue?'.

LEO MCCAREY

■ Miss Bergman was everything that the publicity sheets would have one believe of the majority of film stars (though only the minority qualify): she was unaffected, intelligent, unconceited.

RODNEY ACKLAND

■ Her great quality is that the moment she understands a part, her intellect gives way to emotion. When her emotion takes over, it comes out right.

ANATOLE LITVAK, 1955

■ I didn't do anything I've never done before, but when the camera moves in on the Bergman face, and she's saying she loves you, it would make anybody look romantic.

HUMPHREY BOGART

■ There has never been anything like her.

CARY GRANT

■ One day Ingrid Bergman was making a film in England, and she came over to my hotel and began telling me how terribly upset she was and how worried and miserable. I just looked at her. And she said, 'Oh, Hitch, I know what you're going to say. Don't say it!'. Well, what I was going to say was simply what I always say: 'Ingrid, it's *only* a movie'.

ALFRED HITCHCOCK

■ She's everything a woman should be— she's the kind of woman men aren't afraid of because she's so warm. I feel privileged to be in the same picture as her [*The Cactus Flower*].

GOLDIE HAWN

15

■ [Watching her] taught me more than most people. In one film she had to laugh and then suddenly think 'No, that's no good, I'm going to cry'. And then go back to laughter again. It wasn't completely technical, it was half there as well. She says films are easy.

MICHAEL JAYSTON, 1969

■ I reckon there wasn't a man who came within a mile of her who didn't fall in love with her.

ANTHONY QUINN

■ If possible I admired the woman more than the actress.

LIV ULLMAN

BUSBY BERKELEY (1895–1976)

- You had to watch Berkeley. He was such an expert technician that a number could get totally lost in images.

  ROGER EDENS

JULES BERRY (1883–1951)

- He never knew his lines and filled in with 'hmmms', kept pulling his sleeves up, made big gestures, puffed on his cigarette and somehow landed on his feet. He never did the same thing from one take to another.

  MICHEL KELBER

BERNARDO BERTOLUCCI (born 1940)

16

- Bernardo Bertolucci . . . a mere alert dung-beetle, making a film out of half a dozen masters and *petits-maitres* of cinema.

  JOHN SIMON, 1965

- Bertolucci is not like most directors I've worked with; there's something beautiful, crazy, special about him. He's funny too. He operates like a writer. No-one knows what he's going to do. Several million dollars are riding on him alone. He has the power, he goes ahead, upsets those who plan schedules, takes his own time, follows his own genius.

  STERLING HAYDEN, 1981

JACQUELINE BISSET (born 1944)

- One of the greatest bodies I've ever worked with. But besides that she is rather the opposite, because she is so damned intelligent. It's a strange combination, almost a double personality.

  EDITH HEAD, 1977

- People are inclined to be sceptical about Jacqui because she's so beautiful. But she has that quality of intelligence that goes with the face and makes it something more.

  PETER YATES

JOAN BLONDELL (1909–1979)

- For me the sexiest woman on the screen ever was Joan Blondell.

  GEORGE C. SCOTT, 1970

CLAIRE BLOOM (born 1931)

- She is not a nice-Nellie and she has no inhibitions. She is not as cold as some people say—but she has to be challenged. She is most accomplished and like Maggie Smith she has a great range; she listens and she does it.

  GEORGE CUKOR, 1972

- You can say that Claire and I are on speaking terms. But we're far from being warm friends. It's an arrangement that works out well for our daughter.

  ROD STEIGER, 1972

DIRK BOGARDE (born 1920)

- Bogarde doesn't care to hide his cruel streak. In part this side of his character is instinctive, in part it's a reaction born of the battles he's had to fight, for acceptance as an actor, for acceptance as a homosexual, for acceptance as a writer.

  RICHARD RAYNER, 1983

- On that film [*Accident*] Dirk Bogarde became a very good and valued friend, and he was immensely helpful to me. He took me under his wing and told me a lot about what he learned from working in films, in terms of approach and technique. He gave me tips about lenses, and the amount of projection an actor ought to give according to which lens is being used in a shot.

  MICHAEL YORK

HUMPHREY BOGART (1899–1957)

- As we say here, Bogart can be tough without a gun. Also he has a sense of humour that contains that grating undertone of contempt. Ladd is hard, bitter and occasionally charming, but he is after all a small boy's idea of a tough guy. Bogart is the genuine article. Like Edward G. Robinson, all he has to do to dominate a scene is to enter it.

  RAYMOND CHANDLER

- He brings to the screen directness and ease and the ability to seem an ordinary guy without becoming commonplace.

  CHRISTOPHER SHAW

- A fan came over during dinner one time and Bogey told him to beat it. When the guy got back to his table I heard his companion say, quite happily, 'See, I told ya he'd insult you'.

  NUNNALLY JOHNSON

- I was young and only starting in *To Have and Have Not* when Bogey and I met. Howard Hawks (the producer-director) said he would like to put me in a picture with Cary Grant or Humphrey Bogart. I thought. Cary Grant—terrific. Humphrey Bogart—yuck.

  LAUREN BACALL

- He was a real man—nothing feminine about him. He knew he was a natural aristocrat—better than anybody.

  KATHARINE HEPBURN

- Bogey had everything against him. He had a peculiar name, Humphrey, definitely not in keeping with the character he played. He had a slight lisp. He was not a pretty boy or the conventional leading man. He violated every rule of the movie business. But he was a good actor. He could project. He had tremendous force.

  JERRY WALD

- He was endowed with the greatest gift a man can have—talent. The whole world came to recognise it. With the years he became increasingly aware of the dignity of his profession—Actor, not Star. Himself he never took seriously—his work, most seriously. He regarded the somewhat gaudy figure of Bogart, the Star, with amused cynicism; Bogart the actor he held in great respect . . . He is quite irreplaceable.

  JOHN HUSTON

- Bogey was a rarity among actors in that he was completely honest. He didn't turn his charm on and off to make points. You took Bogey as he was—no other way. That's why, years after his death, the modern anti-establishment youth has made a cult of him.

  JAMES BACON

- [I] hated that bastard.

  WILLIAM HOLDEN

- It took a little while to realise that he had perfected an elaborate camouflage to cover up one of the kindest and most generous of hearts. Even so, he was no

17

soft touch and before you were allowed to peek beneath the surface and catch a glimpse of the real man, you had to prove yourself. Above all, you had to demonstrate conclusively to his satisfaction that you were no phoney.

DAVID NIVEN

■ Bogart's a helluva nice guy till 11.30pm. After that he thinks he's Bogart.

DAVE CHASEN

■ . . . I won't play the sap for you . . . you killed Miles and you're going over for it . . .
. . . I ain't sorry for you no more, you crazy, psalm-singing, skinny old maid . . .
. . . you gotta get up early in the morning to outsmart Fred C. Dobbs . . .
. . . my health. I came to Casablanca for the waters . . .
. . . of all the gin joints in all the towns in all the world, she had to walk into mine . . .
. . . if she can stand it, I can: Play it . . .
. . . we'll always have Paris . . .
. . . here's looking at you, kid . . .
This is just a personal opinion, but I don't think any other star got to deliver as many memorable dialogue lines as Bogart. With Gary Cooper we think 'Yup'. Gable got the famous 'Frankly, my dear, I don't give a damn'. Brando had 'I could have been a contender', and Tracy—I can't come up with a single line to associate with that great actor.

WILLIAM GOLDMAN

■ You'd be having dinner with him and someone would come over and you could just see the tough guy coming on.

JOSEPH L. MANKIEWICZ

■ He had a protective shell of seeming indifference. He wasn't, but he did a lotta

acting offstage. He liked to act tough, liked to talk out of the side of his mouth.

CHESTER MORRIS

■ Bogart represents *the* male myth figure of the war and post-war period of the American cinema.

ANDRÉ BAZIN, 1961

■ What I liked most about him I suppose, was that he was honest, he never minced his words. Believe me, ninety-nine per cent of the people in Hollywood go through life and never say what they mean, but . . . Bogart just wasn't like that, there was no baloney about him.

JAMES WONG HOWE

■ He was an extremely hard-working actor. He'd always pretend that he wasn't, that he didn't give a damn, but that wasn't true. One day I said to him, 'Bogey, you're just a great big phoney'. He put his finger to his lips and grinned at me: 'Sure', he said, 'but don't tell anyone'.

HOWARD HAWKS

■ Bogart was a strange man, I thought, He was nice to me, but not over-nice. I was very young and shy, and he was at the height of his career. . . . my strongest impression of him was—well, I think I should say, a man who was always on his guard.

MICHÈLE MORGAN

■ I found him very professional, very easy. His acting was never hammy, it was very simple—in fact he underplayed, and I think that's the reason why his films stand up so well today. As an actor he obviously had limitations—his range was not that great, but within his range he was the best around.

WILLIAM WYLER

18

- He was one of the very few people who had—and I mean this as a compliment—[the dignity of] a big dog that seems endlessly wise and rather surly. His nostrils catch various fleeting smells and he growls a bit when he finds one of them particularly unpleasant. But if you look at him a certain way, the tail will start wagging grudgingly and he may even get up and amble over toward you.

    PETER USTINOV

- Take Humphrey Bogart. He could never equate the money he was making with what he was doing. He was constantly mocking himself. And that's a good thing, you know what I mean? He was quite a man, Bogart. He was genuinely tough and he was honest.

    RICHARD BROOKS

- Bogart was like Fonda—proud and happy to be an actor.

    KATHARINE HEPBURN, 1981

- Was he tough? In a word, no. Bogey was truly a gentle soul.

    LAUREN BACALL

- . . . there was that very credible virility of guys like Spencer Tracy or Humphrey Bogart. I don't think that I could one day resemble them, but in life and in movies I profoundly admired Bogart, both personally and professionally.

    LEE MARVIN

PETER BOGDANOVICH (born 1939)

- Then Peter Bogdanovich wanted to do it [*The Long Goodbye*] with Robert Mitchum or Lee Marvin. The way he does all his films—as photostats of other films.

    ROBERT ALTMAN

- We had those sparkling, shining Lubitsch comedies of the late 1930s. And now we've seen Peter Bogdanovich crucified for trying to do a Lubitsch kind of comedy with *At Long Last Love*. I had a marvellous time seeing that film. I understood every nuance.

    MEL BROOKS

- You're talking about a man who did something quite extraordinary. He was a film critic. He then went and made *The Last Picture Show*, which won a few nominations for the Academy Award. He was very *resented* for that. Not openly, but somewhere down deep inside, the critics said . . . kill.

    BURT REYNOLDS, 1978

19

RICHARD BOLESLAWSKI (1889–1937)

- He was quite unfitted to make pictures although he put all his poetry and theatrical genius into them. He couldn't endure the tyranny of the studio bosses (who hated him) or the commercial greed. But especially what killed him was the unsatisfactory nature of the pictures themselves. The beauties he put into them were *so* ephemeral, and he was heartbroken with disappointment again and again.

    HUGH WALPOLE

- I thought Richard Boleslawski, who directed *Les Miserables* and, later, *Garden of Allah*, might have been a great director, but he didn't live long enough to prove it. He was a big bear of a man, very sensitive.

    JOHN CARRADINE

BEULAH BONDI (1892–1981)

■ I cannot let pass this short review of a fine and beautifully acted film, *The Southerner*, without reference to the superb playing of the grandmother by Beulah Bondi. It merits at least a couple of dozen Oscars at current rates.

RICHARD WINNINGTON, 1946

SHIRLEY BOOTH (born 1911)

■ In my opinion, Shirley Booth is the finest actress I have ever worked with.

BURT LANCASTER

■ Shirley Booth, the star of *Come Back, Little Sheba*, must retire if we are talking about the highest reaches of her profession, where the grim ladies of Ibsen and the richer ones of Shakespeare hold court. But in the region of sentiment, of domestic tragi-comedy, she is peerless: a chubby, sociable matinée actress, who genuinely loves her audience, and loves their love of her.

KENNETH TYNAN

■ . . . the wonderful Shirley Booth. As in *Little Sheba*, the character is downtrodden and pathetically resilient, tender, anxious, self-deprecating—but it is in no sense a repeat performance [in *About Mrs Leslie*] and if it proves anything, it is simply that this actress excels on a certain emotional wavelength.

JAMES MORGAN

ERNEST BORGNINE (born 1917)

■ Where can we find the great actors we had yesteryear, guys like Tracy and Cooper and Edward G. Robinson? You know, I was talking to Lee Marvin the other day and we agreed that we were the last of a breed. We're the last who had the opportunity of working with these fine actors. I feel very humble. It makes me feel that I've got to try that bit harder.

HIMSELF, 1973

FRANK BORZAGE (1893–1962)

■ [He] was completely sympatico and a joy to work with—we did four films together.

DELMER DAVES

■ One of the kindest and nicest men I have ever worked for was Frank Borzage. He was most patient and tolerant on a Batjac picture he directed called *China Doll*. I had great respect for him.

CATALINA LAWRENCE, 1970

■ Borzage is a wonder. A pinup from his matinée idol days shows a face so trusting, you feel like hissing dire warnings about the ways of the world. But somehow, on the evidence of his films, he kept his benevolence and gentleness right to the end. He must have led a charmed life, or he was the greatest con-man of all time.

BOB BAKER, 1974

CLARA BOW (1905–1965)

■ She had defiance that was a flower of fright. She had a jaunty air of telling you that she didn't care what happened; she could handle it.

WHITNEY BOLTON

■ I liked Clara. A very warm, sweet, generous girl. What great potential! But she wasn't a finisher. . . . Her mind was like a sponge, but she didn't have the concentration or ability to see it through. She was quite ingenuous. People would go into shock over her salty language.

COLLEEN MOORE

■ No-one ever expressed more vividly than Clara Bow the spirit of Scott Fitzgerald's Jazz Age—all the optimism and poignancy and fever to reclaim the life and the years that the war had stolen. Her pout is an unequivocal anticipation of kisses. Her hips roll and sag in undisguised invitation.

DAVID ROBINSON

■ All of Miss Bow's vehicles must overrun with youthful gaiety, and because she has the misfortune to be labelled 'The It Girl', she must be a sort of Northwest Mounted Policeman of sex, who gets her man even if she has to bludgeon him.
. . . The formula is particularly trying when applied to one of the most pleasing stars of the cinema.

RICHARD WATTS JR.

■ She danced even when her feet were not moving.

ADOLPH ZUKOR

■ Clara Bow, with her tousled mane of red hair and intense black eyes, who generated sex appeal and excitement with breathtaking ease.

MAURICE CHEVALIER

■ The embodiment of the independent-minded flapper with bobbed hair and cupid bow lips.

KEN WLASCHIN

■ I can still see her at lunch that vulnerable, ambitious and driven, and, in a way, sensitive, little figure sitting there.

ADELA WHITELY FLETCHER, 1974

CHARLES BOYER (1899-1978)

■ My favourite among my films is *Love Affair*. And shortly before he died Charles Boyer told a reporter that it was his favourite too. The last time I saw *Love Affair*, I said to him, 'You know, Charles, you really were *good* '. 'Ah', he said, 'so you finally looked at *me*'.

IRENE DUNNE

■ Charles Boyer remains my favourite leading man . . . I found him a man of intellect, taste and discernment. He was unselfish, dedicated to his work. Above all, he cared about the quality of the film he was making, and unlike most leading men I have worked with, the single exception being Fred Astaire, his first concern was the film, not himself.

JOAN FONTAINE

■ [*The Cobweb*] I guess I thought it would be a good film—I had Richard Widmark and Charles Boyer as co-stars. One as my husband, one as my lover. As it happens Widmark hated me and Boyer was a drunk. It was a disaster.

GLORIA GRAHAME

21

MARLON BRANDO (born 1924)

■ I saw him in a film about paraplegics [*The Men*] and there was a moment in that when he'd been given some bad news. I watched the way he handled that scene and I thought this man has something.

CHARLES CHAPLIN

■ Actors like him are good but on the whole I do not enjoy actors who seek to commune with their armpits, so to speak.

GREER GARSON

■ ... To my way of thinking, his performance in *On the Waterfront* is the best male performance I've ever seen in my life.

ELIA KAZAN

■ I have the feeling that he believes somewhere along the line he missed something he could have done, something he could have *been*. This sounds strange, but it's as if somebody had put an angel inside of him, and he's aware of it, and it's more than he can *contain*.

EDWARD ALBERT

■ Brando in *Mutiny On The Bounty*, simply took charge of everything. You had the option of sitting and watching him or turning your back to him. The script was written from day to day, the writer discussed it with Brando and they shot it. I thought his performace as Fletcher Christian was horrible.

LEWIS MILESTONE

■ Montgomery Clift was an exceptionally bright man who liked to pretend he wasn't, unlike Brando who likes to pretend he's bright whereas in fact he isn't really.

EDWARD DMYTRYK

■ Brando is not exactly a generous actor, he doesn't give. But he does make demands on you, and if you don't come through then he'll run right over the top of you.

LEE MARVIN

■ Whether the film is good or bad Brando is always compulsive viewing, like Sydney Greenstreet, the vulgarian of all time, or Peter Lorre, or even Bette Davis daring to do *Baby Jane*.

ANTHONY HOPKINS

■ Brando wants to do what you want but he wants people to be honest and not try to manipulate him.

FRANCIS FORD COPPOLA, 1972

■ He lives the life of the actor twenty–four hours a day. His style is the perfect marriage of intuition and intelligence. If he must learn to ride a horse for a movie, he will watch that horse like no one else has watched a horse and when he does the scene he will be both horse and rider.

STELLA ADLER

■ Marlon's the most exciting person I've met since Garbo. A genius. But I don't know what he's like. I don't know anything about him.

JOSHUA LOGAN

■ As an actor, he is a genius, and even when he's dull, he's still much better than most actors at the top of their form. But he has preserved the mentality of an adolescent. It's a pity. When he doesn't try and someone's speaking to him it's like a blank wall: in fact, it's even less interesting because behind a blank wall you can always suppose that there's something interesting there.

BURT REYNOLDS

■ Brando is one of the finest actors we've had in the business, and I'm only sorry he didn't have the benefit of older, more established friends—as I did—to help him choose the proper material in which to use his talent.

JOHN WAYNE, 1973

■ I hated working with Marlon Brando— because he was *not* there, he was somewhere else. There was nothing to reach on to.

JOANNE WOODWARD

22

■ Like Marlon Brando in *Superman*. The greatest screen actor in the history of cinema—perhaps—and he's running around with white hair and a Krypton suit. Just something wrong about that.

JAMES WOODS

GEORGE BRENT (1904–1979)

■ I had such a crush on that man. I found out later that all his leading ladies felt that way about him. We laughed all the time. . . . As a matter of fact, he even asked me to marry him, but I wasn't in a position to accept and I had no thoughts in that direction. He was a wonderful man and a part of my life I'll never forget.

JANE POWELL, 1983

ROBERT BRESSON (born 1907)

■ This bewilderingly chilling director goes his own way, for all the breathing world like some anti-Pygmalion: he takes real people and turns them into statues. The camera all too often persists in a new definition of middle shot, moving dolefully around figures-in-interiors at stomach level, avoiding faces just when one yearns to see them, showing tables, objects.

JOHN COLEMAN

■ There's something in the way Bresson makes films which puts me in mind of a certain French tradition that comes from Racine. . . . I don't really think that I was influenced by Bresson—but I would say that I wish I had been.

LOUIS MALLE

JEFF BRIDGES (born 1949)

■ He's able to dissolve himself in a role by investing his characters with integrity

and truth. Through imagination and instinct, he can metamorphose into almost anybody. Robert Duvall has the same quality. So do most of the great English actors.

ROBERT BENTON

CHARLES BRONSON (born 1921)

■ I think I'm in so many of his pictures because no other actress would work with him.

JILL IRELAND

■ Well, Charlie does things in terms of performance that are hard for a lot of other people to comprehend as being part of an actor's tool, and that is being visually interesting. There is a great poetry in Charlie's face. With just a look, he can suggest moods that are quite interesting. . . . He's always on time; he always knows his lines, and he never misses a mark.

WALTER HILL

■ His characteristic gesture was to show his back to the largest number of people possible. I never heard anybody say he thought Bronson did this to be offensive or hostile or even unfriendly. It was just part of who Charles Bronson is. A very large part.

HARRY CREWS

■ I don't think reviews get to Charlie much, though, unless they're especially personal. In the twenty–five years or so I've known him, he's not changed much. He's his own man. Stays pretty much to himself. If he cares what other people think of him, he doesn't show it.

RICHARD CRENNA

23

- He is a very helpful actor in planning or staging a scene. He gets wonderful ideas, good practical suggestions and I enjoy his contributions. He's a positive force for the good in this grinding work of making a film. He's patient when the work is difficult and he's never satisfied until he's convinced what's been done is right. He's my kind of actor you might say. He's a true loner.

  DON SIEGEL

CLIVE BROOK (1887–1974)

- He had that physical presence and a certain masculine charm that enhanced any actress' presence. Just as he, a gentleman, was a man who always made a woman feel like a lady, he also, as an actor, made any actress playing a scene with him feel like a star.

  DEWITT BODEEN, 1975

- The first time I went out in public with my father . . . I was literally almost killed by a stampede on the pavement outside the theatre: hundreds of people trying to touch my father's clothes, . . . Film stars in the 1930s were godlike, and for their families it was often impossible.

  FAITH BROOK, 1984

JAMES L. BROOKS (born 1941)

- Jim Brooks is crude but smart crude. His sarcasm stings you but it makes you grow. When you're working, no matter how tough you are, you're vulnerable. I don't need to be worshipped; I just need a little respect.

  DEBRA WINGER

LOUISE BROOKS (1906–1985)

- There is no Garbo! There is no Dietrich! There is only Louise Brooks.

  HENRI LANGLOIS

- Today we know that Louise Brooks is not just a ravishing creature but an amazing actress gifted with an unprecedented intelligence.

  LOTTE EISNER

- The performance he [Pabst] extracts from Louise Brooks [in *Pandora's Box*] is one of the phenomena of the cinema.

  PAUL ROTHA

- Louise Brooks is the only woman who had the ability to transfigure—no matter what film—into a masterpiece . . . the poetry of Louise is the great poetry of rare loves, of magnetism, of tension, of feminine beauty as blinding as ten galaxial suns. . . . She is much more than a myth, she is a magical presence, a real phantom, the magnetism of the cinema.

  ADO KYROU

MEL BROOKS (born 1926)

- We are not interested in polite titters, we want the audience rolling on the floor and falling about. Mel works on his feet—it's a hit and miss, hit and miss, hit and miss. Then in the editing he will take out the misses!

  GENE WILDER

- I wasn't taken with *Young Frankenstein*, I thought we did better jokes in High School. I was with an audience, expecting to laugh. There wasn't one and in the end they started to walk out.

  JASON ROBARDS, 1978

YUL BRYNNER (1915–1985)

- When I started shooting *Anastasia* I . . . realised at once that he was shorter. I suggested putting a little block under him. He turned round and said to me: 'You think I want to play it standing on a box. I will show the world what a big horse you are'. Maybe some actresses would have walked out but I just laughed and laughed and I never had a complex about my height after that.

  INGRID BERGMAN

LUIS BUÑUEL (1900–1983)

- The beauty of the photography in *Nazarin* must be emphasised. A Zurbaran or a Goya could have signed his name to this film. Here, at last, we find ourselves on the elusive dividing line where ideas of the beautiful and the ugly recede to give way to a new idea of what one might call the necessary.

  ADO KYROU

- Buñuel is a total solitary person. Very attentive, very polite, not at all contemptuous of people, but not wishing to be encumbered with anything, for he knows that everything goes very quickly, too quickly. He has a horror of waste and lost money. He does not like actors to a great degree.

  MICHEL PICCOLI

- Anti-bourgeois, anti-conformist, Buñuel is as sarcastic as Stroheim, but he has a lighter touch; his world view is subversive, happily anarchist.

  FRANÇOIS TRUFFAUT

- . . . [he] paints madness in his film . . . but it is not he who created it.

  HENRY MILLER

- The two hallmarks of a Buñuel film are peculiar, often sadistic sex; and religious excess, often cruel, and usually viewed with irony. The two are generally intertwined, and the result can be splendidly baroque and bizarre. But, . . . Buñuel has a way of bogging down. . . . he feels obliged to bring in perverse sexuality surreptitiously or marginally— as a dream, an allusion, a surreal fantasy—thus dissipating much of its power and even reducing it to maundering private symbolism.

  JOHN SIMON, 1970

- I think today there are too many directors taking themselves seriously . . . the only one capable of saying anything really new and interesting is Luis Buñuel. He's a very great director.

  LUCHINO VISCONTI, 1975

GEORGE BURNS (born 1896) and GRACIE ALLEN (1902–1964)

- The audience gave her [Gracie] that character. What I call her illogical logic always got the biggest laughs. When we went on for the first time, the audience laughed at her questions instead of my answers. So from then on I gave her all the jokes. I was never a jerk. I wanted to keep on smoking good cigars, so I gave her the jokes.

  GEORGE BURNS

ELLEN BURSTYN (born 1932)

- Yet despite her skills there's something annoyingly facile about Ellen Burstyn. She runs through her emotions too quickly, and none of them seem to stick. Her all-too-flexible face is strangely

25

unmemorable. . . . it's hard to recall what she looks like in-between her movies.

DAVID DENBY, 1975

RICHARD BURTON (1925–1984)

■ There is nothing he can't do. He is a wonder and a joy to watch.

SAMMY DAVIS JR.

■ Richard Burton tends to give cleverly externalised performances in which a nice overlay of melancholy is shot through by flashes of something or other. Here [in *The Taming of the Shrew*] we are treated to the obverse: instead of the customarily weary and sullen Burton, we get an infantile, bellowing, guffawing boor, a cross between Jack the Ripper and Jack the Giant Killer.

JOHN SIMON

■ Richard Burton plays Henry [in *Anne of a Thousand Days*] like a man who has promised to buy another diamond before Easter, using himself like an acting machine that will, if flogged, produce another million dollars.

PENELOPE MORTIMER

■ Whenever I said 'Richard you're overdoing it a bit,' he would say, 'Oh, I'm doing a Burton.' He said, 'Listen, Michael, for twenty years I've had the most famous voice in the world. I just want to make one film without it.' The upshot is he gives a performance like he hasn't given for twenty years.

MICHAEL RADFORD

■ He never fought back, never excused himself, never said the critics were wrong because in his heart he knew they were not. I thought the marriage tore him in two. Fifty per cent of him had wanted to marry Taylor, knowing that fame and fortune would accrue. The other half bitterly resented what he had done. So he drank.

RODERICK MANN

■ While *à deux* with Mrs Taylor–Burton and a beaker of champagne, she remarked that Richard often considered returning to Oxford to become a simple don. This was said with great sincerity and a straight face. Which—since the lady was at the time wearing a stupefying wig made from the scalps of at least nine healthy Italians and a frock costing upwards of $5,000—gave me a poignant vision of donnish simplicity.

CARRIE NYE, 1973

■ In the movies he makes with Liz, he seems not to be trying, almost as if he were embarrassed. He seems often to be thrusting the scene at his wife, to see what she is able to do with it. A sense of 'Don't blame me' prevails . . . In either event, he has been relying on this style rather too heavily lately. In nonclassical parts, he is quickly becoming a byword in dullness, simply because he plays everything down so low that it doesn't count.

WILFRED SHEED

■ The only actor I've ever really had a crush on was Richard Burton. Of course, I never *met* Richard Burton, but I saw *Becket* again a little while ago. He had such a cute voice. I thought he was divine in those early days. Then he started ruining himself. I guess you'd say he was very self-destructive.

IRENE DUNNE

■ My first judgement of Richard was that he was an intellectual snob, arrogant, bombastic and given to pedantry. But he was not a snob or a pedant. He only posed as one. He put it up in front of himself as a security screen, proving to the world that he still had serious standards and values, which in private he feared he was losing, or might even have lost altogether. . .

JOHN DAVID MORLEY, 1984

■ He's like all these drunks. Impossible when he's drunk and only half there when he's sober. Wooden as a board with his body, relies on doing all his acting with his voice.

JOHN BOORMAN, 1984

■ The Burton phenomenon fascinates me as much as anyone, more so perhaps because I was closer to it than most. Yet I was not sure I fully understood my brother, why it was that he attracted (and still does attract) such enormous interest.

GRAHAM JENKINS, 1988

■ I'd have thought he'd leave some of his money to the village, put some in a trust for a scholarship or something.

HARRY REES

JAMES CAAN (born 1939)

■ In another age, the cheerful, swaggering presence of James Caan would have made him the major star he is often said to be. He has just been associated with too many poor movies: you probably wait to see them until they're on TV, when you'll usually find he's the best thing about them.

DAVID DENBY

■ In the title role of *The Gambler*, James Caan is something of a revelation, showing a subtlety and depth in his ulcerous playing that overrides the more predictable moments of conscious masculinity. There is a callousness in his manner which is at first unendearing, but as the film progresses this is shown to be part of a much greater whole.

DEREK ELLEY

■ Caan allows his glistening teeth to wag his entire performance [in *Comes a Horseman*], and there are a few nocturnal exterior long shots in which the whole valley seems to be illuminated solely by the light of those silvery teeth.

JOHN SIMON

■ He's a damn good actor, and we started rolling the more we got into it. He got a lot of laughs playing it perfectly serious. He didn't know he was playing it perfectly serious. He didn't know he was playing comedy . . .

HOWARD HAWKS

27

JAMES CAGNEY (1899–1986)

■ Whether he changed lines (as he frequently did), sat in on story conferences, suggested casting changes, contributed ideas for scene design (as he did for *City for Conquest*), or wrote music (as he did for *Captain of the Clouds*), his impact on the average production was enormous. . . . A 'Cagney vehicle'—in that truly meaningful phrase—became a picture in which the display of Cagney's talents dominated all other aspects of the film.

PATRICK McGILLIGAN, 1973

■ Now, you take a great cinema actor, in my opinion, James Cagney. He went very far. He was very theatrical, very intense, and yet always believable. He riveted the audience's attention. His acting advice was 'Believe what you say—say what you believe'. And that says it really.

GREGORY PECK

■ No one was more unreal and stylised . . . yet there is no moment when he was not true.

ORSON WELLES

■ I learned something from Jimmy Cagney—he taught me quite a lot about acting. Jimmy taught me some things about being honest and not overdoing it. He even affected my work with Brando a little bit. I mean 'Don't show it, just do it'.

ELIA KAZAN

■ And yet so many of the actors that I admire are none of them naturalistic players at all. James Cagney, for example. But the point is that you believed him— and he was *real* , but not realistic. They're different worlds altogether.

MALCOLM MCDOWELL

■ He was typed—typed as exactly the kind of guy our mother tried to push us farthest away from. So for ten years Jimmy makes five pictures a year and all along the same Warner Bros formula— Jimmy is a heel for eight reels, then clean him up in the ninth. You didn't like it, you argue, you're suspended, you get a reputation as a difficult actor—so you usually give in.

WILLIAM CAGNEY

■ James Cagney rolled through the film like a very belligerent barrel.

NOEL COWARD

■ When he hits a friend over the ear with a revolver-butt, he does it as casually as he will presently press the elevator button on his way out. By retaining his brisk little smile throughout he makes one react warmly, with a grin, not coldly and aghast . . . but he possessed, possibly in greater abundance than any other name star of the time, irresistible charm. It was a cocky, picaresque charm; the charm of pert urchins; the gaminerie of unlicked juvenile delinquents.

KENNETH TYNAN

■ I was never a fan of any actor outside of James Cagney. . . I always liked Cagney's style and energy. He was fearless.

CLINT EASTWOOD

■ Jimmy Cagney was the most dynamic man who ever appeared on the screen. He should have won five Oscars, he was so fabulous. He stimulated me to such an extent. I must say that I didn't have to act very much; I just had to react to him because he was so powerful.

VIRGINIA MAYO

■ One knows what to expect and Mr Cagney seldom disappoints: the lightweight hands held a little way away from the body ready for someone else's punch: the quick nervous steps of a man whose footwork is good: the extreme virtuosity of the muted sentiment.

GRAHAM GREENE

■ . . . but Cagney played a man you didn't want to see die. Whether he was right or wrong, he was a guy who could stand up to life and to as many gangsters as would come up against him; he was the toughest guy I'd ever seen.

JOHN CASSAVETES

■ He had excellent instincts, a wider range than just about anybody, and a way of penetrating through to an audience that nobody else had. He had a quality of authenticity. Bogie, for instance, was a big fraud. Jimmy used to call him the Park Avenue tough guy.

PAT O'BRIEN

■ His few breaks for freedom—*Boy Meets Girl* among them—have not been successful, whether through Cagney's fault or our inability to adjust ourselves to seeing him without an armpit holster.

FRANK S. NUGENT

■ It is hard to say what our impression of the total American character would have been without him. He is all crust and speed and snap on the surface, a gutter-fighter with the grace of dancing, a boy who knows all the answers and won't even wait for them, a very fast one.

OTIS FERGUSON, 1939

■ Jimmy not only has a great serenity, such as I've not seen in an actor outside of Walter Huston, he has a great love of the earth and of his fellow man, an understanding of loneliness.

NICHOLAS RAY

MICHAEL CAINE (born 1933)

■ Wonderfully good company, ceaselessly funny and a brilliant actor.

LAURENCE OLIVIER

■ He is without doubt the nicest human being I've ever worked with. I mean, *what a pleasure*! It would be nice if I could only do Michael Caine movies from now on. I'd be very happy.

VALERIE PERRINE, 1985

■ I had a very good idea of what to expect from Michael Caine. He's the pure,

elegant professional: two or three 'takes' and that's it.

JOHN MACKENZIE

■ Caine seems not in the least daunted by acting with a legend incarnate. To say that he matches Olivier in every way is to pay him the highest of compliments.

JAY COCKS

■ Only a special breed of actor can maintain a reputation for excellence despite a slew of such embarrassing credits as *Hurry Sundown, Beyond the Poseidon Adventure, The Island* and, to bring his follies up to date, *The Hand*.

WILLIAM WOLF

PHYLLIS CALVERT (born 1915)

■ I'm a very good actor—I played all those love scenes with Phyllis Calvert and we didn't like each other very much.

STEWART GRANGER

■ She was a nice little woman till she went to Hollywood and either she or her advisers decided she was a big star. Then she was a pain in the neck.

COMPTON BENNETT

FRANK CAPRA (born 1897)

■ Capra has too often mistaken inexperience for innocence.

DAVID FISHER, 1954

■ He was my favourite director. Woody Allen and I once sat in a restaurant and picked five pictures we'd take to an island. And much to my shock, he didn't take a Capra picture, and I took two. He took three Ingmar Bergman movies . . .

BURT REYNOLDS

29

■ Very often I would see the wheels going around and the tricks coming up. It was probably useful, but I used to be aware of the mechanics of it and how you would work toward a gag to get a gag in. I'm sure he'd think the same thing about me. He's a good film-maker.

KING VIDOR

■ Now, if you take someone like Capra who spent a year planning, through production and editing, and at the end of it had one marvellous picture . . . well, by that time I'd shot several—to spend a year on just one picture, why I'd get bored to death.

WILLIAM A. WELLMAN

■ . . . we asked, wasn't Mr Sinatra, like Mr Capra, retiring? He nodded. 'He's getting a little old for what he's trying to do', he said. 'That's all. He's like me. He wants to be No. 1'. He paused once more. 'Being No. 2, for me', he said, 'is like being last'.

CLEVELAND AMORY, 1975

■ Movies for me are a heightened reality. Making reality fun to live with, as opposed to something you run from and protect yourself from. And they used to make them all the time. Frank Capra the most notable. He and John Ford and Preston Sturges had more heart, as filmmakers, than everybody else.

STEVEN SPIELBERG, 1978

CLAUDIA CARDINALE (born 1939)

■ A cameraman's dream—a perfect piece of nature—there is not much you can do wrong in photographing her.

CONRAD HALL, 1966

MARCEL CARNÉ (born 1909)

■ . . . a *petit maitre,* but a true craftsman. He knows what he's doing.

ORSON WELLES

LESLIE CARON (born 1931)

■ A ballet dancer really, but technically good. I called her the sergeant major.

FRED ASTAIRE

■ Even now I feel furious with myself because, whenever there's a still camera pointed towards me, my MGM training makes me smile. I don't like it. You can see it on all the people who came from that era because there was no question of them not smiling for the camera. Even Katharine Hepburn—and God knows she was a dramatic actress—if the camera is on her she smiles.

HERSELF

MADELEINE CARROLL (1906–1987)

■ Madeleine Carroll was the first big international star I directed? I suppose she was, if I think about it. But she never behaved like that. Liked to be one of the boys, the first to say 'Who's for the pub?'.

HAROLD FRENCH, 1983

JOHN CASSAVETES (born 1929)

■ We had a great deal of freedom when John acted. We travelled a lot, and it was fun. But with directing . . . really. I think people don't have all their marbles who prefer directing to acting because you write for three months, you cut for maybe six months . . . He's the *most* terrifying perfectionist about what he wants. As an artist I love him. As a husband I *hate* him.

GENA ROWLANDS, 1974

LILIANA CAVANI (born 1936)

■ And the Cavani [*Beyond Good and Evil*] is garbage. There was a good idea there somewhere in the original material, but Cavani has to twist everything into her own little fantasies. She absolutely hates men, but she didn't even get the woman's part right—so you end up thinking *everyone* in the film is awful. Well, an actor takes what he can get.

ROBERT POWELL, 1977

CLAUDE CHABROL (born 1930)

■ We are unable to enjoy a 'half-experience' because there is no figure with whom we are able to identify for more than a short while, and we cannot happily enter the film because it has too much of the grossness, the play acting and the absurdity that are a part of all our lives. The characters in Chabrol films don't remain within the rules of the game. They affront the audience, they offend it.

MARK SHIVAS, 1964

■ One could say, as a generalisation, that from now on Chabrol aims to knock bourgeois values. The question is: is he knocking them in order to overcome them or to maintain them? I think the latter is more likely.

RAINER WERNER FASSBINDER

RICHARD CHAMBERLAIN (born 1935)

■ You're doing it the wrong way round, my boy. You're a star and you don't know how to act.

SIR CEDRIC HARDWICKE

HELEN CHANDLER (1906–1965)

■ The remarkable discovery is the excellence of Helen Chandler, whose film career is almost wholly forgotten; from her first appearance [in *The Last Flight*], standing graceful and vacant in a bar, holding a set of teeth in a glass on behalf of a man who 'said he was going to biff somebody', her performance maintains a complete conviction in the role of the solemnly dotty lost lady.

DAVID ROBINSON, 1968

31

JEFF CHANDLER (1918–1961)

■ . . . on *Two Flags West*, Jeff Chandler as a relative newcomer to the screen was a tremendous admirer of Joe Cotten as a trained and skilled actor. Many times when Jeff was not in the scenes himself he would be on the set just to watch Joe work. Yet when the picture was finished Jeff was the one who walked off with it. Cotten gave a fine performance but Jeff had the magic.

ROBERT WISE

RAYMOND CHANDLER (1888–1959)

■ If my books had been any worse, I should not have been invited to Hollywood. If they had been any better, I should not have come.

HIMSELF

LON CHANEY (1886–1930)

- Don't step on it [a spider]. It may be Lon Chaney.

  MARSHALL NEILAN

- The most famous ballet stars like Nijinsky, could express every emotion and every shade of meaning in the movements of their bodies. Chaney had that gift. When he realised that he had lost the girl, his body expressed it—it was as though a bolt of lightning had shattered his physical self. Extraordinary really!

  CHARLES LAUGHTON

- The concentration, the complete absorption he gave his characterisation, filled me with such awe that I could scarcely speak to him. [For *The Unknown*] he learned to eat without his hands, and even to hold a cigarette between his toes. He never slipped out of character.

  JOAN CRAWFORD

CHARLES CHAPLIN (1899-1977)

- I have never—Chaplin's apart—seen a good American film.

  ARNOLD BENNETT, 1927

- The only one of us who listened and accepted the role of genius intellectual critics thrust upon him was Chaplin. Sometimes I suspect that much of the trouble he's been in started the first time he read that he was a 'sublime satirist' and a first-rate artist. He believed every word of it and tried to live and think accordingly.

  BUSTER KEATON

- That obstinate, suspicious, egocentric, maddening and lovable genius of a problem child.

  MARY PICKFORD

- One of the worst appreciators of comedy outside of himself and his own genius.

  JAMES THURBER

- If people don't sit at Chaplin's feet, he goes out and stands where they're sitting.

  HERMAN J. MANKIEWICZ

- In a company in which he feels himself at ease he will play the fool with delightful abandon. His invention is fertile, his vivacity unfailing, and he has a pleasant gift for mimicry . . . the unbelievable charm that graces all his actions.

  W. SOMERSET MAUGHAM

- But the best comics are also good actors. Chaplin is a wonderful actor.

  ZERO MOSTEL

- Pathos has nearly ruined Chaplin, who is an artist of genius.

  GRAHAM GREENE

- He had no knowledge of camera direction. His films are completely theatre.

  KARL STRUSS

- For me they are the most beautiful films in the world . . . Chaplin means more to me than the idea of God.

  FRANÇOIS TRUFFAUT

- Charlie Chaplin is a great artist. I don't agree with many of the things he says and does, but he's the greatest artist our motion picture business has ever had, and I'd make a picture with him tomorrow if he wanted to.

  SAM GOLDWYN, 1953

- When he found a voice to say what was on his mind, he was like a child of eight writing lyrics for Beethoven's Ninth.

  BILLY WILDER

32

■ His power to stand for a sort of concentrated essence of the common man, for the ineradicable belief in decency that exists in the hearts of ordinary people, at any rate in the West.

GEORGE ORWELL

■ Chaplin is all content and little form. Nobody could have shot a film in a more pedestrian way than Chaplin.

STANLEY KUBRICK

■ Charles Chaplin, I think, is a bad director. Great comedian, great actor, bad director. Mediocre composer, but nice. Did you like *Countess from Hong Kong*? Did you think that was a well-directed movie?

WARREN BEATTY

■ It [*Modern Times*] was an artistic success, but after that everyone over-intellectualised Charlie's work and consequently he became self-conscious. It harmed him, I think.

PAULETTE GODDARD, 1975

■ The greatest actor living and he is an Englishman. One has been upset that he has not been knighted before. No-one could blame him for leaving England— what a wonderful opportunity he had in America. But he was a glory for England in a foreign country.

RALPH RICHARDSON, 1977

RUTH CHATTERTON (1893–1961)

■ Chatterton couldn't get along with *any* director.

WILLIAM A. WELLMAN

PADDY CHAYEVSKY (1923–1981)

■ Also, I don't think Paddy had ever been involved with a director who wasn't malleable. He would make suggestions, and I would listen courteously, and then disagree.

KEN RUSSELL, 1982

CHER (born 1946)

■ Her comic timing is natural and almost infallible. I'll say so even though she nicknamed me 'the curmudgeon'. Cher thinks all directors are mad and crazy. She's right of course.

NORMAN JEWISON

■ Anyone who could be a personality and wear those clothes and who is also a serious actress has to be schizophrenic. I suppose [she has] a great need to be looked upon as a personality. But I just don't think she wants to take on the look of a serious actress in private life if she doesn't feel like it. It would be phoney. And Cher has a strong detection against the phoney.

PETER YATES

MAURICE CHEVALIER (1888–1972)

■ You're the greatest thing to come from France since Lafayette.

AL JOLSON

■ The whole of him was much bigger than the sum of his various talents. His stylised silhouette, the saucy angle of his straw hat, his smile, the way he moved, sang and talked was not only artistically perfect, but spiritually uplifting to young and old. He radiated optimism, good will and above all the *joie de vivre* that every human being longs for.

ROUBEN MAMOULIAN

33

- M. Chevalier is as enjoyable as ever. There is his smile and also his stare—a stare of discomfort when he is dumbfounded. But whether he is solemn or laughing, he is always engaging.

  MORDAUNT HALL

- The greatest mistake one can make about this great performer is to imagine him a sophisticate: he is essentially an innocent . . . His style abounds in a great knowingness, but it is the knowingness of extreme youth, and we find it oddly affecting, because it announces that here, aged sixty-three, is a man whom experience has not made caustic, whose wisdom is summed up, not in an aphorism, but in a huge cry of joy.

  KENNETH TYNAN

- He was a great actor. he had that indefinable quality that every star has to have—that quality that we performers call audience contact. I think I can explain it best as a kind of magic.

  HERMIONE GINGOLD, 1972

- He was in California at Paramount when I was, and for six months I ate lunch within twenty feet of him. He always ate alone . . . He was sour, scowling, and ill-humoured, as well as a notorious tightwad.

  JAMES M. CAIN

- Say what you like about Chevalier as a Don Juan, perhaps as a sentimentalist, certainly as a man driven by ambition, he still remained quite manifestly likeable. Some accused him of meanness. He certainly saved what he earned; but he also gave generously, especially to homes for run-down actors.

  RICHARD MAYNE, 1972

34

JULIE CHRISTIE (born 1941)

- Julie doesn't like being a movie star. All she wants is to act. If she had her way, she'd like a nice role to play in a film that doesn't require a lot of recognition.

  ROBERT ALTMAN

- She's one of the great actresses in the history of films.

  WARREN BEATTY

- Someone recently said to me, isn't it strange to be a movie star *and* be an actress. I said, that's been going on for years, at least since Julie Christie and *Darling*.

  FAYE DUNAWAY

- Julie has such a wonderful film presence and fulfils everything I admire in a performer in that she—more specifically than almost anyone else—works for the director and recognises that the film is created by the director in the way Jeanne Moreau did for Louis Malle.

  DONALD SUTHERLAND, 1987

MICHAEL CIMINO (born 1943)

- If you don't get it right, what's the point?

  HIMSELF

- As it is, no one in *Heaven's Gate* really connects or interacts with anyone else, and most people still go to movies more for these kinds of connections and interactions than for the comparatively abstract implementation of a director's vision. He [Cimino] is trying to say very big things about history and memory with a very private language. That he may have bankrupted a studio in the process raises other questions that may take a very long time to answer.

  ANDREW SARRIS, 1980

- *Year of the Dragon*, is so lacking in feeling, reason and narrative continuity that it furthers the impression left by *Heaven's Gate*, and even by much of *The Deer Hunter*, that Mr Cimino's insistence on working on a vast and extravagant scale is not matched by an ability to work articulately on any other.

  JANET MASLIN, 1985

- A movie [*Year of the Dragon*] that is often so inept it's funny. Mike, have you thought of driving a bus or becoming a piano tuner or otherwise doing something useful!

  RALPH NOVAK

RENÉ CLAIR (1898–1981)

- His strength lies in being solidly individual, endowed with high gifts which owe remarkably little to other people (any comparison with Chaplin is superficial, since the latter's works spring from so much deeper sources). He is not akin to anyone else in the film world, and his spiritual colleagues are to be found amongst the French 18th–century writers, as his own pleasant writings show.

  JEAN QUEVAL

- [*Les Grandes Manoeuvres* represents] everything I love in my country, everything which links me to it by the deepest and most secret ties . . . Here are clarity and modesty, lucidity and tenderness, irony and elegance . . .

  JEAN DE BARONCELLI

- A real master: he invented his own Paris, which is better than recording it.

  ORSON WELLES

MONTGOMERY CLIFT (1920–1966)

- Monty was the most emotional actor I have ever worked with. And it is contagious.

  ELIZABETH TAYLOR

- He had so much power, so much concentration. Clift was a complicated man, there's no question about it . . . He was a sweet man, Monty, very emotional.

  BURT LANCASTER

- Mr Montgomery Clift gives the performance of his career in *A Place in the Sun*, which is not saying a great deal, since he had already demonstrated in *The Heiress* that he didn't belong on the same screen with first-class actors.

  RAYMOND CHANDLER

- The only time I was ever really afraid as an actor was that first scene with Clift. It was *my* scene, understand: I was the sergeant, I gave the orders, he was just a private under me. Well, when we started, I couldn't stop my knees from shaking. I thought they might have to stop because my trembling would show. I was afraid he was going to blow me right off the screen.

  BURT LANCASTER

- But Montgomery Clift was in the picture [*Red River*] too, you know. And they wanted to give that poor kid an Academy Award so bad that they simply forgot about me. Clift was *acting*, they said. Duke's only playing himself. But hell, I played an *old man* in that. And I was only forty.

  JOHN WAYNE

- Monty was a great talent, whose acting I had always admired. He had extraordinary instincts. . . . His

35

observations about the script were always astute and correct. He would have made a great director, which eventually he wanted to be. 'Would you ever direct yourself?' I once asked him. 'Are you kidding?' he replied. 'As a director, I simply wouldn't put up with all that crap from me.' Monty was having problems then. He was full of all kinds of problems, many of them imaginary.

MYRNA LOY

■ He was a method actor, and neurotic as well. 'I want you to look in a certain direction', I'd say, and he'd say, 'Well, I don't know whether I'd look that way'. Now immediately you're fouled up because you're shooting a precut picture. He's got to look that way because you're going to cut to something over there. So I have to say to him, 'Please, you'll have to look that way, or else'.

ALFRED HITCHCOCK

■ Monty was a tragic character. If there is such a thing as a death wish Monty had it. On *Raintree County* we had a miserable time with him, particularly after the accident . . . He was the most sensitive man I've ever known. If somebody kicked a dog a mile away he'd feel it.

EDWARD DMYTRYK

■ The true originator of the rebellious twentieth century anti-hero was Montgomery Clift . . . not Marlon Brando or James Dean . . . the restrained performer with the inner tension and those ancient, melancholy eyes . . . his presence so unobtrusively strong that it lingered even when he was off-camera.

MARCELLO MASTROIANNI

HENRI-GEORGES CLOUZOT (1907–1977)

■ That red-fanged old marrow-freezer.

PAUL DEHN

JEAN COCTEAU (1889–1963)

■ There will be no half-measures about your response to the Cocteau fantasy *La Belle et La Bête*. You will either find it repellent or enchanting. I found it enchanting, and I use the word fastidiously, since the effect it had upon me was less one of active pleasure than of rapt fascination . . . There is no heart in this film at all. It is absolute magic, diamond cold and lunar bright.

C.A. LEJEUNE, 1947

■ He knew that I was open to his world and wanted to enter it. I had respect and admiration for him which touched him. I was what he would like to have had for a son: only, if I had been, I would have been better than I am. At one point, he wanted to marry my mother so that I could become his son . . .

JEAN MARAIS

HARRY COHN (1891–1958)

■ I had a great fondness for Cohn. Naturally I think he was wrong in firing me but that's beside the point. I think he ran a marvellous studio; . . . He wasn't in the money business, he was in the movie business. I had a chance to have a reconciliation with him and I didn't go. I've always regretted it.

ROBERT ALDRICH

CLAUDETTE COLBERT (born 1905)

- Colbert has supreme command of the comic style [in *Midnight*].

  FRANK S. NUGENT

- . . . she's a terrific lady and a good actress—but she liked to work with script in hand. That did not suit the Master [Noël Coward] at all, he had specifically requested that we be word perfect, so an edginess began between them. They were both right, but when working with Noël you did it his way. The edginess grew. He said, 'Look at Betty—she's been filming, yet knows her part perfectly.' That only made me want to kill myself.

  LAUREN BACALL

- Now Claudette Colbert lived next door and she'd finish a movie on Saturday— we worked Saturdays in those days— and begin wondering what she was doing on Monday. I lacked that terrifying ambition. I drifted into acting and drifted out. Acting is not everything. Living is.

  IRENE DUNNE

- I got along famously with Paulette and Claudette. But they didn't get along with each other. There was one incident about which I always laugh. It concerned an interview with Paulette Goddard. She was asked whom she liked best— Claudette or Veronica. 'Veronica, I think. After all, we are closer in age', she said. Claudette read the interview and flipped. She was at Paulette's eyes every minute, and Paulette fought back with equal vengeance. I smiled.

  VERONICA LAKE

- The smartest, canniest, smoothest eighteen-carat lady I've ever seen cross the Hollywood pike. She knows her own mind, knows what's right for her, has a marvellous self-discipline and a deep-rooted Gallic desire to be in shape, efficient and under control. Her career comes before anything, save possibly her marriage.

  HEDDA HOPPER

JACK COLE (1914–1974)

- Except for those within the profession who are aware of him, he is today practically unknown. But all those familiar with his work acknowledge his wonderful talent and his seminal contribution to dance.

  JEROME ROBBINS, 1984

JOAN COLLINS (born 1933)

37

- She's common, she can't act—yet she's the hottest female property around these days. If that doesn't tell you something about the state of our industry today, what does?

  STEWART GRANGER, 1984

- Jackie Collins is in the front rank of the worst prose producers in the history of the English language. The author of *Hollywood Wives* and eight other novels is to writing what her big sister Joan is to acting.

  CAMPBELL GEESON

RONALD COLMAN (1891—1958)

- Mr Ronald Colman is, I understand, the greatest male exponent of 'sex-appeal' possessed by the modern screen. . . . he seems to me to be a good-looking man who probably goes in first wicket down, in scratch at golf, and would be just about as interesting to talk to on any subject as a University Blue.

JAMES AGATE

■ Beautiful of face and soul, sensitive to the fragile and gentle, responsive both to poetic visions and hard intellect— cultured actor Ronald Colman was born to play the kidnapped foreign secretary who 'understood' his kidnapping [in *Lost Horizon*].

FRANK CAPRA

■ He is the typical strong man of the film [*Clive of India*] without any sense of ethics, wilful and purposeful to a fault, and he manages to convey that notion of the masterful scoundrel, half of whose life is given over to sentimental staring at a lady's picture in a locket and the other half to plundering people just because they happen to be Orientals and foreigners.

SYDNEY W. CARROLL

■ Colman has this beautiful face, and this lovely voice—well you know the voice, it was very famous—and he was a magnificent actor.

WILLIAM A. WELLMAN

■ He was a complete Original, in personality, good looks, diversity and style. He added to this point great self-discipline and an ability to be completely absorbed by a scene, to exclude all distractions while actually shooting, and to be able to relax between scenes. Last but not least, he was never, never late on the set.

JANE WYATT

■ He is an excellent director's dummy. He has no personality of his own, only an appearance, and for that reason he is an almost perfect actor for the fictional screen.

GRAHAM GREENE

SEAN CONNERY (born 1930)

■ Much more attractive without his wig on.

BARBARA CARRARA

■ The best Bonds also had Sean Connery, whose absence is surely felt here, [*The Man with the Golden Gun*]. An actor of considerable resource, Connery played 007 with just the right combination of conviction and detachment. He also had a self-mocking aplomb that would be hard to duplicate. His Bond is definitive.

JAY COCKS

■ . . . and Connery's startling performance provides the dramatic momentum. He has a powerful presence—his physical movements are those of a caged but dangerous animal; and his characterisation is rich in shadings. Connery has given strong performances in the past but his performance in *The Offence* has a depth of feeling that will amaze people who still associate him with James Bond.

STEPHEN FARBER

■ Sean Connery, a scoundrel in gentleman's clothes, a man who took advantage, brought an edge of sexual aggression to James Bond, but [Roger] Moore is a passive, weary, and put-upon Bond.

DAVID DENBY

■ There was nothing much in Fleming's Bond—English, public school, snobbish—that connected with him, but he took the character by the throat and

38

shook some sense into it. It was the disparity between the man and the role that made it so compelling. The slickness, the cleverness, the effete charm were there in the scripts, but Sean's animal power made them seem like decorative accretions thinly concealing a real hero in the old mythic mould.

JOHN BOORMAN, 1987

■ Duke [Wayne] and I have a way of gauging how big a man an actor is: how does he get along with the crew? I told Duke that Sean got along fine, so Duke said, 'Well, I reckon he's going to be all right.'

BRUCE CABOT

■ [On turning down James Bond] I'm a big fan of Sean Connery and I knew one thing, I'm the best Burt Reynolds there is; I don't want to be the next best Sean Connery. . . . there'll be an unsophisticated comedy I can do and I'll do it better than Sean, perhaps. But I could never do Bond better than he did.

BURT REYNOLDS, 1973

■ Well I didn't want to use Omar Sharif [in *The Wind and the King*]! Connery is a terrific actor. His Arab speaks with a Scots accent, but we can assume that he was taught English by a Scotsman. He looks very much like an Arab and, in fact, he looks not unlike the Ayatollah.

JOHN MILIUS

■ He doesn't give a damn for the ancillary assets of being a star. It's not that he's ungrateful. It's just that he's concerned with personal integrity. A hell of a lot of people don't like Sean because of this.

TERENCE YOUNG

ELISHA COOK JR (born 1906)

■ Elisha Cook Jr., lived alone up in the High Sierra, tied flies and caught golden trout between films. When he was wanted in Hollywood, they sent word up to his mountain cabin by courier. He would come down, do a picture and then withdraw again to his retreat.

JOHN HUSTON, 1980

GARY COOPER (1901–1961)

■ Coop just likes people, it's as simple as that.

RICHARD ARLEN

■ Coop was a lovely guy. His sense of humour was kind of within. He'd do something he knew was funny. He laughed inwardly. It was a delight! He'd say things, then chuckle within himself. He was wonderful, low-key, like Fred Astaire, an absolute gentleman. These are quality, quality people. They have their own atmosphere about them. Coop's was very laid back and easy.

TAB HUNTER

■ Naturally I never took my eyes off him during the first few weeks of shooting. He was the ideal movie actor . . . There was something unassailable about him, a dignity which he never lost even in the most commonplace pictures.

LILLI PALMER

■ He was a poet of the real.

CLIFFORD ODETS

■ One of the most beloved illiterates this country has ever known.

CARL SANDBURG

■ He was the most gorgeously attractive man. Bright, too, though some people didn't think so.

PATRICIA NEAL

39

■ Gary Cooper was a very interesting, a very complex man. He was not a simple man at all. I think he was one of the best actors film has ever had. I don't think anybody recognised it, even though he won—I think—two Academy awards. Henry Hathaway . . . said: everything Cooper does is original. He thinks about it. You have to watch it to realise what makes Cooper on film.

WENDELL MAYES

■ When I look into his face I can see everything he is thinking. But when I look into my own face I see absolutely nothing. I know what I'm thinking, but it doesn't show.

GRACE KELLY

■ I loved working with Gary Cooper. Gary was my favourite. He was so terrific looking, and so easy to work with.

JEAN ARTHUR, 1977

■ On the screen he's perfect, yet on the set you'd swear that it's the worst job of acting in the history of motion pictures.

SAM WOOD

■ That fellow is the world's greatest actor. He can do, with no effort, what the rest of us spend years trying to learn: to be perfectly natural.

JOHN BARRYMORE

■ One of the nicest human beings I have ever met.

JOSEF VON STERNBERG

■ The most underrated actor I've ever worked with was Gary Cooper. [He] was a gentle man but strong. They're born with these kind of things—Henry Fonda and Jimmy Stewart are born with it, it's nothing they learned in school or experience, except that they learned to

have confidence. Now there's other actors that learn techniques. They're the worst ones.

HENRY HATHAWAY

■ His great power is in his presence. That guy just represents America to me. He's strong, he's able, he's kind, he wouldn't steal a penny from you, but if you cross his path, he'll kill you. Or at least give you a punch in the mouth. This is what America is, I think.

FRANK CAPRA

■ I loved working with Gary Cooper. People refer to Cooperisms and Cooper tricks, but I always found him to be a tremendous actor.

ROBERT PRESTON

■ Gary Cooper was the first actor to believe you didn't have to mug to act, if you thought of what you were doing, it showed—and he proved he was right.

HENRY HATHAWAY

■ For three days I act rings around him. I have him stopped. Against my acting he can do nothing. I have won every scene. So I look at the rushes. On the screen I am there. Everybody else is there. But what do I see? Nothing, that is , but Gary Cooper.

AKIM TAMIROFF

■ And who in Hollywood could pay honest, humble, 'corn tassel poet' Mr Deeds? Only one actor: Gary Cooper. Every line in his face spelled honesty . So innate was his integrity he could be cast in phony parts, but never look phony himself.

FRANK CAPRA

■ Then we shot the scene and I still said to myself, he doesn't do anything. Then

I saw the rushes, and there he was . . . The personality of this man was so enormous, so overpowering—and that expression in his eyes and his face, it was so delicate and so underplayed. You just didn't notice it until you saw it on the screen. I thought he was marvellous: the most underplaying and most natural actor I ever worked with.

INGRID BERGMAN

■ This young Detroit salesman [in *Desire*] singing unmusically as he drives along, hugging himself over his unexpected conquests, smuggling his cigarettes over the frontier in rolled-up socks like all honest men . . . His quiet, informal style takes the Lubitsch suggestion well. Ordinarily too receptive to be a good actor, he becomes a very good actor in the present film by virtue of this malleability.

C. A. LEJEUNE

■ I also remember, . . . meeting Gary Cooper at a party. I was so impressed that I blurted out that all the stars I had met before had been terrific people. Cooper thought about it for a minute, then said: 'Yes, I suppose we are, the ones who are on top. But watch out for the ones who haven't quite made it, or are past it.' It was valuable advice.

ROCK HUDSON

■ Gary Cooper never understood a thing about real acting but had the most marvellous presence.

JOHN CROMWELL, 1969

FRANCIS FORD COPPOLA (born 1939)

■ Whatever Francis does for you always ends up benefitting Francis the most.

GEORGE LUCAS

■ Still, Coppola is a most stirring example of a man purified by success. I have the feeling that after earning another $7 million or so on *Godfather II* he'll make some movies even more difficult and uncompromising than *The Conversation*, and among them will be a work of art satisfying in all its details.

DAVID DENBY

■ Coppola's talented. I'm pissed that he cut a scene that would have given the audience an insight into my character in *Apocalypse Now*, but he's talented.

ROBERT DUVALL, 1983

■ One of the preview cards at the Coronet screening had scribbled on it: 'Francis you can't win 'em all,' But whoever wrote that was wrong. I can.

HIMSELF

■ I think Francis likes to work in chaos, lot of different things happening at once and a certain amount of panic.

NICOLAS CAGE

■ I don't see why this amount [just over $30 million for *Apocalypse Now*] shouldn't be spent on a morality story, when you can spend it on a giant gorilla, a little fairy tale like *The Wiz* or some jerk who flies up in the sky.

HIMSELF

■ The only thing it recalls is the humourless ferocity of an ego bent on making a movie even though there are no characters, no story, no screenplay and no concepts except those relating to technology and style. As a romantic comedy *One from the Heart* is about as frothy as *2001*.

VINCENT CANBY, 1982

■ Francis Ford Coppola is his own worst enemy. He has such dualities in his mind

41

about success and artistry. He equates success with sell-out and doesn't care to remember that nearly all the really good directors became successful. I think it's that arty bunch in San Francisco who tell him he shouldn't have made *The Godfather* films, but should have stuck to little pictures like *The Rain People*.

PETER BOGDANOVICH

■ Coppola couldn't piss in a pot.

BOB HOSKINS

ROGER CORMAN (born 1926)

■ Roger Corman is a master of exploitation. He's a master in two ways: he makes exploitation pictures and he exploits people. But it's a two-way street. People also exploit him: directors who have never directed before, cameramen who have never shot a feature-length film before, actors and actresses who have never acted before.

JON DAVISON

COSTA-GAVRAS (born 1933)

■ Costa-Gavras is more the classic director of the American cinema of John Ford and those people. His films are a little linear, didactic for a character who is so complex and ambiguous. I love him! We all do, we all call him—Nadine, myself—when we're cutting. He can take any film and find ten more minutes to cut.

JEAN-LOUIS TRINTIGNANT

JOSEPH COTTEN (born 1905)

■ I was a so-called star because of my limitations and that was always the case. I couldn't do any accents. So I had to pretend. Luckily I was tall, had curly hair and a good voice. I only had to stamp my foot and I'd play the lead—because I couldn't play character parts.

HIMSELF

■ You're very lucky to be tall and thin and have curly hair. You can also move about the stage without running into the furniture. But these are fringe assets, and I'm afraid you'll never make it as an actor . . . But as a star . . . but as a star, I think you well might hit the jackpot.

ORSON WELLES

TOM COURTENAY (born 1937)

■ Among Mr Courtenay's many qualities is a very contemporary way of wincing, an engaging ability to register the go-getting insanity of others while transmitting his own brand of humourous, life-saving cowardice . . . Courtenay quite leaps at his chance [in *Otley*] wonderfully bewildered, marvellously frightened, superbly and twitchingly unable not to commit small, dire items of repartee.

JOHN COLEMAN, 1969

JEANNE CRAIN (born 1925)

■ I remember Jeanne Crain as a very pleasant, very shy, and very demure young woman, mother, and wife whose husband was doing very well in some business. She was one of the few whose presence among the theatre-folk I have never fully understood.

JOSEPH L. MANKIEWICZ

JOAN CRAWFORD (1904–1977)

■ She was always so arduous and working so hard at everything; at dancing, on her looks, on her speech and on her carriage. She was dedicated to self-improvement.

DOUGLAS FAIRBANKS JR

■ She was very much the star. I think that's a very important thing to remember about her, that she was in command of what she did. Now, if she was not that confident herself, she certainly gave a damned good performance of somebody that was! . . . She *lived* the life of a star. When you walked into her house, it looked as though a star lived there.

ROSALIND RUSSELL

■ My first impression of Joan Crawford was of glamour.

JAMES STEWART

■ When Joan is all by herself in a bathtub, with just a sponge in her hand, she never takes her hair down and becomes a woman. There's no separation between Joan the woman and Joan the movie star. She is the epitome of what every movie fan thinks a movie star should be like.

RADIE HARRIS

■ I don't blame the daughter, don't blame her at all for writing *Mommie Dearest*. She was left without a cent, living in a motor home in Tarzana, and I doubt she could have written this if it weren't true. One area of life Joan should never have gotten into was children. She bought them. . . . Joan was the perfect mother in front of the public but not behind the front door. . . . Well, I doubt that *my* children will write a book.

BETTE DAVIS

■ I knew Joan [Crawford] during those days. Worked with her and was often at parties at her home; pool parties in the afternoon, when the children were there, and I never saw or heard anything that would give me a clue that the stories were true that the daughter wrote. I think whatever is truth about them has been exaggerated so that it makes her more of a monster than she was.

HENRY FONDA

■ Now there's a formidable lady. Her knowledge of the business of the lighting, is something out of this world.

BRUCE CABOT

■ There is not enough money in Hollywood to lure me into making another picture with Joan Crawford. And I like money.

STERLING HAYDEN

■ Joan Crawford won't venture out of her Fifth Avenue apartment to buy an egg unless she is dressed to the teeth.

HEDDA HOPPER

43

■ I think she is a splendid actress, but I'm a little repulsed by her shining lips, like balloon tyres in wet weather.

JOHN BETJEMAN

■ People automatically think that if you're a star your social calendar must be filled weeks in advance. Not so. I remember once, years ago, when I was going through a depression, I phoned Joan Crawford and I said to her, 'Joan, you've been waiting for the phone to ring too, haven't you?' And she said 'Yes'. So I said 'Let's go and have a meal.' She was delighted to do so. And that was the great and glamorous Joan Crawford.

ROD STEIGER

■ This [*Sudden Fear*] was my favourite Crawford: who, subjected to *Torch Song, Woman on the Beach,* or *Johnny Guitar,* at a tender age could ever hope for a complete recovery?

JOHN RUSSELL TAYLOR, 1967

■ When Joan Crawford came to Warners for *Mildred Pierce* she was a monster. Whatever you suggested she fought tooth and nail. . . . I knew she was terrified that her career might be over, and she had no faith in the project. . . . But I knew that the director Michael Curtiz wanted the clothes simple and above all, no shoulder pads! One day, as a special favour, we went to Joan's house for a fitting. When she discovered we hadn't brought any pads, she kicked us out.

MILO ANDERSON

■ Crawford and Davis were perfect pros on the set of *Whatever Happened to Baby Jane?* until 6pm. Then I'd get a call from Joan asking, 'Did you see what that (bleep) did to me today?' A couple of minutes later Bette would call and ask, 'What did that (bleep) call you about?' First one and then the other. I could count on it every night.

ROBERT ALDRICH

■ While Bette is an *actress* through and through, Joan is more a very talented *motion-picture star*. If Bette has an emotional scene she tackles it completely consciously and when you say 'Cut' she might ask 'Do you think that was a little too much this or a little too much that?' But, when Crawford plays an emotional scene, you have to wait twenty minutes until she comes out of it after you have said 'Cut', because she is still crying or laughing or whatever; she's still going.

CURTIS BERNHARDT

■ Up until the night before shooting on the film was due to commence there was a continued harassment about the possibility of her not showing up. I got a call at two o'clock that very night saying that she wouldn't be there unless her writer could attend to which I responded that if her writer showed up we would not shoot. Looking back, I really think that's the only way you can properly deal with Miss Crawford.

ROBERT ALDRICH

■ Three times a week she'd sit down at a desk just to answer the fans' letters. And the consummate movie star, she dressed the part, played it off screen and on, and adored every moment of it. Her (protean) characterisations were something I adored about her that the executives never understood.

JOSEPH L. MANKIEWICZ

■ Working with Davis was my greatest challenge ever, and I mean that kindly, Bette likes to scream and yell and I just sit and knit. During *Baby Jane* I knitted a scarf from Hollywood to Malibu.

HERSELF

■ Oscar Levant was bright, wise-cracking, with a touch of vicious humour, but always brilliant. To Joan Crawford, who knitted continuously while rehearsing, eating, arguing, looking at rushes: 'Do you knit when you fuck?' There were icebergs on the set of *Humouresque* for days.

JEAN NEGULESCO

■ Why do her lips have to be glistening wet? I don't like her smiling to herself . . . her cynical accepting smile has gotten a little tired . . . She cannot fake her bluff.

F.SCOTT FITZGERALD

■ Ever conscious of her star image and her status (to the point of sometimes lapsing into the royal 'we') Miss Crawford can sound like she's perused too many Reader's Digests, but she's no slouch in the salesmanship department either.

ADDISON VERRILL

■ We made this film, [*What Ever Happened to Baby Jane*] Joan and I in three weeks, that's all the money they would give us to make it with. And Joan one day suggested that we should put up on the set a sign that said, 'With this schedule we haven't got time not to get along'.

BETTE DAVIS

■ [In *Sudden Fear*] after a relentless succession of hard-baked films and shadowy heroines the gargantuan-scale art of Miss Crawford represents, to me at least in these hard times, a good satisfactory evening out at the cinema.

RICHARD WINNINGTON, 1952

■ Poor old rotten egg Joan. I kept my mouth shut about her for nearly a quarter of a century, but she was a mean, tipsy, powerful, rotten-egg lady. I'm still not going to tell what she did to me. Other people have written some of it, but they don't know it all, and they never will because I am a very nice person and I don't like to talk about the dead even if they were rotten eggs.

MERCEDES McCAMBRIDGE

LAIRD CREGAR (1916–1944)

■ His general features inconsistent with the general mold of the fashionable leading man, he was invariably cast as a fiend. Time and time again, Laird would go in and ask the make-up man what fantastic distortions of his face would be

required. The make-up man would invariably answer, 'We want you just as you are, Mr Cregar.'

GEORGE SANDERS

BING CROSBY (1904–1977)

■ Bing Crosby sings like all people think they sing in the shower.

DINAH SHORE

■ Bing Crosby has switched his batting technique (or had it switched for him) in this latest film *Going My Way*. And— would you believe it?—old Bing is giving the best show of his career.

BOSLEY CROWTHER, 1944

■ Crosby's golfer image is entirely appropriate to a man who never seemed to miss the fairway and whose enduring success has more to do with his faultless swing than with physical commitment.

FREDERIC RAPHAEL

■ He was a tough guy. Make one wrong move and he'd never speak to you again.

PHIL HARRIS

■ A lot of people think that Bing was a loner, but Bing was a very loyal friend.

BOB HOPE

■ As I look back, I think he was a very shy, insecure man. The world looked upon him as one of the great talents, he just never saw himself in that light.

DOROTHY LAMOUR

■ I've never met anyone in the profession who was so unconcerned about his work. I don't mean he was unprofessional. Quite the contrary. It's just that once he finished a movie or a performance, that was that. He *never* watched his old movies on TV, always preferring to look at a baseball match instead.

MARY CROSBY

■ He stays in his room when he is working on a new number or planning a show. The casual air is deceptive. He is relaxed but not lazy.

KATHRYN GRANT CROSBY, 1976

■ We worshipped him. What he thought was everything. Of course, he was away a lot on location. Sometimes we didn't see him for months. But when he was home it was like my whole world was there. He was tremendously sensitive and he cared deeply. He just had a rough time showing it.

GARY CROSBY

■ I'd always longed to do a musical and. of course, working with Bing Crosby and Frank Sinatra was simply marvellous. They create a certain excitement and are two very strong personalities. So it was fascinating for me to be in the middle—watching the tennis match go back and forth from one to another with tremendous wit and humour—each one trying to outdo the other.

GRACE KELLY

■ The best way to get along with Bing was to forget first of all that he was Bing Crosby. It was not always easy.

ROSEMARY CLOONEY, 1978

■ Bing had a brilliant mind and an original wit. That casual delivery combined with an unexpectedly wide vocabulary. It was a great device for comedy—and also an effective way of communicating with an audience or with a person.

ROSEMARY CLOONEY

TOM CRUISE (born 1962)

■ He's got a lot of actor's courage. He doesn't mind climbing up there and jumping off. It's nice to watch that.

PAUL NEWMAN, 1987

■ A magnet for women.

TONY SCOTT

GEORGE CUKOR (1899–1983)

■ We were deep into shooting *Gone with the Wind* and very happy with director George Cukor's sensitive approach. But Gable . . . was aching for Victor Fleming, to whom he could relate: Fleming was a man's man . . . Cukor was interested in costumes and jewellery and hairstyles . . . Finally, one horrible afternoon, Gable . . . shouted furiously, 'Fuck this! I want to be directed by a man!' Everybody froze. . . . Cukor stood there trembling and finally made a clumsy, shattered exit. It was obvious that Cukor was finished on this picture.

LEE GARMES

■ He has the ability to make me trust myself.

KATHARINE HEPBURN

■ Mr Cukor is a hard task-master, a fine director and he took me over the coals giving me the roughest time I have ever had. And I am eternally grateful.

JOAN CRAWFORD

■ I learned more about acting from George [while working in *The Women*] than anyone else and through just one sentence. He said, 'Think and feel and the rest will take care of itself.'

JOAN FONTAINE

■ Give me a good script and I'll be a hundred times better as a director.

HIMSELF

TONY CURTIS (born 1925)

■ The stars had this neurosis which goes right to the edge. You have somehow to use this to get performances from these deep-sea monsters. There was this enormous difference between [Lancaster] and Tony Curtis. Tony had a fantastic vanity, but no ego. He could act Burt off the screen, but he will never be a star. He hasn't this granite quality of ego.

ALEXANDER MACKENDRICK

■ A curious combination of the sheikh and the 60s style of star.

PETER EVANS

■ . . . this girl Pamela Mumford was talking about this bloke she fancied who had a Tony Curtis hair-do and telling us how his hair fell in a grease–and–water laden plume in front of his forehead. And all I could think for weeks was oh! that I might have a Tony Curtis so that Pamela Mumford would fancy me too.

RAY CONNELLY

■ Tony Curtis is the white rabbit of show business: always in a hurry.

RODERICK MANN

■ Because I didn't really have a relationship with him he couldn't let me down. I just happened to be one of the last people who hadn't been disappointed too many times. For years I didn't know who Tony Curtis was as much as other people told me who he was.

JAMIE LEE CURTIS

■ I'm not knocking Tony, but he is a pain in the neck to work with. He's such a perfectionist. But I guess it's a very serious picture [*The Boston Strangler*] and the clothes couldn't be handled by just buying a green zipper jacket.

WILLIAM TRAVILLA

■ . . . Tony Curtis was marvellous to work with on *Where is Parsifal?* I'd heard he could be difficult. He was charming, and completely professional. Dressed in a white suit and cowboy hat, for post-synching!, he removed his stetson and gazed at his image on the screen 'What a finely-shaped head', he said to no-one in particular.

TONY SLOMAN

MICHAEL CURTIZ (1888–1962)

■ He was a tyrant, he was abusive he was cruel. Oh, he was just a villain but I guess he was pretty good. We didn't believe it then, but he clearly was. He knew what he was doing. He knew how to tell a story very clearly and he knew how to keep things going.

OLIVIA DE HAVILLAND

■ This [*The Egyptian*] was one of the first films in CinemaScope and he was fascinated with the new process. 'In de nex' shot, you coom from house visper in de ear otter actor secret.'—I went up to Purdom and whispered something in his ear. Curtiz yelled 'Cut!' This was puzzling because I had done exactly as he asked. 'No goot. Dis is Zinemascop, vide shkreen—ven you visper muss be four feet apart.'

PETER USTINOV

- I would normally have been a character actor, but Mike Curtiz gave me the screen personality that carried me to stardom.

  JOHN GARFIELD

- His accent is legend. He used to call Bing 'Binkie', and it was hilarious to hear him call out, 'Binkie, give me one more take.' He said to me one time—I was sitting on a windowsill in a scene— 'Could you give me a little off balance?'

  ROSEMARY CLOONEY, 1978

TIMOTHY DALTON (born 1944)

- I hope he's got a good lawyer.

  SEAN CONNERY, 1987

BEBE DANIELS (1901–1971)

48

- She's a wonderful individual and I can understand why she's tremendously revered in this country [Great Britain]. She's very warm-hearted, and she has a habit of giving—never lost it!

  HAROLD LLOYD, 1970

LINDA DARNELL (1921–1965)

- Experienced, beautiful and nice—a nice person.

  CORNEL WILDE, 1984

- Linda Darnell is the most unspoilt star on the screen—and also the most beautiful.

  KIRK DOUGLAS, 1949

DANIELLE DARRIEUX (born 1917)

- There is an American word that I like very much 'professional' when they said that I was a great 'pro' I considered it the most beautiful compliment that could be paid to me in my career.

  HERSELF

JULES DASSIN (born 1911)

- He has had his good periods, and his lesser ones. He is a good man and that is rare. He has sacrificed a lot to his political beliefs and to me. If he hasn't made many films recently, it's because he devoted himself to the Greek cause and me.

  MELINA MERCOURI

MARION DAVIES (1897–1961)

- I adored her. She was one of the few movie stars who was completely generous, thoughtful of others, unpretentious. She had nothing to gain—she didn't want to be a movie-star, he wanted her to be one, he wanted to show her off. But you see, she took his own viewpoint of himself—she thought he was the great man he thought he was himself. He considered he rated with Napoleon and Gladstone and all the great political figures. So you see it was ideal! She just considered him a very, very great man. On the other hand she had no pretensions—her pet name for him was Droopy Drawers.

  ANITA LOOS

- We began her first picture, *Page Miss Glory*, with considerable misgivings. To make matters worse, Marion fell in love with her costar, Dick Powell. He was a promising juvenile, while Hearst was one of the most powerful men in the country. We persuaded Dick to cool his ardour.

After *Page Miss Glory,* we made *Hearts Divided* with Marion. Neither picture did very well. Marion continued drinking and behind her laughter and gaiety she was a very tragic figure.

HAL WALLIS

BETTE DAVIS (born 1908)

■ My bloody idol.

GEORGE C. SCOTT

■ The greatest actress of all time.

JAMES MASON

■ I loved working with her.

JOSEPH COTTEN, 1970

■ I never know how to react [when people stare at me]. The right way is the way Bette Davis does it. I saw her in a hotel in Madrid once and went up to her and said: 'Miss Davis, I'm Ava Gardner and I'm a great fan of yours.' And you know she behaved exactly as I wanted her to behave. 'Of course you are my dear,' she said 'of course you are'. And then she swept on.

AVA GARDNER

■ Barbara Stanwyck sent me a letter when I signed to direct *'Now Voyager'* 'Dear Irving. You are going to do a picture with Bette Davis. Don't you know there are such things as fresh air and sunshine?'

IRVING RAPPER

■ I even found Bette Davis attractive, when I played Maximilian to her Carlotta [in *Juarez*] and, brillant actress though she is, surely nobody but a mother could have loved Bette Davis at the height of her career.

BRIAN AHERNE

■ Bette Davis taught Hollywood to follow an actress instead of the actress following the camera and she's probably the best movie actress there's ever been.

ELAINE STRITCH

■ The two stars didn't fight at all on *What Ever Happpened to Baby Jane?* There was never an abrasive word in public and not once did they try to upstage each other. Nor did Miss Davis allow her enmity with Miss Crawford to colour her playing of the scenes in which she was supposed to torment her. They both behaved in a wonderfully professional manner.

ROBERT ALDRICH

■ And Jack always took the side of the director. He'd say: 'You are the captain, you run the ship. The authority is yours. I hold you responsible for the actors coming in on time and everything else.' In the case of Bette it was a little different. When Warner heard that Bette wanted to see him, he turned white.

CURTIS BERNHARDT

■ It is always a great pleasure to work with an actress who is so professional. She is eager to do a good job; you never have to tell her what a scene was about—you just have to calm her down once in a while and keep her from becoming over-enthusiastic.

WILLIAM WYLER

■ Margo Channing [in *All About Eve*] became Davis's greatest acting triumph, Margo was vain, vehement and temperamental by turn. Part and player seemed one. Davis had the film's best lines and knew instinctively what to do with them. Her performance bears the true mark of a champion.

HOMER DICKENS

49

- Her performance in *Of Human Bondage* was wickedly good . . . and even the most inconsiderable films seemed temporarily better than they were because of that precise nervy voice, the pale ash-blonde hair, the popping neurotic eyes, a kind of corrupt and phosphorescent prettiness.

  GRAHAM GREENE

- I learnt more from watching Bette Davis than anyone else.

  GEORGE C. SCOTT

- I am fascinated by fearless, courageous women. She was the first woman who challenged the old Hollywood system of packaging and gift wrapping the goods in the way *they* wanted and not the way you might like it.

  FAYE DUNAWAY

- She was Queen Elizabeth and I was Sir Walter Raleigh in *The Virgin Queen*. She was always first on the set, knew her lines, knew exactly what she was doing and never needed extra takes. We enjoyed each other.

  RICHARD TODD, 1987

- You're the luckiest of us all. You started playing older women when you were young. So you never had to bridge the gap.

  CLAUDETTE COLBERT

- When Bette's good, she's real good. When she's bad, she's awful . . . but at least she's not afraid to bat an eyelash.

  JOAN BLONDELL

- When I went to Hollywood to appear with Bette Davis in *Dark Victory*, I was warned about her—she'll upstage you, etc. She couldn't have been more helpful.

  GERALDINE FITZGERALD

- For Bette Davis I wear my diamonds.

  ANNA MAGNANI

- All she had going for her was her talent.

  DAVID ZINMAN

- What a wonderful, wonderful actress Bette is. She's made such a great contribution to our business . . . Bette is a fascinating, warm, considerate person, and during *Right of Way* whe was absolutely exhilarating from the first to the last day.

  JAMES STEWART

- Whatever Bette had chosen to do in life she would have had to be the top or she couldn't have endured it.

  GARY MERRILL

- By the pure power of imaginative acting she gives a performance as vivid and inspiring as any star display of personality—on a infinitely deeper level of truth. [In *Jezebel* she] truimphantly proved her point that a woman's face can be appealing and moving even when not preserved in peach-like perfection.

  FREDA BRUCE LOCKHART

- Seldom has Miss Davis been more mannered than she is here [in *Mrs Skeffington*]. There is not, I imagine, a single pose or gesture, or trick of speech in her performance that has not been laboriously worked out and worked over. Nothing I should say, comes from the heart; everything from the shrewd, lively brain. This is a triumph. not of art but artifice, but it is none the less a triumph.

  C. A. LEJEUNE, 1945

- I'll never forget Bette Davis. She sent me a bowl of gardenias on the first day's shooting of [the remake of] *Of Human*

50

Bondage, with a note stating she hoped the role would do as much for my career as it did for hers.

ELEANOR PARKER

■ I was riveted by Bette Davis who was a marvellous teacher.

PAUL SCOFIELD

■ And we've got some great actresses, too. Miss Jane Fonda, Shirley MacLaine. Bette Davis is now a freak-out—oh well I guess she's always been a freak-out.

TENNESSEE WILLIAMS

■ She was still totally in command, knew exactly what she was doing and precisely how [*The Anniversary*] had to be altered to suit her. I did eventually pluck up the courage to go over and congratulate her on a scene towards the end of the shooting, and she seemed genuinely touched; she said up to then the highest compliment she'd heard on the set was 'Print it'.

SHELIA HANCOCK

■ The great lesson I learned from Bette was her absolute dedication to getting everything just right. She used to spend hours studying the character she was going to play, then hours in make-up ensuring that her physical appearance was right for the part. I have always tried to put the same amount of work into everything I've done.

OLIVIA DE HAVILLAND

■ Bette Davis was and is every inch a lady—polite, mannerly, gracious, even self-effacing. I know it's goatish of me to say it, but Miss Davis was, when I played with her [in *Kid Galahad*], not a very gifted amateur and employed any number of jarring mannerisms that she used to form an image. In her early period

Miss Davis played the image, and not herself, and certainly not the character provided by the author.

EDWARD G. ROBINSON

■ Now Davis is a tough old broad and you fight. But when you see what she puts on the screen you know that it was worth taking all the bull.

ROBERT ALDRICH, 1976

■ Until you're known in my profession as a monster you're not a STAR. Don't smile at this, it's a very serious point; I've never been a monster, I've never fought for anything in a treacherous way. I've never fought for anything except for the good of the film and not always for just what I was doing in it.

HERSELF

■ When they offered me that part opposite her, I didn't want to do it. I thought, ... what if all my illusions were broken? But I couldn't resist the temptation ... she's no pussycat—she's just a great and independent artist and I loved every minute working with her.

GENA ROWLANDS, 1980

DORIS DAY (born 1924)

■ The only real talent Miss Day possesses is that of being absolutely sanitary: her personality untouched by human emotions, her brow unclouded by human thought, her form unsmudged by the slightest evidence of femininity ... until this spun-sugar zombie melts from our screen there is little chance of the American film's coming of age.

JOHN SIMON, 1964

■ Doris Day is a dear girl, a kind girl, and a Christian Scientist. We used to hold

51

what amounted to Christian Science sessions on the set (or so it seemed to me), when all the lights would be put out and the director could be heard telling Doris *sotto voce* 'God is in the studio, God is in the flowers, God is on the set . . .' At which point I would wander away and sit down to ponder life and death.

REX HARRISON, 1974

■ That face that she shows the world—smiling, only talking good, happy, tuned into God—as far as I'm concerned, that's just a mask. I haven't a clue as to what's underneath. Doris is just about the remotest person I know.

KIRK DOUGLAS

■ I loved working with her. We used to call her Miss Sparkle Plenty because she was so vivacious.

VIRGINIA MAYO

52

■ She thinks she doesn't get old. She told me once it was her cameraman who was getting older. She wanted me to fire him.

JOSEPH PASTERNAK

■ Doris has an unerring instinct as to her moves, motives and impact . . . She also has impeccable comedic timing; which is the quality I most admire in a performer. To play with her is elevating. She makes you want to give all you've got to a scene, to rise to her level. I also feel that Doris has an enticing sexual quality that is there but subliminally.

JACK LEMMON

■ When I think about all the performers I've been associated with over the course of my 50-odd years [in showbusiness], when I think about natural talent I'd have

to rate ladies at the forefront—Doris Day and Judy Garland.

BOB HOPE

■ It's true that Doris can come on strong but, like most people who come on strong, what she's really saying is 'Help me.' And if you help her, everythings just fine.

ROCK HUDSON

■ What a comedienne she is! The trouble we had was trying not to laugh. Doris and I couldn't look at each other. You know, that sweet agony of laughing when you're not supposed to? That's what we had. The second film we made together, *Lover Come Back*, was even worse. I think they added two weeks to the shooting schedule because of our laughter.

ROCK HUDSON

■ I have nothing but the best to say about Doris Day. She was wonderful to me, really lovely. She sent flowers when I started and remained friendly and attentive. As I've said, it's difficult when you start stepping down. You fight so hard to get to the top and then you realise it's time to gracefully give in a little. Doris, who was riding high then, never played the prima dona. I appreciated her attitude enormously.

MYRNA LOY

JAMES DEAN (1931–55)

■ Dean was so real. I believed he was the real person, that he wasn't acting . . . See I never thought Rock Hudson was real. Or any of the guys in the forefront then—Gregory Peck, Paul Newman and them.

BRUCE DERN

I had realised that, for a successful collaboration, he needed a special kind of climate. He needed reassurance, tolerance, understanding.

NICHOLAS RAY

A cult following . . . developed for James Dean, whose actual stardom lasted— from the premiere of *East of Eden* to his fatal car crash—only 5 months and 20 days.

HARRY HAUN

We never became lovers, but we could have—like that.

SAL MINEO

The conflict between giving himself and fear of giving in to his own feelings . . . a vulnerability so deeply embedded that one is instantly moved, almost disturbed by it.

NICHOLAS RAY

This [*Rebel Without a Cause*] is the first time in the history of motion pictures that a 24-year-old boy, with only one movie to his credit, was practically the co-director.

JIM BACKUS, 1955

I don't mean to speak ill of the dead, but he was a prick. Pardon my French. He was selfish and petulant, and believed his own press releases. On the set, he'd upstage an actor and step on his lines. Arrogant. But let him alone and he was brilliant. Nobody could touch him.

ROCK HUDSON

Jimmy was the most talented and original actor I ever saw work. He was also a guerrilla artist who attacked all restrictions on his sensibility. Once he pulled a switchblade and threatened to murder his director. I imitated his style in art and in life. It got me in a lot of trouble.

DENNIS HOPPER

He seems to have become a sort of cult now, but not one that has much to do with the reality of who he was. I've never understood why people get together to keep alive the memory of a dead actor: he was gifted, sure and exciting and wonderful to work with, but there was also a terrific neurosis there.

JULIE HARRIS

All in all, it was a hell of a headache to work with him.

GEORGE STEVENS

Dean was a curious guy, very much a loner. I remember I had a very heavy tripod that I was using with a View camera . . . Jimmy . . . would go out on Sundays to shoot pictures . . . He asked me—quietly—if he could borrow my tripod and I said yes. So, he would always co-operate with me, but was very hostile to everybody else.

RUSS MEYER

Dean's body was very graphic; it was almost writhing in pain sometimes. He was very twisted, . . . as if he were cringing all the time. . . . Dean *was* a cripple anyway, inside—he was not like Brando. People compared them, but there was no similarity. He was a far, far sicker kid, and Brando's not sick, he's just troubled.

ELIA KAZAN

Dean is still alive. All young actors tend to think of Dean as something they've just discovered. He's always been around. He always will—and he'll always

53

be young. That's the reason we all relate to him.

DENNIS QUAID

■ Maybe he's lucky he died when he did. I saw *East of Eden* the other night. His performance now is so stereotyped. All the bad imitations have destroyed James Dean. But when you see Brando in that famous cab scene in *On the Waterfront*, that's still breathtaking.

ANTHONY HOPKINS

■ No, when I finally met Dean it was at a party, where he was throwing himself around, acting the madman. So I spoke to him ... He listened to me. He knew he was sick. I gave him the name of an analyst, and he went. At least his *work* improved.

MARLON BRANDO

54

GLORIA DE HAVEN (born 1924)

■ [On being rivals]. No, not at all. We were just kids. Gloria and I were friends, and we're still best friends today—my husband and I were recently on a cruise with her, she's a lovely woman. But you never realise that you have become a star, you don't really know what that is. You just report for work at the studio each day.

JUNE ALLYSON

OLIVIA DE HAVILLAND (born 1916)

■ We're getting closer together as we get older, but there would be a slight problem of temperament. In fact, it would be bigger than Hiroshima.

JOAN FONTAINE

■ If ever there was a born actress it is Olivia de Havilland. Her diction is superb. She can deliver a line with any inflection a director wants, as accurately as if it were played on a piano.

MERVYN LE ROY

■ Olivia de Havilland is a lady of rapturous loveliness and well worth fighting for.

ANDRE SENNWALD

■ Her face was so beautiful, all I could do was stand and stare.

ERNIE PYLE

■ Olivia was wonderful in *To Each His Own*. Nobody else could have played it as well as she did, to be so beautiful and innocent in the beginning, then grow to be a bitch and finally the lonely Miss Norris. Olivia is a very flexible actress. She listens to what you have to say, and she will do her best to do it as you want it.

MITCHELL LEISEN

CECIL B. DEMILLE (1881–1959)

■ His handling of crowds, masses of people, his organisation ability was fantastic; but I don't think he knew a damn thing about acting. He couldn't tell you the first word about how to play a scene. Never did. He set it up camera-wise, you see, and there is nothing you can do but read the lines and go to the spots he tells you to go.

RAY MILLAND

■ He was no director. He didn't know what to tell us. I think the only man DeMille ever envied was Hitler. His early work is often suprisingly intimate, even delicate and in the case of a satirical comedy like *Why Change your Wife?*, full of delightful

sly wit which pre-dates Lubitsch's
American comedies by several years.

JOHN GILBERT

- Cecil B. DeMille
rather against his will,
was persuaded to leave Moses
out of *The Wars of the Roses*.

NICHOLAS BENTLEY

- I was very fond of him. I never saw him
direct an actor; his speciality was the
camera. He simply hired the best actors
he could get and let them do their job.
He didn't interfere with them unless
something was drastically wrong.
DeMille's speciality was the camera, the
pageantry.

JOHN CARRADINE

CATHERINE DENEUVE (born 1943)

- Catherine is modest and reserved. As an
actress she is overwhelmingly sincere—
I can assure you, she reduced us all to
tears more than once. She was
wonderful. But the moment I said 'Cut'
she would forget the despair and start
talking about something else—she knew
anything else would have mortified me.
Catherine Deneuve gave herself body
and soul to this film—she gave it
everything she had.

NADINE TRINTIGNANT

- Soon my shy adolescent had blossomed
out into a hard-headed woman
ruthlessly in control of her own life.

ROGER VADIM

- At the beginning . . . not an extraordinary
actress. But she has become a formidable
one, subtle, full of nuance, sensitive,
intelligent. I love working with her.

JEAN-LOUIS TRINTIGNANT

ROBERT DE NIRO (born 1943)

- To me he is a hero in many respects, and
when you meet him and you know him
a bit, he's a simple, honest and
honourable man. So I said 'Just be
yourself'. This was terrifying for him. He
actually tried to make the part [in *Brazil*]
more difficult than was necessary. All I
could do was try and make him
comfortable and confident, so that he
could be closer to himself.

TERRY GILLIAM, 1985

- Mystique, in partnership with
romanticism, has always been a key
component of stardom but there is a
calculated mystique about De Niro that
undermines romance. De Niro is too
volatile and self-absorbed for that. He is
the negative side of stardom but he's a
great actor and a brilliant technician.

ADRIAN TURNER

55

- And even now I still know of nobody
who can suprise me on the screen the
way he does—and did then. No actor
comes to mind who can provide such
power and excitement.

MARTIN SCORSESE, 1987

- He's very low key and concentrated
when he's working. The thing that gets
in the way of his work is people staring
at him. So what you have to do on the
set when he's working is to get people
who are just going to gawk out of his
eyeline. With the other actors he's very
tuned, very responsive.

BRIAN DE PALMA, 1987

- I like him. There's often this tendency
with actors when they're asked to play a
villainous part to send little signals to the
audience that say, 'I'm not really like

this,' De Niro doesn't. He knows it's a performance, so he can be as villainous as the part calls for. He appears very little in the film [*The Untouchables*] but you always know he's there.

SEAN CONNERY

■ Sure, a class-A bastard. After the sneak preview in San Francisco, Bobby said to me in the car, 'I don't mind being a bastard, as long as I'm an interesting bastard'.

LIZA MINNELLI

■ Bobby needs somebody to watch over him. He doesn't even know enough to wear a coat in the wintertime. When we did *Bloody Mama* he didn't even know how much money they were paying him. I found out how little it was and insisted they at least give him some expense money.

SHELLEY WINTERS, 1975

■ The thing is, De Niro has made very few errors in any of his choices. That burden weighs heavily on him each time he has to decide what to do. Certainly, he's extremely careful with someone like Roland Joffe or myself, directors he hasn't worked with before.

ALAN PARKER

■ I can never recognise him from one movie to the next, so I never know who he is. To me he's just an invisible man. He doesn't exist.

TRUMAN CAPOTE

■ De Niro has shown me only kindness. He's a real friend. He's helped me shop for my wife's and my kid's Christmas presents. He's invited me round to meet his granny and he's come to my house for a pot-luck dinner. That really knocked

56

my wife out. I think she was finally impressed with me.

BOB HOSKINS

■ He is a Method actor. I think it would be fair to say he's much slower than I am. As a man, Bob dislikes making a decision. And acting is a whole line of decisions. You make a decision everytime you play a line—do I play it like this or like that? . . . But what I saw was a man trying many areas and now and again something would *really* work.

JEREMY IRONS, 1986

SANDY DENNIS (born 1937)

■ The part [in *Who's Afraid of Virginia Woolf?*] calls for a simple, dull girl who gradually uncovers a cache of hysteria, only to revert to superficial wholesomeness again. Miss Dennis acts, from beginning to end, demented, but demented in the most simperingly phoney way, so that the always tenuous boundary between the worst kind of method acting and raving madness disappears altogether.

JOHN SIMON

BRIAN DE PALMA (born 1941)

■ I have a reputation as an action director because I know how to kill, how to shoot people, how to spill blood.

HIMSELF

■ Mr De Palma has made a career out of ripping off Hitchcock and he has been treated much more kindly than Hitchcock was in his last days.

I. A. L. DIAMOND

- De Palma can't make movies about sex or ones that tackle 'serious' issues or themes because narrative trickery and manipulative dexterity are his almost exclusive concerns. As with much of the work of Steven Spielberg, his movies come at you on the surface and they tend to resonate there as well.

  ANDREW RISSIK

GERARD DEPARDIEU (born 1948)

- Fills the space like a young Marlon Brando. He has an extraordinary intensity.

  BERNARDO BERTOLUCCI, 1975

VITTORIO DE SICA (1902–1974)

- He was somebody who wanted to make life a 24-hour pleasure.

  MANUEL PUIG

- Probably, then, the qualities which set Vittorio de Sica apart even from his brilliant fellow Italian directors are his respect for the instinctive human dignities and honesty in refusing to disguise the hopelessness of poverty.

  MARGARET HINXMAN, 1949

- Yes I liked *Bicycle Thieves*, but even that, is it not a bit . . . a bit literary as it sees the world?

  LUIS BUÑUEL

- *Bicycle Thieves* is a good picture. I like very much. But some concession to sentimentality. A little concession. *Umberto D* never. Nothing. Without compromise. But it was too early. Many pictures of mine this way. Now is a great success. Then, nothing. Oh, a little. The intelligentsia accept *Umberto D*. But the

audience—no, nothing. Too early. Too early.

HIMSELF, 1971

MARLENE DIETRICH (born 1901)

- There was an impressive poise about her (not natural as it turned out, for she was an exuberant blubber when not restrained) that made me certain that she would lend a classic stature to the turmoil the woman in my film would have to create. Here was not only a model . . . designed by Rops, but Toulouse-Lautrec would have turned a couple of handsprings had he laid eyes on her.

  JOSEF VON STERNBERG

- You won't believe it but the lady is extremely funny.

  MAXIMILIAN SCHELL, 1985

- Not only do I think the lady speaks a little less than the absolute truth, but I consign her protests to the suspect file, along with her professed contempt for her film career.

  JACK TINKER, 1978

- In your voice we hear the voice of the Lorelei; in your look, the Lorelei turns to us. But the Lorelei was a danger, to be feared. You are not; because the secret of your beauty lies in the care of your loving kindness of the heart. This care of the heart is what holds you higher than elegance, fashion or style: higher even than your fame, your courage, your bearing, your films, your songs.

  JEAN COCTEAU

- The more she talks the more you begin to respect Garbo. When she had nothing more to say, she got the hell out of town. But Dietrich plunged on, sewing herself

57

into tortuous gowns and singing the same old songs ... now she's bored, humourless and cranky.

REX REED, 1973

■ I dined with Princess Margaret and Tony *and* Marlene! A curious evening. I didn't feel exactly a warm glow between the two ladies.

NOËL COWARD

■ She has an honesty and a comic and tragic sense of life that never lets her be truly happy unless she loves. When she loves she can joke about it, but it is a gallows humour.

ERNEST HEMINGWAY

■ Marlene, the most glamorous of all, she was also one of the kindest.

DAVID NIVEN

■ She's devoid of graciousness; she's rude to everybody. She's hard of hearing. She's got an old lady's stoop. She insults nearly everybody who gets near her. She's a complainer; she's impossible to satisfy. I think she behaves like an idiot. ... She gets more mileage on less talent than anyone I know.

EARL WILSON

■ One afternoon Dutchy invited Bianca [his mother] to her cabin, offered her a glass of champagne and showed her a book on lesbian lovemaking ... 'In Europe it doesn't matter if you're a man or a woman' Marlene explained, 'We make love with anyone we find attractive'.

BUDD SCHULBERG

■ Most women, according to an old joke, have gender but no sex. With Dietrich the opposite is very close to the truth. She has sex, but no particular gender.

Her ways are mannish: the characters she plays love power and wear slacks, and they never have headaches or hysterics. They are also quite undomesticated. Dietrich's masculinity appeals to women, and her sexuality to men.

KENNETH TYNAN

■ I always thought that I was a very bad actress. Everyone says that it [*The Blue Angel*] is my best film, that that's what I did best, that I was perfect in it, and it's thanks to that that I'll be remembered, but I've always thought it very mediocre.

HERSELF

MATT DILLON (born 1964)

■ I wasn't sure if I was going to encounter a teen idol or a professional, but I'm happy to report that Matt is a professional. He's very dedicated, very conscientious. He is very concerned about being a good actor and I think he's going to be around for a long time.

RICHARD CRENNA, 1986

WALT DISNEY (1901–1966)

■ Of all the studios in Hollywood, it was Walt Disney's where the workers had to go on strike. Disney himself is a charming fellow; ... and he is operating what is by Hollywood standards a sweatshop ... to think he can be the magician who makes ten million children laugh and wonder, and at the same time employ men who can't be sure the kids of their own will have the good clothes to go to school.

OTIS FERGUSON

■ Too many people grow up. That's the real trouble with the world, too many

58

people grow up. They forget. They don't remember what it's like to be 12 years old. They patronise, they treat children as inferiors. Well I won't do that.

HIMSELF

■ He was one of the great innovators in film. One of the things I liked was—when talkies came in, a lot of the timing of silent films went out of the window and nobody made those marvellous slapstick comedies any more because there were only verbal jokes. But Disney kept on making those wonderful cartoons for at least another ten years so he kept the whole idea of film comedy and narrative through image alive. People don't realise that they owe an enormous lot to him.

MICHAEL POWELL

ROBERT DONAT (1905–1958)

■ Robert Donat's performance [in *The Citadel*] is absolutely magnificent. It is an obvious comparison to compare him with Paul Muni; for the selfless absorption in the part which they both achieve is one of the major necessities of the cinema at its best. Donat is absolutely convincing from beginning to end, and the Muni comparison becomes all the more apt when we see him defending his faith before the Medical Council—the same sort of greatness, the same sureness of purpose.

BASIL WRIGHT, 1939

■ He is the only actor I have ever known who had a graph of his character development charted out on the wall of his dressing room.

KING VIDOR, 1973

■ Robert was a very complex personality— but a very simple man, if you understand.

But how can you describe someone you were so close to?

RENEE ASHERSON

■ This [in *Goodbye Mr Chips*] is the most magnificent performance I've ever seen on any screen. Not a false motion—not a wasted gesture. He is the greatest actor we have today.

PAUL MUNI

■ Donat says that the five greatest performers, in his opinion, are Charlie Chaplin, Spencer Tracey, Paul Muni, Greta Garbo and Deanna Durbin.

ED SULLIVAN

■ Robert Donat was one of the greatest actors of his generation, and probably the most unlucky. The gods gave him every grace and every gift but one, good health.

CAMPBELL DIXON

59

KIRK DOUGLAS (born 1916)

■ Kirk would be the first to tell you he's a difficult man. I would be the second.

BURT LANCASTER, 1987

■ Kirk was civil to me and that's about all. But then Kirk never makes much of an effort toward anyone else. He's pretty wrapped up in himself. The film I made with Kirk, *Young Man With a Horn* was one of the few utterly joyless experiences I had in films.

DORIS DAY

■ A lithe, barrel-chested six-footer who impressed me enormously. He has a jauntiness, a self-confident grace that commanded attention . . . I went backstage to talk to him. I found him quiet, softspoken, but bursting with energy and animal magnetism.

HAL B. WALLIS

■ We both came from, sort of, well, shall we say, humble beginnings. We were both young, brash, cocky, arrogant. We knew everything, were highly opinionated. We were invincible. Nobody liked us.

BURT LANCASTER

■ Kirk Douglas, he's tough too; the people who *are* good, are the ones that can be difficult. I remember one day we had to stop filming on *The War Wagon* to do a special promo film with Wayne when Ronald Reagan was standing for Governor. Kirk, at that time was a Democrat, I think that now Kirk is a Reagan-man.

BURT KENNEDY, 1985

60

■ I don't mean to sound like I studied humility with Kirk Douglas, but most of the stunt films that I've done I think will hold up, and it'll be long after I'm out of the business.

BURT REYNOLDS

■ He fits into being an advertising man and a driving, ruthless person better than Brando could have. You would always suspect Brando. Kirk's awfully bright. He's as bright a person as I've met in the acting profession.

ELIA KAZAN

■ Virtue is not photogenic. What is it to be a nice guy? To be nothing, that's what. A big fat zero with a smile for everybody.

HIMSELF

■ Boastful, egotistical, resentful of criticism.

SHEILAH GRAHAM

■ In this film [*The Vikings*] every day I did a large number of action scenes and reaction shots. But something bothered me: the cameras always seemed a good way off and Douglas somehow managed to find himself in close-up. When the film came out, I was so far away I had difficulty recognising myself. Alone Douglas's smile had the right to the close-ups.

ERNEST BORGNINE

MICHAEL DOUGLAS (born 1944)

■ He's full of charm and humour, but don't ever cross him! He's a very strong man— with the accent on strong—and had to claw his way out from under his father's giant shadow. I was glad that he didn't direct at the same time ... As it was, I really had his attention when we were in the mud together, deep in the Mexican jungle.

KATHLEEN TURNER, 1985

■ I alway wondered why I never saw on film what I saw for real. He's a vulnerable man, but he always played macho. In this he plays a loser and it was a real conflict for him to reveal that vulnerability. He kept saying—'Lemme *do* something!'

ADRIAN LYNE, 1988

■ It's great to play a part which they compare to the best your father's done. I'm a tremendous fan of his; he's got 12 performances that are classics. But I didn't try to be a clone. Now people say, 'Oh, he does have that quality his dad has, but he can also do light comedy, he can do sensitive young men, he can do action pictures, he can do killer guys.'

Suddenly, you've worked yourself up to the top of the pecking order and you say to yourself, okay, this is going to be fun ...

HIMSELF

■ He was a little lazy, he came to the picture [*Wall Street*] with a bit of a Hollywood attitude, and I don't work that way. I work fast, no re-shooting, not much margin for error. He didn't cotton to that school of making pictures so we had some problems and I got tough with him. I think I brought out the angry side of him. I wanted a kid of Kirk Douglas in this movie. Where the hell's your father? You're a wimp! You're a Mister Nice Guy! Then he got on top of it quick, hot, and he was good.

OLIVER STONE

BETSY DRAKE (born 1923)

■ Betsy was a delightful comedienne, but I don't think Hollywood was every really her milieu. She wanted to help humanity, to help others help themselves.

CARY GRANT, 1973

MARIE DRESSLER (1869–1934)

■ She was the biggest star of her time. She ruled in musical comedy and in low comedy. As time went on she acquired a kind of peculiar distinction, a magnificence. She was a law unto herself. She'd mug and carry on—but she knew how to make an entrance with great aplomb, great effect.

GEORGE CUKOR

■ Poor Marie. *Tugboat Annie* was her greatest film, but it was also her last film.

When we made it, in 1933 she was dying of cancer, and she knew it. Annie was a part she desperately wanted to play. She could only work three hours a day, because of her physical condition. She was in constant pain, and the pain mirrored itself on her face, on her bearing, but never on her professionalism when the camera was rolling.

MERVYN LEROY, 1974

KEIR DULLEA (born 1936)

■ Keir Dullea and gone tomorrow.

NOËL COWARD

MARGARET DUMONT (1889–1965)

■ She was a wonderful woman. She was the same off the stage as she was on it— always the stuffy, dignified matron. And the funny thing about her was she never understood the jokes. At the end of *Duck Soup*. ... Margaret says to me, 'What are you doing Rufus?', And I say 'I am fighting for your honour, which is more than you ever did.' Later she asked me what I meant by that.

GROUCHO MARX

FAYE DUNAWAY (born 1941)

■ When I got here I walked in thinking I was a star and then I found I was supposed to do everything the way she says. Listen, I'm not going to take temperamental whims from anyone ... I just take a long walk and cool off. If I didn't do that, I know I'd wind up dumping her on her derriere.

ROBERT MITCHUM

61

- She was a gigantic pain in the ass. She demonstrated certifiable proof of insanity.

  ROMAN POLANSKI, 1977

- But I've been very lucky. I've worked with all the actors I wanted to work with. I adore Faye Dunaway, I love her and I feel she's one of the most underrated actresses, I think she's brilliant.

  FRANK PERRY

- Of the present day, Faye Dunaway is very difficult.

  BETTE DAVIS, 1987

- Put simply, she has that twice-as-big quality . . . She belongs up there with the greats: Hepburn, Davis, Garbo.

  PADDY CHAYEVSKY

- Faye carries a cloud of drama round with her . . . There is something in her at hazard.

  ELIA KAZAN

- I never met anyone with such a demoniacal drive to succeed as a movie star.

  ESTELLE PARSONS

- She's a 20th century fox, a calculating lady who repels even as she attracts.

  BART MILLS

- Of all actresses, to me only Faye Dunaway has the talent and courage to be a real star.

  JOAN CRAWFORD

- Faye Dunaway says she is being haunted by mother's ghost. After her performance in *Mommie Dearest*, I can understand why.

  CHRISTINA CRAWFORD

- I used to take Faye's side [when she was quarrelling with Polanski], because she's one of the few women in whom I can confide. I'd say 'Faye, I want you to know exactly why I'm not with you in this particular instance'. A waste of time. She'd always interrupt me in the middle of the sentence.

  JACK NICHOLSON

IRENE DUNNE (born 1904)

- Irene Dunne today is virtually the same woman that millions of moviegoers fell in love with over 30 years ago. She is funny, brilliant and yet somehow wistful . . . Having just seen all of her 'lost' films. I can say with certainty that Irene Dunne's film career was one of the few which fulfilled all of its possibilities, giving American motion pictures an actress of classic beauty, humour and intelligence.

  DAVID CHIERICHETTI

- Underrated on every count.

  JOHN CROMWELL, 1969

- Nothing is instinctive, everything she does is very carefully thought out, she knows her camera and lighting as well as any cameraman, she knows every movement, every intonation, every nuance. She's a first-class craftswoman. . . . but instead of being dull and perfect, she's absolutely enchanting and perfect.

  DOUGLAS FAIRBANKS JR

- She was an excellent actress, much more used to the Hollywood scene that I was. She too went her own way, and tactfully used the director, as I later learned to do myself, to her own advantage; she listened to what he had to give, and discarded it or used it, as she wished.

  REX HARRISON, 1974

■ Dunne was a brilliant actress and her comedy timing was impeccable. She played it straight, instead of playing it for laughs as some comediennes do.

CARY GRANT

DEANNA DURBIN (born 1921)

■ When she sings, there is no sense of the footlights about it. She sings for music, not for show. She isn't one of those sopranos who expect the audience to pay out on the high notes. Her singing, which must have been magnificently taught her, is still, praise heaven, cool, clean, and scholarly.

C. A. LEJEUNE, 1939

■ I met Deanna Durbin and liked her very much. She is a charming girl and was then in the stage between girlhood and womanhood, just married, and particularly ravishing. I was very excited. I had all the Durbin pictures run through for me and those made by Koster were certainly the best. However I had no gift for that style and [The Amazing Mrs Holliday] was, quite rightly, finished by people who know the job better.

JEAN RENOIR, 1954

■ I loved working with her ... she was fascinating. She was a good enough actress and still sang like an angel.

JOHN GREEN, 1947

■ The modern Jenny Lind.

LAWRENCE TIBBETT

■ I was always mad about Deanna. I admired her work enormously. Then she disappeared suddenly. Whatever became of her?

GRACIE FIELDS

■ Realising that she can't sing all the time, and seeking something to fill the gaps, her pictures' producers have hit upon the daring scheme of letting her natural bloom of youth suffice. And so Miss Durbin's eyelashes are of a normal length and her lip-rouge unobtrusive. She is given opportunity to be sweet and spirited; she is guarded from being cute.

CECELIA AGER

■ Her sparkling personality, lyrical voice and wholesome countenance charmed audiences more than anxious to adore her. She inspired American youth and helped promote the advance of culture by bringing works of musical masters to the screen.

GENE RINGGOLD

■ There is no doubt any longer of Miss Durbin's immense talents as an actress; any undertones that there are in this amusing, astute and sentimental tale [Three Smart Girls Grow Up] are supplied by her.

GRAHAM GREENE

ROBERT DUVALL (born 1931)

■ Duvall was strange. First of all he was and is a great actor. You could ask him to do a scene five, six times and he'd do it exactly the same way every time ... But, on the other hand, there would be delays, like we had to wire up a whole house, and he'd just get restless ... He'd get mad.

BRUCE BERESFORD

■ Perhaps never before in the history of American movies have there been so many first rate leading actors ... the most consistently surprising and

63

rewarding of the lot, Robert Duvall . . .
Now it's time to recognise Robert Duvall
as one of the most resourceful, most
technically proficient, most remarkable
actors in America today . . . When I say
'one of. . .' I don't mean to weasel out of
anything. At this moment, having just
seen Mr Duvall in *The Great Santini*, I
think he may well be the best we have.
The American Olivier.

VINCENT CANBY

■ Duvall is such a great pro. Before we
started shooting he knew all his lines by
heart. He always came to the set fully
prepared and meticulously researched,
whereas Brandauer is the kind of actor
who believes he will produce something
unique when the camera starts rolling.
At times it was difficult to blend their
two styles, but I think the end result [in
The Lightship] is very satisfying.

JERZY SKOLIMOWSKI

CLINT EASTWOOD (born 1933)

■ I think there's a parallel in my career and
Clint's. We both have a particular
audience that is loyal to us no matter
what the critics say. With Clint, they want
him to rip the bad guy's face off.

BURT REYNOLDS, 1978

■ On first meeting, he's one of the nicest
people you ever met. But I can't say I
know him well. We talked a couple of
times and had a meal together. I liked
him. I think you'd have to be around for
a year before you saw his ugly side,
assuming he has one.

NORMAN MAILER, 1984

■ Hardest thing in the world is to do
nothing and he does it marvellously.

DON SIEGEL

■ He appears to do nothing and does
everything, reducing everything and
everybody . . . like Mitchum and Tracy.

RICHARD BURTON

■ Clint Eastwood is no publicity manager's
invention; he came after the decline of
the studios, and no studio invented him
or helped him edge to the top. He is very
modest about his success, and grins
engagingly: 'Any actor going into
pictures has to have something special.
That's what makes a star while a lot of
damn good actors are passed by.'

DEWITT BODEEN

■ He's even-tempered—a personality trait
not much in evidence among directors.
The crew is totally behind him and that
really helps things go smoothly.

WILLIAM HOLDEN

■ As a director, Eastwood is not as good
as he thinks he is. As an actor, he is
probably better than he allows himself
to be.

RICHARD SCHICKEL

■ He played a nameless man, a silent,
malevolent anti-hero cowboy who
moved across the screen with a sinister
but deadly grace. Dressed in a poncho
and chewing on the butt of a black
cigarillo he earned himself the reputation
as the most violent character in movies.

MERIEL McCOOEY

■ Gary Cooper was perhaps more a man
of instinct than Clint, but they both
project one thing beautifully: pure
Americanism. In that respect, Clint
belongs to the great tradition of American
stars—men like John Wayne, James
Stewart, Henry Fonda, Spencer Tracy,
Clark Gable and, of course, Gary Cooper.

64

Off screen Clint is articulate and intelligent, not quiet or laconic like the cowboys and GI's he plays in films.

TELLY SAVALAS

BLAKE EDWARDS (born 1922)

■ A man of many talents, all of them minor.

LESLIE HALLIWELL

DENHOLM ELLIOTT (born 1922)

■ I amended the actor's cliche to 'Never work with children, animals or Denholm Elliott'.

GABRIEL BYRNE

EDITH EVANS (1888–1976)

■ Dame Edith Evans who knows [in *The Last Days of Dolwyn*], like a witch, how to drain her face and voice of everything she has learnt from fashion, and start, from innocence, all over again.

C. A. LEJEUNE

DOUGLAS FAIRBANKS (1883–1939)

■ Whenever Douglas Fairbanks entered he caused quite a stir; buoyed by his sudden rise to fame after only two pictures, he seemed charged with electricity. His wife, calm and gentle, seemed undisturbed even when her exuberant husband did handstands or leapt over the sofas to amuse his appreciative Algonquin audiences. Because he had never outgrown a small boy's penchant for showing off, he was rarely referred to as Douglas or Mr Fairbanks; it was always Doug.

FRANCES MARION

■ He has such verve. He can use his body.

D. W. GRIFFITH

■ Fairbanks' glory, the mystery of his visual imagination, is that he could throw away all the text book tricks on the make-shift apparatus of ordinary life. To Fairbanks the limb of a tree suggests a hocks-off; a narrow lane with high walls is a risky, but workable, set of parallel bars; a spear is a pole to vault with . . .

ALISTAIR COOKE

■ Douglas Fairbanks was make-believe at its best, a game we youngsters never tired of playing, a game—we are convinced—our fathers secretly shared. He was complete fantasy, not like Disney's which has an overlayer of whimsy and sophistication, but unashamed and joyous. Balustrades were made to be vaulted, draperies to be a giant slide, chandeliers to swing from, citadels to be scaled.

FRANK S. NUGENT

■ A little boy who never grew up.

MARY PICKFORD

■ He had extraordinary magnetism and charm and a genuine boyish enthusiasm which he conveyed to the public.

CHARLES CHAPLIN

DOUGLAS FAIRBANKS JR (born 1909)

■ The trouble with Douglas Fairbanks Junior is that he likes everything he sees and he sees everything.

CLEMENCE DANE

FRANCES FARMER (1913–1970)

■ Frances Farmer had a warrior quality which never permitted her to give in or

65

compromise herself. She could have acquiesced along the way, but she never did. She had to take everything head on.

JESSICA LANGE, 1985

JOHN FARROW (1904–1963)

■ The director [on *John Paul Jones*] was John Farrow, beside whom Julien Duvivier was really an angel of goodness. He was really a nasty man, not especially with me, but I have rarely seen a sadist of such magnitude. He was the father of Mia and Tisa Farrow, whom I knew when they were little. He was quite a good-looking man but the spirit of evil, looking to antagonise everybody.

MICHEL KELBER, 1981

■ We had no script discussions. In fact he gave me almost no direction at all. God forbid I should miss a cue! Then he would snarl, 'You know your lines, don't you?' I resolved not to fight with him. It would only have made things worse. And he was not very pleased with the other actors, either. Certainly he did not make my list of favourite directors.

LANA TURNER, 1982

■ John was one of those directors who got phobias about people. He would dislike certain ones and he'd deliberately bitch up the scene, because he didn't like the actors working in it. He couldn't stand George Coulouris, couldn't stand him. Consequently we had to make up our scenes ourselves more or less.

RAY MILLAND

MIA FARROW (born 1945)

■ A black moonchild, like Lilith. Her sex is not here [pointing to his groin], but in the head, like a wound in the middle of the forehead.

SALVADOR DALI

■ All turned in and vulnerable, a child with a highly energetic brain. From the neck up she's eighty.

SHIRLEY MACLAINE

■ Trying to describe Mia is like trying to describe dust in a shaft of sunlight. There are all those particles. Her conversation is clotted.

RODDY MCDOWALL

■ People have a tendency to look at Mia and say look at those funny clothes and the way she acts and the things she talks about. Compared, let's say, with Debbie Reynolds she's some kind of freak. But I think that Mia is the straight one. I think that Debbie Reynolds is the freak.

ANDRE PREVIN, 1969

■ Hah! I always knew Frank [Sinatra] would wind up in bed with a boy.

AVA GARDNER

■ It is difficult to gauge a star's breaking point, but Mia and I could not have gone on as we had begun. Fortunately there was no need to. She is shrewd. Her instincts are perfect. Once she had the idea, she was a rewarding working partner.

JOSEPH LOSEY, 1979

RAINER WERNER FASSBINDER (1946–1982)

■ It is unbelievable that, at an age of twenty-eight, Fassbinder has written and directed more for film, theatre, and television than most directors achieve in their entire lives. His knowledge of people, and his ability to formulate this knowledge artistically is most remarkable.

CHRISTIAN BRAAD THOMSEN, 1974

■ Rainer's a little shit, but one can't help liking him. He can be so generous, yet he seems to feel this need to work in a permanent state of quarrel.

PETER ZADEK

■ He has a certain merit. It is very difficult, after all, to make any film in Germany at all. I don't agree with what he said about me, but what he said is of no importance.

CLAUDE CHABROL

ALICE FAYE (born 1912)

■ Alice, dear Alice . . . Wouldn't it be nice if all the people in the world had as much joy in their lives as I had in making those six pictures with you?

DON AMECHE, 1984

■ I've only good things to say about Alice Faye.

HENRY FONDA

■ Alice is a darling. Everybody loves her.

BETTY GRABLE

■ [With] Alice Faye . . . you'd move the camera in on a close-up and you'd imagine she was the greatest singer in the world. You know, Alice Faye at that time, she'd sing a song on the screen and the next morning it sold a million copies. Technically, she wasn't a particularly good singer but she was one of those unusual song salesmen on the screen, she knew how to sing the song to sell it.

JULE STYNE

■ Alice had a quality, a feminine warmth that none of the other girls seemed to have at that time, not Betty Grable or any of them; and for that reason I think she was a star. There was a certain warmth to her, a simplicity that made her very valuable, I think.

WALTER LANG

■ I'd rather have Alice Faye introduce my songs than anyone else.

IRVING BERLIN

■ Not only is she my favourite actress, she is a favourite person.

HENRY KING

FEDERICO FELLINI (born 1920)

■ More than anything else, *La Strada* suggests a director striving to be a poet when he is not; the insistence on bare and desolate landscapes, the Chaplinesque mime of the waif, the constant intervention of 'picturesque' episodes—all these reflect Fellini's desire to load his story with atmosphere and symbols of profound meaning. But the 'meaning' isn't there.

GAVIN LAMBERT

■ To me, you are like Jesus Christ. I shall never meet anyone else like you in my lifetime.

LINA WERTMULLER

■ He's gifted like others are gifted today. In truth, he suffers from being a little provincial boy. His films are like the dreams of a country boy imagining what it's like to be in the big city. His greatest danger: to be a very great director with precious little to say.

LUCHINO VISCONTI

67

■ Federico Fellini says he likes to work out his fantasies in movies.

ROGER CORMAN

■ His films are a small-town boy's dream of a big city. His sophistication works because it is the creation of someone who doesn't have it. But he shows dangerous signs of being a superlative artist with little to say.

ORSON WELLES

JOSÉ FERRER (born 1912)

■ He has all the signs of being a good comedian, but those evil fairies at his Puerto Rican christening bestowed on him short legs, a too large nose, small eyes, a toneless singing voice and a defective sense of timing. It is extraordinary to me that an actor with his years of experience should still, after six weeks playing, misjudge his effects and talk through laughs.

NOËL COWARD

■ José Ferrer, you're too good an actor to have to stoop that low.

BEATRICE LILLIE
[on his role in *Moulin Rouge*]

JACQUES FEYDER (1885–1948)

■ I owe him everything.

MARCEL CARNÉ

SALLY FIELD (born 1946)

■ To watch her work on a role from the beginning, building it carefully step-by-step, is inspirational.

ROBERT BENTON, 1985

■ Sally is one of the best, perhaps *the* best, actress I've ever worked with. Her rushes on *Norma Rae* were so good that I found myself crying over some of the more dramatic scenes. She's simply astounding.

MARTIN RITT

■ She's tough, she's gritty, she's got a great sense of humour and she gets prettier every day.

BURT REYNOLDS

■ Watching this actress give life to a woman of grit and guts, of humour and compassion, without worrying about the consequences, is the kind of marvellous experience we don't often see in movies. In *Norma Rae* Sally Field can be identified as a major Hollywood resource.

VINCENT CANBY

SHIRLEY ANN FIELD (born 1938)

■ One of the best English actresses of her time.

DAVID PUTTNAM

GRACIE FIELDS (1898–1979)

■ Gracie Fields really does represent a common denominator for those millions of English folk who like humour and sentiment of the type known as homely. Her personality is not merely powerful; it represents an intimacy with each audience which can arise only out of the true traditions of English music hall.

BASIL WRIGHT, 1937

■ I found her very interesting, an actress with three selves, London, Lancashire, and Imperial. But the London Miss Fields is an accomplished comic actress who comes on as an agreeable surprise; and there are mysterious glimpses of a gaunt and rather grim woman who isn't pretty and doesn't care.

CYRIL CONNOLLY

■ Gracie was a wonderful person really and I think one of the most wonderful things about her was that she had absolutely no conceit. She never behaved in any way at all like a famous person. And yet in many ways I think she led a sad life really. She had everything—this marvellous applause, this marvellous acclaim—and yet she had nothing, no family of her own and not enough love. She was a very dominating personality with practically everybody except her menfolk and I consider that she allowed them to dictate to her.

LILIAN AZA

W. C. FIELDS (1879–1946)

■ As Egbert Souse, the hero of this subversive epic [*The Bank Dick*], Fields portrays a character absolutely free of every virtue, major or minor. He drinks, smokes, lies and cheats; hates children, old ladies and pillars of society; is opposed to work, thrift, honesty—and still emerges from the picture enormously likeable.

JOHN McCARTEN, 1949

■ A creative genius. I have only to see his face to laugh.

JOHN BETJEMAN

■ His comedy routines appeared spontaneous and improvised, but he spent much time perfecting them. He knew exactly what he was doing every moment, and what each prop was

supposed to do. That 'my little chickadee' way of talking of his was natural.

BING CROSBY

■ The Talkies brought one great comedian, the late, majestically lethargic W. C. Fields, who could not possibly have worked as well in Silence; he was the toughest and most warmly human of all screen comedians, and *It's a Gift* and *The Bank Dick*, fiendishly funny and incisive white-collar comedies, rank with the best comedies (and best movies) ever made.

JAMES AGEE

■ He was an isolated person. As a young man, he stretched out his hand to Beauty and Love and they thrust it away. Gradually he reduced reality to exclude all but his work, filling the gaps with alcohol . . . He was also a solitary person. Years of travelling alone around the world with his juggling act taught him the value of solitude and the release it gave his mind.

LOUISE BROOKS

■ His main purpose seemed to be to break as many rules as possible and cause the maximum amount of trouble for everybody.

ROBERT LEWIS TAYLOR

■ He was really born to play [Mr Micawber], . . . that rare combination of the personality and the part. He was charming to work with, his suggestions and ad libs were always in character. There was a scene in which he had to sit at a desk writing, and he asked me if he could have a cup of tea on the desk. When he got agitated, he dipped his pen into the teacup instead of the inkwell.

GEORGE CUKOR

69

■ Fields quiescent and smouldering is funnier than Fields rampant and yelling. He played straight men to a malevolent universe which had singled him out for seige and destruction. He regarded the conspiracy of fate through a pair of frosty little blue eyes, an arm flung up to ward off an imminent blow, and his shoulders instinctively hunched in self-protection.

KENNETH TYNAN

■ The great man, the omnipotent oom of one of the screen's most devoted cults, brings with him some new treasures, as well as a somewhat alarming collection of wheezes which, ten years ago in the vaudeville tank towns, must have seemed not long for this world. But somehow when Mr Fields, in his necessary search for comic business, is forced to strike up a nodding acquaintance with vintage gags, they seem to become almost young again.

ANDRE SENNWALD

■ I remember the first day I worked with him. He was due at 9, and came in at 11, and he'd had quite a night the night before, I guess. I was supposed to say 'Good morning pater,' and kiss him. So in the rehearsal he apologised, because you could smell the alcohol, and I said 'Mr Fields, on you it smells like Chanel No. 5' and he said 'Honey, you're in!'.

UNA MERKEL

PETER FINCH (1916–1977)

■ I consider Peter Finch and James Mason the two best English actors of the 1960s. But I never understood Finch. How could he do something as beautiful as *Sunday, Bloody Sunday*, but also make all that

other shit? I mean he could read, couldn't he?

ALAN BATES

■ Everybody adored Peter so much that he would just come on to the set and everyone would start smiling.

VIRGINIA MCKENNA

■ You're acting! Don't act! I don't act, that's why I'm a star.

ERROL FLYNN

ALBERT FINNEY (born 1936)

■ It's irritating for actors always to remain identified with their first famous role, but there's something in Albert Finney which made him particularly memorable as Arthur Seaton in the film of *Saturday Night and Sunday Morning*. His acting seems to be a perpetual struggle of violent, joyous energy to release itself from a dour, cramping inarticulacy, preferably in flamboyant horseplay or clowning.

RONALD BRYDEN, 1967

■ And take a boy like Albert Finney, whom I consider a tremendous talent; but he doesn't seem too interested in what he's doing, which I find puzzling and appalling when you're that good. No, the system today doesn't seem to me to be geared to providing new lasting greats. There'll be a continuous turnover; a lot of temporary fame.

ROBERT RYAN, 1970

EDDIE FISHER (born 1928)

■ The reason I drink is because when I'm sober I think I'm Eddie Fisher.

DEAN MARTIN

ROBERT FLAHERTY (1884–1951)

- There were really three Robert Flahertys: man, myth, and moviemaker. To judge the third, it would be helpful if we had never heard of the first two—if we could bring to the criticism of his films the same innocent eye that he brought to his film subjects. The man is dead. The myth must die. The films will live.

  RICHARD CORLISS, 1978

LOUISE FLETCHER (born 1934)

- Louise had the strength to do it subtle [her role in *One Flew Over the Cuckoo's Nest*]. She didn't go for cheap exaggeration. It was the most difficult part in the picture. I was afraid that, surrounded by all those spectacular performances, she would get lost.

  MILOS FORMAN

ERROL FLYNN (1909–1959)

- He was a better actor than his publicity gave him credit for. I shared his house, his fights, his liquor and his girls. He was a real man with terrific looks. What happened to him, of course, was that he took to the dope—in fact, he was registered over here in England as an addict—and that destroyed him. God, if he were alive today do you realise that he would be sixty-one . . . and probably still a star.

  BRUCE CABOT

- I had a very big crush on Errol Flynn during *Captain Blood* (1935). I thought he was absolutely smashing for three solid years—but he never guessed. Then he had one on me but nothing came of

it. I'm not going to regret that—it could have ruined my life.

  OLIVIA DE HAVILLAND

- He wasn't an admirable character, but he was a magnificent male animal, and his sex-appeal was obvious . . . It seemed not to matter whether he could act. He leapt from the screen into the projection room with the impact of a bullet.

  HAL WALLIS

- He was one of the wild characters of the world, but he had a strange, quiet side. He camouflaged himself completely. In all the years I knew him, I never really knew what lay underneath, and I doubt if many people did.

  ANN SHERIDAN

- Errol Flynn was a joy, a lovely man, and most of the talk about him is nothing but rumour by people who didn't even know him. He loved to talk about how much he could drink and the women he'd made love to, but most of it was just the rationalisations of a disappointed moralist. He was the hardest-working, most down-to-earth actor I ever worked with.

  HENRY KING

- Flynn was a magnificent specimen of the rampant male. Outrageously good looking, he was a great natural athlete who played tennis with Donald Budge and boxed with 'Mushy' Calahan. The extras, among whom I had many friends, disliked him intensely.

  DAVID NIVEN

- You know Flynn, he's either got to be fighting or fucking.

  JACK L. WARNER

- Flynn was a great guy but he hated the head of the studio, Jack Warner, and all

71

the front office. When Jack Warner would come on the set Flynn would walk off. He didn't like the top brass but he loved the crew and the crew thought he was a helluva lad.

FRANK WESTMORE

■ Everybody used to think that he didn't give a damn about being an actor, ... I think just the contrary was true ... I always felt that Errol was like the Don Juan character himself, trying to prove himself constantly, ... he may have been an incipient homosexual, he certainly never practised it. ... he's the first man I ever heard talk about his mother in a scurrilous manner. Loved his father, detested his mother.

VINCENT SHERMAN

■ He seemed very nice though rather silly and fatuous.

SCOTT FITZGERALD

■ You knew where you were with Errol— he always let you down.

DAVID NIVEN

■ He was not an actor of enormous talent— he would have admitted that himself— but in all those swashbuckling things he was beautiful.

BETTE DAVIS, 1987

HENRY FONDA (1905–1982)

■ Once when a good man was wanted, a man of obvious integrity, a 'non-actor' in appearance who could act everyone else off the screen, they used to say 'Fetch Fonda'. Now they say it when a big man's wanted, a man you believe could rule the world or a sizeable slice of it.

ISABEL QUIGLEY, 1964

■ But my father does things as an actor that I couldn't do. He played on stage in *Mister Roberts* for four years. His wife died during that time, and other personal tragedies came in his life. But there's not one person who won't say that he was just as good on closing night as opening night. I could never do that.

JANE FONDA

■ I have never known an actor with such craft, with such professional seriousness; such a pleasant man, full of humour, so reserved and so keenly quick-witted.

SERGIO LEONE

■ I dig my father. I wish he could open his eyes and dig me.

PETER FONDA

■ He is a better actor than almost anyone you like to name in Hollywood, yet when you come down to it he has not played anything like a wide variety of roles in his seventy or so films. His quality has been demonstrated rather by the intelligence and authority with which he has explored various aspects of one basic attribute: decency.

JOHN RUSSELL TAYLOR

■ [He] seems to be vouchsafing his emotion and talent to the audience in tiny blips ... Fonda's entry into a scene is that of a man walking backward, slanting himself away from the public eye.

MANNY FARBER, 1966

■ I think there's a scream inside Hank that's never been screamed, and there's a laugh that's never been laughed.

SUSAN BLANCHARD
(Fonda's 3rd wife)

■ If I can be like Henry Fonda, then I look forward to ageing, to sixty and beyond—

72

and not just because Hank finally won the Oscar that *he* deserved. *He* was a good character actor and a good actor in the American tradition of playing variations on oneself.

PAUL NEWMAN

■ Henry Fonda's mind, his dedication to his art, and his brooding, sad face have always been great influences in my life. No matter what our differences, Fonda is a part of me, and I'm a part of him. May he live forever, for when Fonda smiles the theatre shines.

JOSHUA LOGAN, 1988

JANE FONDA (born 1937)

■ In our big scenes together [in *On Golden Pond*], Jane became very emotional. There's a moment when she's groping to find the right relationship with her dad, and I'm not sure what she's up to. When it was over, I could see Jane was proud. She pointed to the film crew—by that time everybody was crying—and whispered to me, 'I guess they all had problems with their father'.

HENRY FONDA, 1981

■ Jane's person is more specific than most of us. She's well disciplined and knows what she wants and where she's going and works objectively to apply all her information to that intention. With Jane, the character and force is embodied in her persona and it's a lovely, delicate and self-depreciating human.

DONALD SUTHERLAND, 1987

■ She's a romantic pro-Leninist. Unfortunately she's lost her sense of humour. One day I called her Jane of Arc. She didn't laugh at all.

ROGER VADIM

■ Ibsen says everything five times [in *A Doll's House*], so three times in the film was more than enough. Jane wanted it said all five times.

JOSEPH LOSEY

■ I liked her passion. And her professionalism. You know, Jane worked for years as a silly ingénue on the stage in New York and, I mean, she was laughable at first. But she stayed with it and slowly, carefully learned her craft.

ROY SCHEIDER

■ She wanted to meet me! She'd seen the movie and thought I had an incredible presence and was interested in knowing who that guy was. It was more curiosity than business. She said, 'What does it feel like to have what's happened to you happen?' And I said, 'You're a huge star, what do you mean?' And she said, 'Babes, what's happened to you doesn't happen to many people.'

JOHN TRAVOLTA

PETER FONDA (born 1939)

■ In *The Trip* I started to get fed up. I was fed up because Peter Fonda was a star and I wasn't. And Peter couldn't act. I'm sorry, man, he just can't act. He never bothered to sit and learn. He never studied. And he just kind of larked out. Now I don't begrudge the fact that he has talent. But he's not an actor, by any stretch of the imagination.

BRUCE DERN

JOAN FONTAINE (born 1917)

■ If Joan Fontaine does not presently attain real stardom, this is because she looks,

73

behaves and dresses [in *Suspicion*] like that extraordinarily unfashionable thing, a lady. And by that I mean the properly nurtured daughter of gentlefolk. Whether her unspoiled looks, natural charm and very considerable acting abilities will compensate for the absence of lacquered nails, smeared mouth and all the dreary messes of the beauty parlour, the public must decide.

JAMES AGATE

■ With her Dresden doll-like delicacy, and her cool, elegant manner, aristocratic Joan Fontaine should have been a ranking international cinema star for much longer than the World War II period.

JAMES ROBERT PARISH

■ I married Joan Fontaine, sister of Olivia de Havilland, young, pretty, gay and utterly charming—and no actress, thank God, or at least so I thought until the fifth day of our honeymoon in the Oregon woods, when my dream was abruptly shattered by a phone call from David Selznick offering her the lead in his picture, *Rebecca*. We rushed back to Hollywood, where she was launched into orbit as a big new motion picture star.

BRIAN AHERNE

■ She pranced in one day when we were shooting *Frenchman's Creek* [in 1944] and said she was sorry for being so difficult, but after all, the whole picture rested on her shoulders and it was a heavy responsibility. The whole company of distinguished British actors was so insulted they refused to work with her and we lost a lot of time patching that one up.

MITCHELL LEISEN

■ I dreaded working with Joan Fontaine again [in 1951], but the first day, she came up to me during a break and she said she was just doing it for the money, she wasn't out to prove anything any more, and she would act it whatever way I told her. And that's just what she did; she couldn't have been more delightful and fun to work with. We had a ball doing it.

MITCHELL LEISEN

■ Joan is very bright and sharp and can be cutting. She said some things about [my marriage] that hurt me deeply. She was aware there was an estrangement between us . . . I swore that I would never reconcile with Joan until she apologised.

OLIVIA DE HAVILLAND

BRYAN FORBES (born 1926)

■ Bryan Forbes is what is called Out There a 'hyphenate'. He is a writer-director. Since he got his first directing job, he has written every movie he's been involved with. (I didn't know it then, but he would totally rewrite *Stepford* too. Almost totally. The last quarter of the movie is mine. I think he would have changed that, too, but he ran out of time).

WILLIAM GOLDMAN

HARRISON FORD (born 1942)

■ Harrison possesses magnetic qualities. He is capable of filling a room with his personality. If he'd been a plumber and came to fix your tap, he's a person you'd notice. We provoke each other. It's no cosy fireside chat.

PETER WEIR, 1986

74

■ Often when Harrison read a line, it was a different reading than I anticipated, but it worked. Somehow, it was more inspiring or original than what I had in mind.

ROMAN POLANSKI, 1988

■ He is a remarkable combination of Errol Flynn in *The Adventures of Don Juan* and Bogart as Fred C. Dobbs in *The Treasure of Sierra Madre*.

STEVEN SPIELBERG

■ To me, Harrison Ford is Allie to his fingertips . . . Allie Fox [in *The Mosquito Coast*] is an unusual man and [he] portrays him in all his complexity.

PAUL THEROUX

JOHN FORD (1895–1973)

■ I only did one Ford film with Duke, *Fort Apache*, but I knew 'the family' well enough to know that Duke was very often Ford's whipping boy. Ward Bond was a Ford whipping boy, too. But both of them knew Ford well enough to know they were being used, and they didn't let it get to them. Walter Brennan couldn't take it. He said he'd never work for Ford again, and never did.

HENRY FONDA, 1973

■ The set was anything but tranquil on a Ford picture. Ford believed that acting is a competitive thing. That it's good to be tense, good to be suspicious of other actors. His direction would be mostly asides, whispers . . . In a Ford film you were never exactly sure of what was going to happen next. And this is the way he wanted it.

JAMES STEWART

■ I liked working with Jack Ford very much; he and I were great friends. But he was as unsuited to that material [for *Mary of Scotland*] as a director as I was unsuited to Mary of Scotland as an actress.

KATHARINE HEPBURN

■ Marvellous but loony, tearing out pages of the script everywhere.

ANNE BANCROFT

■ He was so egomaniacal. He never would rehearse, didn't want to talk about a part. If an actor started to ask questions he'd either take those pages and tear them out of the script or insult him in an awful way. He loved getting his shot on the first take, which for him meant it was fresh. He would print the first take—even if it wasn't any good.

HENRY FONDA

■ John Ford is still the most Brechtian of all film-makers, because he shows things that make people think, damn it.

JEAN-MARIE STRAUB

■ Orson Welles was once asked which American directors most appealed to him. 'The old masters,' he replied. 'By which I mean John Ford, John Ford and John Ford.' Well, I studied *Young Mr Lincoln*, for example. As I say, Jack Ford had a big influence on me.

ELIA KAZAN

■ One time I called him John and he told me that only his enemies called him John. 'Call me Jack,' he'd say. . . . Well, it's a funny thing with Jack: socially, you never wanted any part of him. He just wasn't that pleasant. For one thing, he was a reformed alcoholic; he didn't drink and he didn't think anybody else should.

75

He also liked to play cards, but if you won you were a no-good son of a bitch.

WILLIAM CLOTHIER

■ While Wayne and Ford are nothing like the pals they have been painted, they do have a mutual respect for one another as artists. In the main, Ford thinks of Wayne as a lucky stiff with a minimum of talent but a lot of drive in his acting. Wayne thinks Ford is a mean, artful, old perfectionist who would kick his own mother down a flight of steps, if he thought it would get a laugh from the neighbours.

JAMES HENAGHAN

■ Oh, Ford was a peculiar man. You had to know how to handle him. Actors were terrified of him because he liked to terrify them. He was a sadist.

JOHN CARRADINE

■ Shakespearian is a word for *The Quiet Man*.

LINDSAY ANDERSON

CARL FOREMAN (1914–1984)

■ *High Noon* was . . . the most un-American thing I've ever seen in my whole life. The last thing in the picture is ole Coop putting the United States marshal's badge under his foot and stepping on it. I'll never regret having helped run Foreman out of this country.

JOHN WAYNE

GEORGE FORMBY (1904–1961)

■ Formby was mean as mean can be, but I must say that at the end of about the third picture, he did give me a pair of gold cufflinks. One of his problems was

that his wife Beryl was on the set day in and day out, because she was terribly jealous of him. On one occasion, she was whisked off with appendicitis for some time, and then George was quite a different character—very nice.

RONALD NEAME

BOB FOSSE (1927–1987)

■ Fosse, I think, came to a high point in his life, with an Oscar, a Tony and an Emmy, and asked himself, Do they think I'm really that good? They don't know I'm really a sham, a hoax, a phoney, a lousy human being, not much of a friend to anybody and a flop . . . they don't know I'm covered with flop sweat. That's an expression Bob uses a lot—flop *sweat*.

ROY SCHEIDER

ANTHONY FRANCIOSA (born 1928)

■ I'll never forget the night I brought my Oscar home and Tony took one look at it and I knew my marriage was over.

SHELLEY WINTERS

JOHN FRANKENHEIMER (born 1930)

■ I don't think John really understands dramatic values; he's more or less mechanically inclined: lenses and cameras and that. All that's my job; he ought to worry about the story and the actors.

JAMES WONG HOWE

■ He went from boy–wonder to has–been without ever passing through the stage of maturity.

NEIL SINYARD

JEAN GABIN (1904–1976)

■ A great actor gives us an enhanced sense of our own humanity and in that respect, I suppose, Gabin was surpassed by Raimu. But at his best, Gabin was the most magnetic actor the screen has ever known.

GEOFFREY MINISH, 1977

■ Gabin is not an actor whom one asks to portray the hero of any story. For he himself, anterior to all stories, is a hero, and it is to this hero that the imagination of the scenarist should be devoted. Gabin would never be able, no matter what the script, to portray any destiny other than his own. And that destiny? It involves an enraged outcry against the universe, and the defeat or death of Gabin ...

ANDRÉ BAZIN

■ Jean Gabin was mysterious enough, secret enough, but he was a great actor, and it's always agreeable to work with a great actor. When you're working with people of talent, as for *En Cas de Malheur*, matters go very easily.

EDWIGE FEUILLÈRE

CLARK GABLE (1901–1960)

■ In the old days there were an immense number of stars, today only a handful. You talk about stars, you mean yesterday. People like McQueen aren't like *they* were. There's not the same kind of awe. I've seen women faint when they met Gable face to face, and men cry. There's no thrill today.

EDWARD DMYTRYK, 1975

■ Women liked Gable best when he played a heavy with a grin.

HOWARD HAWKS

■ Can you imagine what being kissed by him meant to me?

MARILYN MONROE

■ It was the joy of your life to know Clark Gable. He was everything good you could think of. He had delicious humour; he had great compassion; he was always a fine old teddy bear ... In no way was he conscious of his good looks, as were most of the other men in pictures at that time. Clark was very un-actory.

JOAN BLONDELL

■ He was the epitome of the movie star— so romantic, such bearing, such friendliness.

ELIZABETH TAYLOR

■ Yeah, Gable was the greatest male ever on the screen. Valentino may have been the greatest women's actor. But men liked Gable and women liked Gable. He had them all.

CLARENCE BROWN

■ Clark Gable was the only real he-man I've ever known, of all the actors I've met.

JOHN HUSTON

■ Clark Gable was highly professional. He was a bigger star than we could create today. I was just a mini-star when we did *Gone with the Wind*. I was afraid to talk to him. People can't understand it now, but we were in awe. Clark Gable didn't open supermarkets.

OLIVIA DE HAVILLAND

■ I was so happy to be within two feet of him.

CLAUDETTE COLBERT

■ Gable made villains popular. Instead of the audiences wanting the good man to get the girl, they began wanting the bad man to get her.

NORMA SHEARER

■ [Rhett Butler] was one of the best roles ever offered in Hollywood and my screen character saw himself emerging from the film as a dashing-type fellow. But I said no. I didn't see myself as quite that dashing, and later, when I saw Clark Gable play the role to perfection, I knew I was right.

GARY COOPER

■ He was America's dream of itself, a symbol of courage, indomitable against the greatest of odds. But he was also a human being, kind, likeable, a guy right out of the life all around the fans who worshipped him. Gable was the boy-man, without arrogance, but plenty of fire and spunk, a gay, daring, dashing blade.

BEN HECHT

■ Naturally I looked at him. 'God damn brat,' he said. 'You've ruined every one of my birthdays. They bring you out from behind the wallpaper to sing that song, and it's a pain in the ass.' Do you know, I've only begun to like him today . . . now that he's levelled with me?

JUDY GARLAND

■ When Clark Gable left MGM, the only one who said goodbye was the old guy at the gate. Gary Cooper, Cary Grant and Katharine Hepburn were all box office poison at different times. So it's not what you are in Hollywood—it's what people *think* you are.

ROBERT STACK

■ Clark made you believe whatever he was playing. He had that God-given thing: a theatrical personality, the ability to communicate with the audience, which all the training in the world cannot give you. The public caught it in Clark Gable the first time he walked on the screen.

DAVID O. SELZNICK

■ Favourite leading man? Oh, Clark Gable! No question about it. With him, I enjoyed myself so hugely that I felt a little guilty! Gable was delightful. The most perfect kisser I have ever worked with.

ANNE BAXTER

■ I loved that man. I wish we could have met when we were both young and about the same age, but I guess it probably wouldn't have worked out. When you're both famous, it's a double problem—even when you're famous in different ways, like Arthur [Miller] and I were.

MARILYN MONROE

■ They tell me they're going to make a film about Clark Gable. Who will play him: Burt Reynolds? Well, there's a man sufficiently sexy. Like Michael Caine, Marlon Brando, Sean Connery or Roger Moore, but the real magic has gone. Marlon is much too secret and Sean can't console himself for not being a second Laurence Olivier. I mean, Roger and Michael are absolutely adorable, but they're not in the same class as Cooper or Gable.

SHELLEY WINTERS

ABEL GANCE (1889–1981)

■ The visual resources of the motion picture have never been stretched further than in Abel Gance's *Napoleon*. The picture is an encyclopaedia of cinematic effects—a pyrotechnical display of what the art of the silent film was capable of in the hands of a genius. Few of the experiments have been carried further—even by Gance himself. He admits he has made no progress since this picture was completed.

KEVIN BROWNLOW

GRETA GARBO (born 1905)

- Her intelligence and grace were revealed in all her Silent films, from *The Torrent* to *The Kiss*. Her immense power bursts forth for the first time in *Anna Christie*.

ROBERT E. SHERWOOD, 1930

- Garbo will be forgotten in ten years, and as an actress her memory will be dead when Helen Hayes', Lynn Fontanne's and Katharine Cornell's are beginning to grow greener.

CLAIRE BOOTHE LUCE, 1932

- One leaves the cinema after *Camille* uncertain for the moment where familiar bus routes pass, unwilling to dissipate the awed and uplifted certainty that one has been in the presence of greatness.

DEREK PROUSE, 1955

- There have been two great personalities in movies in the last forty years. One was Valentino. The other was Greta Garbo. Today, without having made a film since 1940, she is still the greatest.

CLARENCE BROWN, 1963

- Extremely well behaved and disciplined. She was unique—a creature born for the screen. She knew when to quit, she just sensed it. She is much too intelligent to want to try to come back now.

GEORGE CUKOR, 1972

- The most inhibited person I have every worked with.

ERNST LUBITSCH

- What, when drunk, one sees in other women, one sees in Garbo sober.

KENNETH TYNAN

- This being, at one and the same time real and inaccessible, rouses all desire. With impunity she smiles, parts her lips, puts her head back, half closes her eyes. She is there, alive, offering herself to thousands of men. But if one of them were suddenly to rush forward in a fit of madness, he would find nothing but an empty cloth, his arms would clasp nothing but emptiness . . . Oh, that beautiful face, that perhaps one evening (how often have I dreamed of it!) will appear again on the screen before the fascinated masses in the cinemas of the whole world.

FRANÇOIS MAURIAC

- She was a provocative girl. I found working with her an extraordinary experience. She wasn't a trained actress—and she was aware of that herself—but she had extraordinary intuitions, especially in the realm of erotic experience. Her acting made you feel that here was a woman who knew all there was to know about all aspects of love.

MELVYN DOUGLAS

- She must think that I am trying to imitate her, but there is nobody like Garbo. I am new to the screen, but I think she is the greatest star in the world. She has a magic quality which will survive bad pictures—and even age . . .

MARLENE DIETRICH

79

- I'm a legend because I've survived over a long period of time and still seem to be master of my fate. I'm still paddling the goddamned boat myself, you know ... whereas Garbo has always been a mysterious sailboat who disappeared over the horizon the moment she felt she couldn't cope. She represented a kind of elusive beauty, and she felt, I think, that when that elusive beauty started to fade she would wave goodbye and disappear.

  KATHARINE HEPBURN

- I liked her; she was nice, very beautiful. As an actress, she gave you very little. In other words, it was a love affair between her and the camera. In fact, when working with her, one felt she was doing nothing really, that she wasn't even very good, until you saw the results on the screen ...

  MAUREEN O'SULLIVAN

- There are actresses who have more acting ability, but Garbo had a guarded mystery about her, and was enchanting to work with. She had the most beautiful nose and face, and you could read on it all the thoughts that came to her. Her ability to project what was within was unique. She was really wonderful and should not have let one bad picture disturb her. Most of us have had many bad pictures.

  CHARLES BOYER

- Co-starring with Garbo hardly constituted an introduction.

  FREDRIC MARCH

- Subtract Garbo from most of her films, and you are left with nothing.

  RICHARD WHITEHALL

- She is the true immortal. Other legends and other goddesses crumble and fade into loveable or laughable antiques; but Garbo, miraculously, remains.

  DAVID ROBINSON

- Every man's harmless fantasy mistress. She gave you the impression that, if your imagination had to sin, it could at least congratulate itself on its impeccable taste.

  ALISTAIR COOKE

- The saddest thing in my career is that I was never able to photograph her in colour. I begged the studio. I felt I had to get those incredible blue eyes in colour but they said no. The process at the time was cumbersome and expensive, and the pictures were already making money. I still feel sad about it.

  WILLIAM DANIELS, 1969

- But the marvel of her appeal lay far deeper than the outward beauty of a wonderful bone structure and sensitive photogenic face. Rarely had the West been privileged to see such spiritual depths as were manifest in Garbo's performances ... Few Western women, if any, have ever rivalled her artless emotional profundity. Without that genuine, tragic soulfulness, she would have created little more impression than Dolores del Rio, a gardenia without scent ...

  CECIL BEATON

- She turned one day to the director and she said, 'Is it necessary for that man to be here?' It was the cameraman! She didn't even recognise him, it was just a man standing there looking at her. She was destroying herself and becoming emotional and she didn't want anybody to see her doing these things.

  HENRY HATHAWAY

80

■ And in the first five minutes of the film, [*Anna Karenina*] when the smoke artfully provided by the train clears away and reveals the Garbo's face, you might just as well pick up your hat and go home if you too can't guess the end. Before she has even chosen her lover, her look tells you it doesn't much matter who he is, they all go the same way home.

ALISTAIR COOKE

■ When Conrad Nagel steps into her box at the opera [in *The Mysterious Lady*], she pretends it's a mistake, but her gestures tell us otherwise. They are more open than usual, maybe even reckless: she brazenly drapes her arms on the chairs behind her as she speaks to Nagel, exaggerating the arc of her breasts, and we realise that this Garbo is not tired but tiger-tense in anticipation of her noble, vulnerable prey.

RICHARD CORLISS

■ Whatever your personal reaction to Garbo may be you cannot deny that this Swedish lady has power. You can't ignore her. She is in some ways like Katharine Hepburn—rough, strong, ruthless, a mass of pure ore that can be worked and refined. In certain moods it is possible to be proof against Hepburn. You can be tired, lethargic, captious, and Hepburn won't touch you. But Garbo compels your attention, whatever your mood.

C. A. LEJEUNE

■ Garbo went through a great deal to get a scene right. She worked out every gesture in advance and learned every syllable of dialogue exactly as written. She never improvised, and I respected her for that.

GEORGE CUKOR

AVA GARDNER (born 1922)

■ She can read a script and immediately give you a completely lucid explanation of its merits and faults.

STANLEY KRAMER, 1959

■ As I watched her on that set [of *The Killers*], I was intrigued. I sensed a basic, fundamental thing about her, an earthiness bordering on the roughneck, even though she was at pains to conceal it. Some time later I met her again and tried to make a conquest. I was completely unsuccessful. No midnight swims, no weekends . . . no Huston.

JOHN HUSTON, 1980

■ In the film *Mayerling* (1968), Ava played my mother; in *Harem*, she's my wife! I tell her the next time she will be my daughter. I'm obviously ageing faster than she is. She looks like a million dollars.

OMAR SHARIF, 1987

■ One of the most generous and warm-hearted of people.

ANTHONY ANDREWS

■ Today marked the worst behaviour I've yet seen from that curious breed I make my living opposite. Ava showed up for a late call, did one shot (with the usual incredible delay in coming to the set) and then walked off just before lunch when some Chinese extra took a still of her. She came back after a painful 3-hour lunch break . . . only to walk off, for the same reason.

CHARLTON HESTON

■ Ava has been completely victimised by the kind of life she has led, and as a result has become the kind of person she is today.

ARTIE SHAW

- Ava herself was charming. She's a real movie queen, really exciting; lovely looking, too, with marvellous legs. When she crosses the screen, you're bound to follow her.

  GEORGE CUKOR

- She was her customary self, as amiable as an adder . . . Both Elizabeth Taylor and Ava are as spoiled as medieval queens. They expect men to fall at their feet, and they are accustomed to being catered to and having everything done for them.

  HELEN LAWRENSON

- Ava Gardner's famous temper caused 'some sticky moments'. She's a great trouper, we overcame all that. She's an old friend, with the command and control of the authentic star. Ava's a *gent*!

  GEORGE CUKOR

82

JOHN GARFIELD (1913–1952)

- Garfield's deep-set eyes over the flame of a match.
  'How long you staying?' (he asks).
  'I'm flying to Germany in the morning.'
  'I'd like to go along! I don't have a passport.'
  'To Germany?'
  'You still got a lot of Nazis? I'm a Jew.'
  'Don't know, they're quiet for the moment.'
  'Ours are deafening, it evens things out.'

  HILDEGARD KNEF

- Julie, dear friend, I will always love you.

  CLIFFORD ODETS

JUDY GARLAND (1922–1969)

- How good she is! She is no Venus, let us admit—but how delightful is her smile,

how genuine her emotion, how sure her timing, and how brilliantly she brings off her effects.

JAMES AGEE, 1942

- She has only to open her throat and send her voice pleading and appealing up to the roof, to leave no doubt that talent like hers is independent of age and appearance.

  KENNETH TYNAN, 1954

- With a talent like Miss Garland's it's tragic that she didn't cherish it and take care of it.

  BETTE DAVIS, 1970

- In some of her films . . . she showed talent which was very comic and touching. Touching because she played with a bright smile and a great spirit, while the situation was rather dramatic, even tragic perhaps. She had in fact a quality which can only be compared to Chaplin's heartbreaking quality . . . always optimistic, always gay, always inventive, against poverty, against desperate situations—and that's when Judy is at her best.

  JAMES MASON, 1970

- There wasn't a thing that gal couldn't do—except look after herself.

  BING CROSBY

- When she started [in *I Could Go on Singing*], the real tears came and I realised she was not even sticking to the script. She was just pouring her heart out to us. . . . I knew that I had to shoot it then, because it would never happen again. We got in as close as we could and took it. . . . When we wrapped up the last shot, Judy just stood there and yelled: 'You'll miss me when I'm gone!' and marched off. We never saw her again and, of course, we did miss her.

RONALD NEAME, 1970

■ She was just simply wonderful. She danced beautifully, learned beautifully. She was very adept at whatever she did. Really in fine form. We were all set to do another picture together, but she got sick and that was the end of that.

FRED ASTAIRE, 1974

■ The most talented woman I ever knew was Judy Garland. She was a great great comedienne and she could do more things than any girl I ever knew. Act, sing, dance, make you laugh. She was everything. I had a great affection for her. Such a tragedy. Too much work, too much pressure, the wrong kind of people as husbands.

BING CROSBY, 1976

■ I used to try and see Judy Garland whenever I could. She was one of the first who knew how to build a song, take it to its climax and then draw back.

BARBARA COOK, 1986

■ I never had any problems with Judy . . . But Judy loved to growl, loved to *pretend,* and when she heard I was assigned to *Easter Parade* she said 'Look sweetie, I'm no June Allyson, you know. Don't get cute with me. None of that batting-the-eyelids bit, or the fluffing the hair routine for me, buddy! I'm Judy Garland and just you watch it!'

CHARLES WALTERS

■ She was the very best there was. In our profession, no one could command an audience the way she did. Of course, she had the most marvellous training. At MGM there were so many people to tell

her what to do, how to make the best of herself . . . Tragic? Oh yes.

TONY BENNETT, 1987

■ It was the only tacky thing I knew MGM do. Letting her go. They should have closed it [*Annie Get Your Gun*] down till she was ready.

HOWARD KEEL

■ The finest all-round performer we ever had in America was Judy Garland. There was no limit to her talent. She was the quickest, brightest person I ever worked with.

GENE KELLY

■ She was a friend of mine—a trying friend, but a friend . . . This is what I tell myself: She did everything she ever wanted to do. She never really denied herself anything for me. See, I say, she had a wonderful life—she did what she wanted to do. And I have no right to change her fulfilment into my misery. I'm on my own broom now.

LIZA MINNELLI

■ Judy Garland was the most exciting sheer talent I ever worked with. She was so unpredictable, very child-like, very difficult to work with at times, but the rewards were immense.

NORMAN JEWISON

■ Judy Garland was trouble. She was also probably the greatest female performer the world has ever known—so we just had to weather it. We never knew if she was going to show up for a performance. She always did, eventually, but we often had to hold up the curtain for her.

LEW GRADE

■ I worked a great, great deal with Judy and never had one minute's trouble . . .

83

Could there be a better actress than Judy was? She was a real honest to God musical theatre performer. Sang like an angel. A great showman. Hell of a dancer, and a heart-rending actress!

JOHN GREEN

JAMES GARNER (born 1928)

■ If men only knew what's appealing to a woman is how a man makes her feel about herself. Jim is funny and dear, and he laughs at my jokes. That's what makes Jim sexy; it doesn't change with years.

SALLY FIELD

GREER GARSON (born 1908)

■ As an Irish servant in a rich Scottish household [in *The Valley of Decision*], she is alive, vivid and charming, and suggests how really good she might be under better circumstances. If she were not suffocated and immobilised by Metro's image of her—and, I'm afraid, half-persuaded of it herself—I could imagine her as a very good Lady Macbeth . . .

JAMES AGEE

■ Very bright. Fantastically beautiful. Very much the lady. She was a great Irish wit. There are actors who work in movies. And then there are movie stars. She was a *movie star*.

TERESA WRIGHT

VITTORIO GASSMANN (born 1922)

■ He's a monster . . . Nature has made him prodigiously gifted and that's not always a blessing. His monstrous technical ability make him neglect to go deeper

into the roles he plays. All the same, what an actor!

LUCHINO VISCONTI

RICHARD GERE (born 1949)

■ I'm always trying to find diplomatic ways to talk about Richard and the movie *An Officer and a Gentleman*. I liked him before we started but that is the last time I can remember talking to him.

DEBRA WINGER, 1987

■ Richard Gere's role (in *The Honorary Consul*) is obsessive and everything, all the action, stems from him. Without him, nothing really moves. I look upon him as a sort of James Dean of the 80s, maturer and older, perhaps, but still moody and with a definite aura and personality that comes across.

JOHN MACKENZIE

■ Cinema has always had its male sex symbols but Richard Gere is nevertheless quite a new phenomenon. Combining the sultry Latin appeal of Rudolph Valentino, the moody vulnerability of James Dean and the sexual charisma of Marilyn Monroe, his sudden entry into Hollywood stardom has reached new heights.

SALLY HIBBIN

■ As the chief luxury item [in *American Gigolo*], Richard Gere is thoroughly self-centered, which is probably right for the character. Physically, the mixture of tenderness and roughness, strength and grace, is perfect, but here, as in his other movie roles, Gere never really develops a character. This actor lacks a strong sense of his own identity.

DAVID DENBY

■ Richard Gere has taken his shirt off in every movie he's made. He's falling out of his clothes.

CHRISTOPHER REEVE

■ Gere plays the kind of guy who's saying 'I wanna get laid and you're gonna get laid whether you like it or not'. I'm the kind of guy who says 'Please'.

CHRISTOPHER REEVE

GIANCARLO GIANNINI (born 1942)

■ . . . an extraordinary actor. Till now [in *Innocente*] (1976) he has only worked in films unworthy of him.

LUCHINO VISCONTI

CEDRIC GIBBONS (1893–1960)

■ MGM's class or standard was largely due to Cedric Gibbons' influence on the sets and décor; his high standards were matched by Douglas Shearer's recording and the other departments.

MAUREEN O'SULLIVAN

MEL GIBSON (born 1956)

■ It was not difficult for me to imagine what it was like to be hopelessly in love with Mel. It was wonderful for me to play opposite him. I didn't have any idea how much emotional range he had.

DIANE KEATON

■ The most exciting thing that's come into my life as an actor and a friend. He's a very special human being.

RICHARD DONNER

■ Any film [*Lethal Weapons*] which contrives to get both of its leading men stark naked within the first five minutes has got to have a lot going for it. Danny Glover is no physical wreck, even when he's upped his real age by a decade to play a 50-year-old. But when your other piece of bare-ass is Mel Gibson, then you score *maximum points*.

ANNE BILLSON

■ Mel is the new Australian. He is going to be a very good star. He is quite different from the Australian everyone knows—the kind Rod Taylor represents.

PETER WEIR

■ Mel is the most gorgeous man I have ever seen.

SIGOURNEY WEAVER

■ I haven't seen a star with his sex appeal and style since Paul Newman.

FREDDIE FIELDS

JOHN GIELGUD (born 1896)

■ I'm in two minds about doing this sort of thing. *Arthur* was an extraordinary success and gave me a new, young public which had never seen me on the stage. But then I made another film of the same kind called *Scandals* which was a terrific flop in America, a total disaster. If you play too many cameos people begin to think you're in every film that comes up and they get sick of you. I would like to do just really good parts. And yet cameos are so much less of a responsibility. I've only been really proud of two things I've done in the last few years. One was *Providence*, the film I made with Alan Resnais and the other was *Brideshead*. It was a small part, but effective.

HIMSELF, 1983

- Resnais fucked me. Put Johnny G. in and, well, you can forget about me. Wipe the screen. No one, and I mean *no one*, upstages Johnny G. So I was a bit pissed off. But it [*Providence*] was a good movie.

  DIRK BOGARDE, 1983

JOHN GILBERT (1895–1936)

- In the time of Hollywood's most glittering days, he glittered the most. There were no enemies in his life. He was as unsnobbish as a happy child. He went everywhere he was invited. He needed no greatness around him to make him feel distinguished. He drank with carpenters, danced with waitresses and made love to whores and movie queens alike. He swaggered and posed but it was never to impress anyone. He was being John Gilbert, prince, butterfly, Japanese lantern, and the spirit of romance.

  BEN HECHT

- MGM released the 'most sizzling movie' ever made on their lot, *The Flesh and the Devil,* starring Greta Garbo and Jack Gilbert. The reaction of the audience was exactly what the theatre owners had prayed for—a new heartthrob. Sparks which they thought the death of Valentino had extinguished turned Gilbert into a veritable Roman candle. A couple of weeks following the ballyhoo over the picture, Gilbert picked up Rudy's laurels, and long queues of women persisted in following him wherever he went.

  FRANCES MARION

LILLIAN GISH (born 1896)

- I do not say that this little girl is as great an actress as Sarah Bernhardt. For all I know she may not be able to speak the President's American. What I do know is that in this one picture *Broken Blossoms* she ranks with the world's great artists ... It is curious that this plain little American girl should give the world an exact image of the great actress in far-off youth.

  JAMES AGATE

- Miss Gish had a place in the world of movies comparable to that in the theatre of a Sarah Bernhardt or an Eleanora Duse.

  BOSLEY CROWTHER

- Her career is proof of the fact that the entire history of the feature film is contained within a lifetime.

  KEVIN BROWNLOW

- I think the things that are necessary in my profession are these: Taste, Talent and Tenacity. I think I have had a little of all three.

  HERSELF

- I told her that I'd been nominated and how sorry I was that she wasn't [both for *The Whales of August*]—for everyone thought she would be, it was surely her last chance for a major Oscar. And she said 'It could be worse. Suppose I'd been nominated and lost to Cher?'.

  ANN SOTHERN

- She might look fragile, but physically and spiritually she was as fragile as a steel rod. Nobody could sway her from her self-appointed course. With a Botticelli face, she had the mind of a good Queen Bess, dictating her carefully thought-out policies and ruling justly, if firmly.

  FRANCES MARION

86

JEAN-LUC GODARD (born 1930)

- *A Bout de Souffle* seems to me the most original, insolently gifted and shattering work the young French directors have yet produced.

  PENELOPE GILLIATT, 1961

- Godard's thoughts about politics may be no more profound or original than those of the next man.

  PENELOPE HOUSTON, 1966

- After the first film I said never again, not with him. He's not an easy man . . . You never know what the film will be like even after the shooting. He takes the materials into his editing kitchen and, like a great cook, what he serves up bears no relation to what he started with, because he has added his imagination, his pain and his intelligence.

  NATHALIE BAYE

PAULETTE GODDARD (born 1911)

- It was her honesty I liked.

  VERONICA LAKE

- I always liked working with Paulette. She was not a brilliant actress, she had no sense of timing and everything about her playing was mechanical and contrived. But nobody knew it better than she did, and she was completely honest about it; she is the most honest actress I ever knew. She worked her ass off trying to give it all she had, and in the end, her performances were quite all right.

  RAY MILLAND

JAMES GOLDMAN (born 1931)

- I tell you though, if you look at a film like *All The President's Men*, well any one of two dozen directors could have made that movie, only very few writers could have written it—Goldman was amazing because everyone knew the pay-off: Nixon's out. It would be just like making *Psycho* and over the opening credits showing Tony Perkins taking off his wig!! And he did it.

  BRUCE ROBINSON

SAM GOLDWYN (1882–1974)

- He came to see me one day after he had seen the rushes for *Porgy and Bess*. He was full of praise, particularly for the photography. So I said: 'Why don't you tell Leon Shamroy, the photographer?' He was only standing a few paces away. And Goldwyn said: 'Why should I tell him? I pay him enough!'

  OTTO PREMINGER, 1972

ELLIOTT GOULD (born 1938)

- Very often you see American monsters created by the audience. Oh, they do have something, but it's only one dimension. What I want from the actors in my pictures is an ability to express the second and third dimensions, an ability to put the part together inside themselves and then materialise it. I want to get it from their faces, from their eyes, from their movements. I can see that Gould has it.

  INGMAR BERGMAN, 1970

- He's a lot of fun in the tub [in *Move*].

  PAULA PRENTISS

- He's an excellent actor, the character he plays [in *Little Murders*] has a kind of brooding intensity that Elliott doesn't

87

have. He had to work very hard for that. But he was completely successful.

ALAN ARKIN

■ He was the first person to teach me to enjoy acting. He never throws a tantrum, never gets into a snit.

CANDICE BERGEN

■ He knows exactly what he wants and how to get it.

ROBERT ALTMAN

EDMUND GOULDING (1891–1959)

■ He did something that drove actors crazy. He'd get out there and act out everybody's roles for them—even the women! And we were supposed to imitate him. We wanted to give our own interpretations.

JOAN BLONDELL

■ He concentrated on attractive shots of me—in other words, gave me the 'star' treatment. It was the first time I had had this. I was always a member of the cast— a leading member—but not made special in the way Goulding made me special in this film. *And* in the last scene in chiffon, a large beautiful picture hat, and a glamorous hairdo, I looked *really* like a 'movie star.'

BETTE DAVIS

BETTY GRABLE (1916–1973)

■ She's a friendly, likeable person, with indomitable good humour, unassuming and frank.

HELEN LAWRENSON, 1969

■ She'd murder you. I remember once I got her angry on the set. She stormed over

and said, 'You know why I'm doing this picture? I thought they said Dan Duryea!'

DAN DAILEY

■ She was not only one of the biggest box office attractions of all time, but her work symbolised that era of gaudy Technicoloured escapism for which millions craved in World War II when she became the most celebrated pin-up girl of all time . . .

TOM VALLANCE

STEWART GRANGER (born 1913)

■ This [*The Man In Grey*] is his first film part of any size. His screen technique is entirely undisciplined. He throws away, with a prodigal nonchalance, the sort of moments veterans have taken years to achieve. As a star performer, he is still quite brilliantly bad. I don't know any British actor I would sooner sign as a prospect.

C. A. LEJEUNE, 1943

CARY GRANT (1904–1986)

■ I told him how much I envied him because as the suave, charming, gifted man he is, he makes all his pictures in places like Monte Carlo, London, Paris, the French Riviera, and I made mine in deserts with a dirty shirt and a two day growth of beard and bad food.

ROBERT RYAN, 1970

■ I mention the story of the magazine editor who sent him a telegram reading: 'How old Cary Grant?' to which Cary is said to have replied: 'Old Cary Grant fine. How you?' That story has been attributed to different people over the years. I wish I could say it was true, but it's not.

RODERICK MANN, 1974

■ Everyone thinks of him affectionately because he embodies what seems a happier time . . . We didn't want depth from him; we asked only that he be handsome and silky and make us laugh.

PAULINE KAEL, 1975

■ I'm getting older too, dear. The only one who isn't is Cary Grant.

GRACE KELLY, 1978

■ The champion.

MARLENE DIETRICH

■ I learned many things working with Cary Grant. He has such tremendous concentration. Many actors do not have the courage to stand still. Cary Grant knows how to concentrate, how to look directly at you, but always with great relaxation.

SOPHIA LOREN

■ *The Awful Truth* was, I believe, his first major comedy role, and I could sense his reticence behind the bright spirits . . . As I watched Cary working each day I marvelled at the excellence of his timing—the naturalness, the ease, the *charm*. Cary was wonderful in the film; it's my favourite comedy performance of his.

IRENE DUNNE

■ To women he is Hollywood's lone example of the Sexy Gentleman. And to men and women, he is Hollywood's lone example of a figure America, like most of the West, has needed all along: a Romantic Bourgeois Hero.

TOM WOLFE

■ These pictures [the comedies of the late 30s] did much to establish the Cary Grant we know and love 45 years later: the comic actor in high polish, plowing through all manner of screwball commotion with unassailable suavity, emerging from many an ordeal-by-slapstick with dignity tattered but intact. He had only to repeat this formula for the remainder of his career . . .

HARRY HAUN

■ Grant can milk more meaning out of a look, or a turn of his head, or just standing still, than most Hollywood hams can bludgeon out of fifty lines of dialogue.

GEORGE JEAN NATHAN

■ Cary Grant was famous in his films for trying to get other people in the scene to do the expository talking. Grant was a brilliant listener, and often scenes would be shifted to suit him. He was no fool. If you *can* give the exposition to a secondary character, *do* it. It's just another way of protecting the star.

WILLIAM GOLDMAN

■ Cary is marvellous, you see. One doesn't direct Cary Grant, one simply puts him in front of a camera. And, you see, he enables the audience to identify with the main character. I mean by that, Cary Grant represents a man we know. He's not a stranger.

ALFRED HITCHCOCK

■ They are trying to show he's a great lover, but they'll never prove it to me.

ZSA ZSA GABOR

■ Our relationship on *A Touch of Mink* was amiable but devoid of give-and-take. For somebody who is as open and right out there as I am, it was hard at first

89

to adjust to Cary's inwardness. Not that he wasn't friendly and polite—he certainly was. But distant. Very distant.

DORIS DAY

KATHRYN GRAYSON (born 1922)

■ She's a beautiful woman. A good friend. Fun to be around.

HOWARD KEEL

PETER GREENAWAY (born 1942)

■ Greenaway is a great comedian. What no one seems to have realised is that Peter Greenaway is the real Woody Allen. Let me clarify that. He is the film-maker that Woody Allen would like to be, in the sense that his stuff is an elaborate, absurdist and extremely intellectual joke.

BRIAN DENNEHY

90

SIDNEY GREENSTREET (1879–1954)

■ Sidney Greenstreet only had two favours to ask. One was that we shouldn't change even a comma in his dialogue when he'd learned it, and the other was to be sure that the rest of the actors gave him the correct cues. Greenstreet wanted a lot of rehearsal. Lorre just wanted to go ahead and shoot it. But he did everything with a sense of fun and he would always agree to rehearse for Greenstreet.

DAN SIEGEL, 1973

■ Poor Sydney! He never did live down the Fat Man. I don't think he ever did a picture later in which that evil, hiccuppy laugh wasn't exploited. He was a very fine, versatile actor, within his physical limitations.

MARY ASTOR, 1975

JOAN GREENWOOD (born 1921)

■ When it comes to holding her own with a large and brilliant cast, there is no one to equal Joan Greenwood. Nor does she *have* to resort to those mocking, wicked affectations in order to do so.

PETER JOHN DYER

■ That formidable enchantress.

FRANK MARCUS

JANE GREER (born 1924)

■ A more charming, talented and gracious person I shall never know.

RUDY VALLEE

D. W. GRIFFITH (1875–1948)

■ Griffith remains an enigma terribly outdated; . . . he brought a sense of time and a unique visual scope to the screen, but . . . this visionary director could not recognise his flaws and could not listen to others. The mystery of the lonely rejected Griffith of later years still haunts Hollywood, and piques the interest of the younger generation.

ALBERT JOHNSON, 1954

■ The whole industry owes its existence to him.

CHARLES CHAPLIN

■ Nothing essential has been added to the art of the motion picture since Griffith.

RENÉ CLAIR

■ Among the most repellent elements in his films (and there are such) we see Griffith as an open apologist for racism, erecting a celluloid monument to the Klu

Klux Klan, and joining their attack on Negroes in *The Birth of a Nation*.

S. M. EISENSTEIN

■ It's true, I sometimes called him David. Even so, I might have *said* David, but I always *thought* Mr Griffith. He was a born general. His voice was a voice of command. It was resonant, deep and full.

LILLIAN GISH

■ We do not want now, and we never shall want the human voice with our films. . . . Music—fine music—will always be the voice of the silent drama.

HIMSELF, 1924

FILIPPO DEL GUIDICE (1892–1961)

■ He believed that the industrial tail was wagging the artistic dog, and he set about trying to free the creative talent from business worries and interference. He rightly declined to be described as a producer, and attempted—as 'Administrator'—to keep Wardour Street away from Denham. In this process he fell into a trap which his own character laid for him. In fact he was trying to go from one extreme to the other, and he gave his film-makers such a heady draught of self-importance that they were soon understandably giddy.

PETER PRICE

ALEC GUINNESS (born 1914)

■ He cut my part [in *The Scapegoat*] into such shreds that my appearance in the final product made no sense at all. This is an actor who plays by himself, unto himself. In this particular picture he plays

a dual role, so at least he was able to play with himself.

BETTE DAVIS

■ The whole presence of the man is guarded and evasive. Slippery sums him up; when you think you have him, eel-like, he eludes your grasp. He looks unmemorable. Were he to commit a murder, I have no doubt that the number of false arrests following the circulation of his description would break all records.

KENNETH TYNAN

■ He's an actor, that fellow, a superb actor. But over and above that he does his homework. However idiosyncratically I saw Alec playing a part, I would be very, very cautious about criticising it, because I know that every point about it would be backed by a complete marshalling of all the available evidence. He really does his homework.

LAURENCE OLIVIER

91

SACHA GUITRY (1885–1957)

■ He loved art and beautiful women; he was a tireless worker; he could even, when he felt like it, be a moralist. He will probably hold his place in the years to come—a minor place though by no means a negligible one—not among the creative artists but among the great entertainers of the theatre and cinema. He had, in the highest degree, wit; and in France this covers a multitude of sins.

LOUIS MARCORELLES

YILMAZ GÜNEY (1937–1984)

■ Güney's films are raw, angry and uncompromising . . . Posters of Güney are sold in Istanbul alongside posters of Eastwood, Dean and Brando and he has a similar intensity. As a director ... it sometimes seems as if the Mexican Buñuel had been crossed with Satyajit Ray, with a dash of Pasolini and Leone ... his films are accurate and, indeed, prophetic accounts of the problems that face his marvellous, terrible country.

ADRIAN TURNER

GENE HACKMAN (born 1931)

■ When acting is done well it is an extraordinary craft, and there are some who approach it like a job. It is breathtaking and inspiring to see someone like Gene Hackman, who is absolutely unpretentious and has never gone through the imbecilities and self-aggrandisement of other actors.

CANDICE BERGEN

■ When you're on top, you get a sense of immortality. You feel you can do no wrong, that it will always be good no matter what the role. Well, in truth, that feeling is death. You must be honest with yourself.

HIMSELF

■ Gene Hackman's good to work with. We really work *together*, y'know? He gives a lot and he likes it when you give. It's hard to find actors you actually deal with, and he *deals* with you.

MATT DILLON

ANN HARDING (1901–1981)

■ ... the pretty and highly regarded Ann Harding, a woman of great charm, integrity and beauty.

LAURENCE OLIVIER

JEAN HARLOW (1911–1937)

■ I'd seen her in *Public Enemy* and *Hell's Angels*, where she was so bad and self-conscious it was comic. She got big laughs when she didn't want them. Then I saw *Red Dust*—and there she was, suddenly marvellous in comedy. A tough girl and yet very feminine, like Mae West. They both wisecrack, but they have something vulnerable, and it makes them attractive.

GEORGE CUKOR

■ I'd have liked to have gone to bed with Jean Harlow. She was a beautiful broad. The fellow who married her was impotent and he killed himself. I would have done the same thing.

GROUCHO MARX

■ Well, the scene required me to embrace her. I think she kind of subdued the acting a bit because we were only rehearsing but not the kiss! When it came to kissing—Harlow was the greatest. And Hollywood being what it was, we did the scene over and over again. They were ... happy days.

JAMES STEWART

■ You know, she never wore underclothes and she was walking past the guys on *Public Enemy* one day and Cagney said 'How do you hold those things up?' and she said 'I ice them.' And she was very serious.

JOAN BLONDELL

■ She chatted gaily, 'The newspapers sure have loused me up, calling me a sex-pot! Where'd they ever get such a screwy idea?' One look at Harlow and whether you were male or female you could get no other idea; she was the Scylla and

92

Charybdis of sex, from her provocative come-hither expression to the flowing lines of her beautifully proportioned body.

FRANCES MARION

■ She didn't want to be famous. She wanted to be happy.

CLARK GABLE

■ A square shooter if ever there was one.

SPENCER TRACY

ED HARRIS (born 1950)

■ Luckily Ed doesn't give a damn about image making, and that is crucial here [in *Sweet Dreams*] because the audience has to like and heartily dislike him at the same time. We certainly don't whitewash him. In no way is it a Robert Redford performance.

KAREL REISZ, 1986

RICHARD HARRIS (born 1932)

■ Richard can't help it if he's known in the business as 'the horizontal champ' can he? When it comes to doing anything dangerous on the set, he's usually found flat on his back. I'm a far better cowboy than he is. But then, to be fair, I'm a younger man. And I'm prettier. And I have more hair than he has.

OLIVER REED

■ Richard is very much the *professional Irishman*. I found him a somewhat erratic personality and an occasional pain in the posterior. But we certainly never feuded.

CHARLTON HESTON

REX HARRISON (born 1908)

■ Of course, he's a monster, but I love him. He has such humour about himself. At least with me, I can send him up, but I don't think anyone else should try.

HAROLD FRENCH, 1983

■ Rex Harrison was in a strange kind of mood [in *Midnight Lace*] no doubt because his wife, Kay Kendall, had died. He had very little time for me or anybody else, as far as I could tell; he did his job and that was it.

MYRNA LOY

■ The most brilliant actor that I have ever worked with. I've liked others very much more.

ANNA NEAGLE

■ Darryl wanted Huston [to direct *Dr Doolittle*], but I figured there was already enough temperament with Rex without getting Huston involved.

ARTHUR P. JACOBS

■ The bastard of all time if he wants to be.

CHRISTOPHER CAZENOVE

93

■ Rex is marvellous, but impossible . . . bad at human relationships . . . The only enduring relationship Rex had was with his basset-hound Homer. Rex loved Homer.

ELIZABETH HARRIS HARRISON

■ He's the actor I've learnt most from. Whenever I used to think about how I would play a part I would first think how Rex would approach it.

DIRK BOGARDE

■ Why do I always pick the tough ones?

ARTHUR P. JACOBS
[On apes, animals—and Rex Harrison]

RAY HARRYHAUSEN (born 1920)

■ Long after we are all gone, his shadow-shows will live through a thousand years in this world.

RAY BRADBURY

- Ray Harryhausen! A magic name to those who know of the wonders he has wrought. Creator of cyclops and pterodactyl, dragon and god.

  JOEL UMAN

WILLIAM S. HART (1870–1946)

- Bill Hart was dynamic. He was deeply emotional, having the uncanny ability to project his feeling to audiences. His impact on women, whether teenager or dowager, was powerful, even though his profile was something less than Greek and his expression about as warm as chiseled granite.

  WALTER SELTZER

- He was the actor I loved the most. Although the scenarios of the first westerns were less complicated than those of today, he had a fastidiousness and a professional conscience without parallel to see that each line of the script was minutely respected . . . He was a gentleman of the kind not found today.

  ADOLPH ZUKOR

94

LAURENCE HARVEY (1928–1973)

- Acting with Harvey is like acting by yourself—only worse.

  JANE FONDA

- The tales I can tell of working with him are too horrendous to repeat.

  LEE REMICK, 1970

- I think I shall risk the halibut. It can't be too awful, can it? After you've lived with Laurence Harvey, nothing in life is ever really too awful again.

  HERMIONE BADDELEY, 1981

HURD HATFIELD (born 1918)

- America's least known great actor.

  ARTHUR PENN

HENRY HATHAWAY (1898–1985)

- It's hard work under a director like Henry Hathaway. Guys like that are actors' enemies. He told Glen Campbell, 'When I call action, tense up, goddamn it.' When he told me to tense up, I said, 'Don't give me that Martha Graham shit. Don't pose me'.

  ROBERT DUVALL, 1983

- He insisted on doing [the scene] his way. I insisted on doing it my way. . . . Finally, on the 86th take, I cracked and did it his way. When it was all over, he came up to me and said, 'Kid, there's one thing I can promise you: you'll never work in this town again.' And I didn't. Not for eight years. It was Hathaway himself who hired me, for *The Sons of Katie Elder* in 1964.

  DENNIS HOPPER

RONDO HATTON

- He was the only horror film star to play monsters without makeup.

  DENIS GIFFORD

HOWARD HAWKS (1896–1977)

- *Land of the Pharaohs* is in the mainstream of Hawks' work: a clearly defined group, here the captive race; a young man's development through experience to maturity; the instant sexual antagonism so common in Hawks' comedies; the way in which the pyramid comes to obsess the Pharaoh . . . the consequent stiffening of the characters into inflexibility.

ROBIN WOOD

JACK HAWKINS (1910–1973)

■ Watching Jack Hawkins in *Gideon's Day*, there is nobody else, I said to myself, really nobody who can with such a three-dimensional effect draw for us the reliable chap, conscientious but no tortoise, harassed but wryly surmounting frustration. Particularly the reliable policeman; Mr Hawkins does a special line in policeman.

DILYS POWELL

GOLDIE HAWN (born 1945)

■ She was landed with an idiot giggle, a remorseless inclination to squeak and if a brain hummed behind those dumbfounded eyes the secret never leaked out.

DONALD ZEC

■ Goldie is a knock-out girl. Honest as a child's stare and full of fun and giggles.

RODERICK MANN

■ In the fullest possible meaning of the word she is so nice.

PETER SELLERS

■ Goldie is one of the sharpest ladies I've ever worked with. She doesn't miss a thing. She's my greatest audience. She laughs at all my stories, and in the right places, too.

BURT REYNOLDS

■ Ditsy, my eye, she's the brightest dumb blonde since Queen Boadicea sliced Roman kneecaps.

VICTOR DAVIS

■ Goldie does something that none of the other actresses can do. She has a whimsy and a comedic ability that no one else has. We can all imitate her, but we can't get near it. I don't think that Goldie has yet branched out as much as she would like to dramatically, because she's such big box office doing what she does.

SALLY FIELD, 1985

■ Everyone knows the woman is super-talented. She is also a saint. *Protocol* was a difficult production with lots of locations, a big cast and a tight schedule. Goldie was wonderful throughout.

HERBERT ROSS

SUSAN HAYWARD (1918–1975)

■ Susan Hayward was an ice queen—very like Grace Kelly that way. When we'd be standing ready to shoot our scenes she was so silent and remote. It was so different from working with an actress like Barbara Stanwyck who, when we were waiting to go into our scenes for *The Bride Wore Boots*, would whisper, 'Come on, Bob. You know you'd like to fuck me. Admit it.'

ROBERT CUMMINGS

■ You aim at all the things you have been told that stardom means—the rich life, the applause, the parties cluttered with celebrities. Then you find that you have it all. And it is nothing, really nothing. It is like a drug that lasts just a few hours, a sleeping pill. When it wears off, you have to live without its help.

HERSELF

■ I learned a lot from that lady. I learned more about my trade, about presence in front of the camera, by watching her.

95

She acted like it was nothing, with no effort.

RORY CALHOUN

RITA HAYWORTH (1918—1987)

■ High in the hierarchy of stars who don't even have to pretend to act is Rita Hayworth, who might be called the Betty Grable of the intellectuals. She sways her scattered millions of ecstatics by remote emotional-erotic control; and no such thing as a story is ever allowed to interfere

RICHARD WINNINGTON, 1946

■ Miss Hayworth, who plays in this picture [*Gilda*] her first straight dramatic role, gives little evidence of a talent that should be commended or encouraged. She wears many gowns of shimmering lustre and tosses her tawny hair in glamorous style but her manner of playing a worldly woman is distinctly five-and-dime.

BOSLEY CROWTHER, 1946

■ She was so sweet and hard-working. She asked me to watch her work out her dance routines and go over her lines with her. . . . I'd tell her little things and she'd whisper, 'Don't tell the director, please'. She was so modest and affectionate.

EDWARD EVERETT HORTON, 1970

■ A great dancer but a different style to me.

FRED ASTAIRE

■ Few women have more willingly and deftly submitted to becoming the passive material out of which a myth can be created, and this fact, added to her rather remarkable qualifications, goes a long way toward explaining her success.

WINTHROP SARGENT

■ Every man I've known has fallen in love with Gilda and wakened with me.

HERSELF

■ Rita Hayworth is not an actress of great depth. She was a dancer, a glamorous personality and a sex symbol. These qualities are such that they can carry her no further professionally.

GENE RINGGOLD

SONJA HENIE (1912–1969)

■ Anyway, Henie was very difficult to work with. She wouldn't listen to you, and she would rather do what she wanted to do. Anytime she got into a good spin, she would stay in it for 5000 years . . . I think everybody thought that her real reason for stalling was that the next day we would be going into overtime and she was already getting a fortune, and this way she'd get even more. I think she was the highest-priced star at the studio, in the country even.

HERMES PAN

PAUL HENREID (born 1907)

■ He looks as though his idea of fun would be to find a nice cold damp grave and sit in it.

RICHARD WINNINGTON, 1946

AUDREY HEPBURN (born 1929)

■ Audrey Hepburn receives the sort of star treatment MGM used to give to Garbo, and, while the results are never comparably rewarding, she does preserve her extraordinary freshness and vivacity.

KAREL REISZ, 1954

■ I would not have chosen Audrey Hepburn myself because Jane Eyre [the film was never made] is a little mouse and Audrey is a head-turner. In any room where Audrey Hepburn sits, no matter what her makeup is, people will turn and look at her because she's so beautiful.

JAMES MASON, 1970

■ She is a truly romantic creature. She doesn't just profess good manners—she is really well mannered at all times. She is not driven in her career but she gives full value and she is never indifferent.

GEORGE CUKOR, 1972

■ Titism has taken over the country. But Audrey Hepburn singlehanded may make bozooms a thing of the past. The director will not have to invent shots where the girl leans forward for a glass of scotch and soda.

BILLY WILDER

■ After so many drive-in waitresses in movies—it has been a real drought—here is class, somebody who went to school, can spell and possibly play the piano. . . . She's a wispy, thin little thing, but you're really in the presence of somebody when you see that girl. Not since Garbo has there been anything like it, with the possible exception of Bergman.

BILLY WILDER

■ As a result of her enormous success, she has acquired that extra incandescent glow which comes as a result of being acclaimed. Her voice is peculiarly personal. With its sing-song cadence, that develops into a flat drawl ending in a child-like query, it has a quality of heartbreak.

CECIL BEATON

■ I knew that Audrey wanted to make the picture and that sooner or later they would come round . . . So, I told my agents to forget all other projects for me. I was waiting for Audrey Hepburn. She asked for me, and I was ready. This could be the last and only opportunity I'd have to work with the great and lovely Audrey and I was not missing it. Period.

FRED ASTAIRE

■ . . . Audrey Hepburn is utterly captivating: while her voice is no more than adequate, she dances charmingly with Astaire, though with a hint of insecurity in solo passages. The occasional artificiality of her screen personality does not, on the whole, obtrude itself.

DAVID VAUGHAN

■ Miss Hepburn, I've just seen *Roman Holiday* and although I wanted to hate you [because I was contractually prevented from doing it] I have to tell you that I wouldn't have been half as good. You were wonderful.

JEAN SIMMONS

■ She's a *lady*. When she participates in the Academy Awards, she makes all those starlets look like tramps. Thank you for your class, Audrey, you're quite a lady. If anyone said anything derogatory about her, I'd push them in the river.

VAN JOHNSON

■ A great lady. It's quite an achievement to spend that long in Hollywood and not become a Hollywood product. She always manoeuvred around that—and that takes intelligence. She was always her own person.

DAVID NIVEN

97

■ She's a tomboy and a fine comedienne. You'd never think of her being able to do my type of comedy. But she can. She has great energy, frail as she looks. But, well, she's so beautiful, so ethereal, it would be sacrilege to put her through it.

LUCILLE BALL

KATHARINE HEPBURN (born 1907)

■ She is [in *Little Women*] divine—no other word for it.

HUGH WALPOLE, 1953

■ [*The Philadelphia Story*] is above all Hepburn's film. Without her, it would have been much less. She is at her most dazzling; perhaps no actress can manage artificial comedy with such assurance and wit, and her temperament—vital, glittering, delicately exaggerated—is unforgettably displayed.

GAVIN LAMBERT, 1961

■ Katharine Hepburn is the most extraordinary *person* I've ever met in my life. And I must say if she became President of the United States we would all be at peace for the rest of our lives. She has tremendous integrity, a superb sense of humour, self-discipline, courage, generosity. And above all she is a great professional.

ANTHONY HARVEY, 1969

■ Fellini came down to visit [Giulietta Masina] looking like a god. I was sitting with Danny Kaye having a quiet glass of champagne when Kate suddenly started attacking Fellini, saying that he and Picasso started out all right but that they had both sold out. It was a rare moment, an extraordinary experience.

RICHARD CHAMBERLAIN, 1972

■ She was always testing me. Kate's an old-fashioned star who makes demands of old-fashioned protocol—flowers, meetings, dinners—and argues constantly in front of the crew. Of course, I'd make another film with her in a minute. This time, though, I'd give her a pair of boxing gloves.

BRUCE GILBERT, 1981

■ It was a magical summer for both of us. We worked together as though we'd been doing it all our lives. Kate is unique—in her looks, in the way she plays, most of all in herself. I love Kate for playing with me in this film. Other movies have had a lot of meaning for me . . . but *On Golden Pond* is the ultimate role of my career.

HENRY FONDA, 1981

■ Miss Hepburn seemed to me someone who took infinite pains to secure the effect which she wished to portray. Her acting has for me the quality of determined incandescence. In all her pictures she ploughed a lone furrow, but she was an undisputed mistress of the plough.

ROBERT MORLEY, 1987

■ She has a face that belongs to the sea and the wind, with large rocking-horse nostrils and teeth that you just know bite an apple every day.

CECIL BEATON

■ I think the nicest thing that has happened to me this summer has been getting to know Kate much better. She has great quality and I am devoted to her.

COLE PORTER

■ Well, we just got used to working together. She butts in, and I don't mind,

98

and I pick it up when she leaves off. We just got used to working together, that's all.

SPENCER TRACY

■ This dame is terrific—and expert in her craft and so electrifying on set that if you don't watch out, you're likely to wind up as part of the scenery.

BOB HOPE

■ What I learned from her was simplicity. She's a living example that stardom doesn't have to be synonymous with affectation or ego.

CHRISTOPHER REEVE

■ Katie was a wonderful gal. She's a strange person but I've always admired her greatly . . . She was the kind who would come in and look at sets and say, 'I've got just the thing at home for this,' and bring it in next day . . . So she was in on everything and Spence would kid the life out of her saying 'Shut your mouth—go back where you belong in vaudeville'.

WALTER LANG

■ As an actress she's a joy to work with. She's in there trying every moment. There isn't anything passive about her; she 'gives'. And as a person, she's real. There's no pretence about her. She's the most completely honest woman I've ever met.

CARY GRANT

■ I can't imagine Rhett Butler chasing you for ten years.

DAVID O. SELZNICK

■ The most completely thorough, driving, constantly-seeking actress with whom I've been associated. . . . she's never really satisfied; she never stops thinking about what she's doing and about what everybody else is doing . . . She is a marvellous woman who has a capacity for many emotional areas, and she has a great talent. She can trigger an emotional truth at precisely the right time. I don't know what she draws on; it's a deep, deep well.

STANLEY KRAMER

■ I idolise . . . Katharine Hepburn. She has this marvellous defense of womanhood. She's gracious. She loves men. But she also sticks up for her rights.

ANNE JACKSON

■ There are women and there are women—and then there is Katie. There are actresses and actresses—then there is Hepburn. A rare professional-amateur, acting is her hobby, her living, her love. She is as wedded to her vocation as a nun is to hers, and as competitive in acting as Sonja Henie was in skating. No clock-watching, no humbug, no sham temperament.

FRANK CAPRA

■ She was a one-man woman, Kate. There was never anyone but Tracy.

JOHN HUSTON

■ She makes dialogue sound better than it is by a matchless clarity and beauty of diction, and by a fineness of intelligence and sensibility that illuminates every shade of meaning in every line she speaks.

GARSON KANIN

■ I *worship* that bloody woman. I've never enjoyed working with anyone so much in my whole life, not even Burton. There were no problems, not a one.

PETER O'TOOLE

99

WERNER HERZOG (born 1942)

- If Fassbinder was the *enfant terrible* of the new German cinema, Werner Herzog has surely earned the right to being its wild man. Too fly for a primitive, he yet shows in his best films a ferocious innocence, the kind of driving candour that is always verging on the ruthless. His world is peopled with eccentrics and obsessives, mirrors—it often seems—of his own churning concerns. At worst, the proper study of Herzog becomes Herzog.

  JOHN COLEMAN

- [He has] a selfconscious, anti–audience approach.

  ARTHUR KNIGHT

- And as the *Fitzcarraldo* bandwagon lumbers on [in Les Blanke's documentary on its making], with Herzog transformed into a parody of himself—the director who has problems with God rather than his producers. [Blank's method] mostly consists of letting Herzog speak for himself, with the result that his hackneyed 'visionary' image is soon replaced by an absurd paranoia . . .

  STEVEN JENKINS

CHARLTON HESTON (born 1923)

- Heston's the only man who could drop out of a cubic moon, he's so *square*. We never got on. The trouble is with him he doesn't think he's just a hired actor, like the rest of us. He thinks he's the *entire* production. He used to sit there in the mornings and clock us in with a stop-watch.

  RICHARD HARRIS

- And I got to really like the guy. A lot of people told me that I wouldn't like him,

but I liked him. And he tried very hard. I mean *Will Penny* is far and away the best thing he's ever done.

BRUCE DERN

ALFRED HITCHCOCK (1899–1980)

- Hitchcock is a genius. I dislike the word. It has been overworked to the point of paralysis. But no other epithet is possible when one thinks of all that 'Hitch' stands for, and sums up the various qualities he has brought to this his latest remarkable hotch-potch of screen attack.

  SYDNEY W. CARROLL

- [Hitchcock] sensed that I thought the whole atmosphere of filming was, to say the least, uncongenial compared to that in the theatre . . . I well remember him saying 'Actors are cattle'. I can see now that he was trying to jolt me out of my unrealistic dislike of working conditions in the studios and what he thought was a sentimental reverence for the theatre.

  MICHAEL REDGRAVE, 1955

- You can see from the way he uses actors that he sees them as animated props. He casts his films very, very carefully and he knows perfectly well in advance that all the actors that he chooses are perfectly capable of playing the parts he gives them, without any special directorial effort on his part. He gets some sort of a charge out of directing the leading ladies, I think, but that's something else.

  JAMES MASON, 1970

- I had a great time with Hitchcock. . . . He tells you on the set what moves he wants. The only major direction about acting he gave me on the film, however, was when I was listening to what somebody else was saying in a scene, and he pointed out that I was listening with my mouth open—as I often do—and he thought it would look better shut.

SEAN CONNERY, 1973

■ He is a man who doesn't show much emotion. His face very seldom expresses anything except a kind of withdrawal mixed with concentration. He is very silent, morose, and often looks his age. But when you speak about movies, suddenly the mask falls, he comes very much alive, he gesticulates, and suddenly you have the feeling that you are talking with a very young man because he is full of life and enthusiasm.

PHILIPPE HALSMAN, 1976

■ Not one thing was left for the moment of shooting before it was finalised. He did it all in advance. I remember seeing him sitting in his chair beside the set on the second day of shooting, and he looked very down. And I said, 'Hitch, what's the matter?' And he said, 'Oh, I'm just so bored. . . . I've done it all. Now all I have to do is tell you where to go, and tell the cameraman where to go.'

FARLEY GRANGER, 1979

■ He was macabre. When I was a little girl he sent me a gift of a replica of my mother Tippi Hedren in a coffin. That was his idea of a joke. He had a sick sense of humour. After that, mother never worked for him again.

MELANIE GRIFFITH, 1987

■ Hitch relished scaring me. When we were making *Psycho*, he experimented with the mother's corpse, using me as his gauge. I would return from lunch, open the door to the dressing room and propped in my chair would be this

hideous monstrosity. The horror in my scream, registered on his Richter scale, decided which dummy he'd use as the Madame.

JANET LEIGH

■ Any American director who says he hasn't been influenced by him is out of his mind.

JOHN FRANKENHEIMER

■ I think the last two decades of Hitchcock's career were a great waste and sadness. He was technically as skillful as ever. But he had become encased in praise, inured to any criticism. Hitchcock himself had become *The Man Who Knew Too Much*.

WILLIAM GOLDMAN

■ He is the one who distilled the essence of film. He's like Webster. It's all there. I've used a lot of his grammar.

BRIAN DE PALMA

101

■ Hitchcock's oeuvre will live longer than that of anyone else because each of the films that compose it was made with such art and such care that it's able to rival the most attractive new work in movie houses and on television sets today. Even those who don't consider themselves cinephiles especially know five or six Hitchcock films practically by heart from having seen them several times.

FRANÇOIS TRUFFAUT

DUSTIN HOFFMAN (born 1937)

■ There are a few, and only a very few, young actors whom I suspect will be around for quite a while, and I'm hard put to name them. Dustin Hoffman is a peculiar example. The kid is a good actor, but certainly a character actor. ... it's hard to tell what the star appeal is.

ROBERT RYAN, 1970

■ He's energised and the greatest combination of the generous and the selfish that ever lived. He wants to be the greatest actor who ever was.

MERYL STREEP, 1983

■ Hoffman has always been very sexy to me, because he's so bloody talented. And that kind of talent, that kind of energy, that sort of burning inside is hot. That's exciting.

SALLY FIELD, 1985

■ Dustin Hoffman is the kind of officer who has to take the hill no matter how many bodies are left at the bottom. I told his wife [after *Tootsie*] I'd never work again for an Oscar-winner who was shorter than the statue.

LARRY GELBART, 1986

■ He is a consummate actor who has consistently offered some of the most magnetic and fascinating moments in screen history ... Yet for all his extraordinary talent, there are those directors and producers within the Hollywood establishment, as well as a fair number outside of it, who wouldn't work with Hoffman to save their celluloid souls. The man, it seems, drives a hard bargain. 'Yes, that's true. I'm not easy to work with'.

CARMIE ARMATA

■ These drab-looking people like Dustin Hoffman —can you believe any girl looks at Dustin Hoffman and gets a thrill? I can't.

RUTH WATERBURY

■ Hoffman has the reputation of being a difficult man to work with, but the result

of his perfectionism has made him an exciting and surprising personality.

RONALD BERGEN

■ If you argue with him on something, he wants his point and he wants his way. Finally, if you say, 'All right, we'll do it *your* way,' he'll say, 'No—I don't want to do it my way until you *like* doing it my way.' It's not enough to *give in* to him, you have to *like* what he wants, too!

TERI GARR

■ But Dustin Hoffman is very much a star, and he has to be dealt with.

WILLIAM GOLDMAN

■ One of the joys of the movie was working with Dustin; he has one of the most wonderful acting minds I've ever worked with.

ROBERT REDFORD

■ I believe ... that he has talent. He ought to get away from this rather nervous character that he's played since *Midnight Cowboy*. Then we'd really be able to see that he's a complete actor.

MARLON BRANDO

■ Finally, there is Dustin Hoffman [as Lenny Bruce], again asserting his claim to being today's great character leading man. His mimicry of Bruce's onstage mannerisms is uncanny, but what is awesome is the range of emotion he commands in the intimate scenes. Loving and loveless, adolescently joyful or darkly sadistic, paranoid and fearless, aggressive and pitiful, he gives a complex and mercurial performance. He alone makes *Lenny* worth seeing.

RICHARD SCHICKEL

■ He's an actor, in the truest sense of the word. He sets himself marvellous acting challenges, then pulls them off. He's not content to play the same role, with slight variations, in every film, which can be lucrative, but tedious.

VANESSA REDGRAVE

■ But he was extraordinary [in *Tootsie*]. When someone asked me if I found it distracting playing opposite someone in drag, I said it had never occurred to me he was in drag. He actually became that woman.

JESSICA LANGE

■ I don't understand this Method stuff. I remember Laurence Olivier asking Dustin Hoffman why he stayed up all night. Dustin, looking really beat, really bad, said it was to get into the scene being filmed that day, in which he was supposed to have been up all night. Olivier said, 'My boy, if you'd learn how to act you wouldn't have to stay up all night.'

ROBERT MITCHUM

PAUL HOGAN (born 1940)

■ 'Hoges' is a natural, a gifted, unwimpish comedian with often unexpected reservoirs of charm. Like the greats— Keaton, Chaplin, Stan and Ollie—he moves with amazing feline grace.

GEORGE PERRY

JUDY HOLLIDAY (1922–1965)

■ She was intelligent and not at all like the dumb blondes she so often depicted ... She didn't give a damn where the camera was placed, how she was made to look, or about being a star. She just played the scene—acted with, not at. She was also one of the nicest people I ever met.

JACK LEMMON

■ Even at their daffiest, Holliday's actions carried pathos and vulnerability—a yearning quality that went right to your heart. Like all great comediennes, she was truly a great actress. Dumb blondes are by definition, shallow: Judy gave them depth. She did it with right-on-the-money timing and attention to detail. She was a surpassingly intelligent woman (as was Monroe) and therein lies the clue: one has to be smart to play dumb.

DOUGLAS MARSHALL

■ With a voice which might be a siren-call from a cement-mixer and a face which reacts like a seismograph to the very breath of an idea, it is a matter of wonder at times that one so mentally defenceless should be allowed out at all. But ... we are persuaded that innocence is its own protection and that to create such an impression of resolute simple-mindedness Miss Holliday must be a very clever actress indeed.

DEREK GRANGER, 1954

■ My, I like Judy Holliday! She looks like a Monet model. And she's so—so *defenceless*. I like defenceless people. They're the best.

KATHARINE HEPBURN, 1954

■ I could have played the part [in *Born Yesterday*], but I could not have given the performance Judy Holliday did.

JEAN ARTHUR, 1972

STANLEY HOLLOWAY (1890–1982)

■ Even so, I cannot think how far it [*Champagne Charlie*] would have got

103

without the controlled flamboyance of Stanley Holloway as the Great Vance. This is a delicious performance by an actor who is Britain's best film discovery of the war years.

RICHARD WINNINGTON, 1944

BOB HOPE (born 1903)

■ The film character that Hope generally chooses for himself in films is, when we meet his real-life counterpart, usually unlikeable. He is mean, avaricious, cocky, and a thorough coward. Yet in Hope's hands we love him, because although on the surface he is a smart aleck he invariably gets the sticky end of the lollipop, and very rarely the girl.

VERONICA HITCHCOCK, 1970

104

■ Nearly everyone is capable of authentic humour—conscious or unconscious—once or twice in a lifetime. Some highly gifted people can be genuinely funny once a week, and an occasional comic genius such as Bob Hope can be funny every day.

TAY GARNETT, 1973

■ If I wanted to have a weekend of pure pleasure, it would be to have a half-dozen Bob Hope films and watch them, films like *Monsieur Beaucaire* and *My Favourite Brunette*. It's not for nothing that he's such a greatly accepted comedian. He is a great, great talent, a guy who has been able to combine a thin story with great jokes.

WOODY ALLEN

■ There is a man.

JOHN STEINBECK

■ Bob Hope is one of the funniest men alive. He can double you up with bright quips and dazzling sallies. But how many of his jokes can you recall five minutes after *The Bob Hope Show* goes off the air?

BUSTER KEATON

■ It's not enough just to get laughs. The audience has to love you, and Bob gets love as well as laughs from his audiences.

JACK BENNY

■ You spell Bop Hope C-L-A-S-S.

LUCILLE BALL

■ Hope? . . . he's got more money *on* him than I have.

BING CROSBY

■ Bob Hope will go to the opening of a phone booth in a gas station in Anaheim, provided they have a camera and three people there. He must be a man who has an ever-crumbling estimation of himself. He's like a junkie—an applause junkie. Christ, instead of growing old gracefully or doing something with his money, be helpful, all he does is have an anniversary with the President looking on. He's a pathetic guy.

MARLON BRANDO

■ Hope? Hope is not a comedian. He just translates what others write for him.

GROUCHO MARX

ANTHONY HOPKINS (born 1937)

■ Anthony Hopkins is one of the better actors alive, in my estimation. Hopkins is the natural heir to Olivier. I don't see anybody in England who can come closer to Larry. If Tony Hopkins can keep his health and keep working, he will become the Olivier of the Eighties.

GEORGE C. SCOTT

MIRIAM HOPKINS (1902–1972)

■ Although I liked Miriam Hopkins' performance [in *The Lady With Red Hair*]— she conveyed the hysterics and tenseness of a temperamental stage actress very effectively—she was terribly difficult to work with. In fact, she was so tense that it overlapped into real life.

CURTIS BERNHARDT, 1969

■ Most of her guests were chosen from the world of the intellect, and they were there because Miriam knew them all, had read their work, had listened to their music, had bought their paintings. They were not there because a secretary had given her a list of highbrows.

JOHN O'HARA

■ Miriam Hopkins and I didn't exactly get on. I mean, she was murder! Her great tragedy was jealousy. Oh boy! There was a scene in that movie where I have to shake the daylights out of her. And I was really ready for that scene. As I walked on to the stage one of the technicians whispered in my ear, 'Let her have it!'

BETTE DAVIS, 1984

DENNIS HOPPER (born 1936)

■ Dennis is a demonic artist, like Rimbaud. Nothing matters but his work.

BROOKE HAYWARD

■ That sound you hear is of cheque-books closing all over Hollywood . . . Dennis Hopper has blown it. His directorial debut may have been adolescent; his second movie [*The Last Movie*] is puerile. Formless, artless, it is narcissistic but not introspective, psycho but not analytic— a shotgun wedding of R. D. Laing and the Late Show.

STEFAN KANFER

■ A madman! Great performance. But a total madman! Incredibly unpredictable. You just never knew what he was going to say. It certainly wasn't going to be the script. It never was! Sometimes, it bore *no* relationship to the script at all and you were left there thinking of something to say as you couldn't use your own lines anymore . . .

JOHN HARGREAVES

LESLIE HOWARD (1893–1943)

■ Leslie Howard was wonderful. He'd come on the set, have a quiet walk through in rehearsal and then he would repeat a shot again and again—even his eyelashes would be in the same place at any given moment, yet his performance was never mechanical. He had the most wonderfully controlled technique I have ever seen.

ANTHONY ASQUITH

■ Howard was more than just a popular actor. Since the War he has become something of a symbol to the British people.

C. A. LEJEUNE

■ It is amazing how hopelessly wrong Leslie is in *Pygmalion*. However, the public will like him and probably want him to marry Eliza, which is just what I don't want.

BERNARD SHAW

■ Leslie Howard was a darling flirt. He'd be caressing your eyes and have his hand on someone else's leg at the same time. He was adorable. He was a little devil and just wanted his hands on every woman around . . . He just loved ladies.

JOAN BLONDELL

105

TREVOR HOWARD (1916–1988)

- I believe Trevor Howard has quite a nice, gentle riposte to unwanted attention. Someone saw him in a bar once and said 'Are you Trevor Howard?' 'Yes', he replied, 'When I'm working I am'.

  CHARLES DANCE, 1987

- Simply a private man, married to an enchanting wife. He was also the greatest screen actor Britain has ever produced.

  BRIAN BAXTER, 1988

- An enormously versatile and powerful actor. He was a star who had no pretensions, something rare in an actor. It was a shame that despite his stage successes, Howard had chosen to concentrate on film work in later years. He was torn between the two mediums. He was a generous man and he had beautiful manners. He was also Bohemian and wild, which was fun.

  JOHN GIELGUD

- He became one of the finest actors we have ever had. One of the greatest, and a lovely man with it.

  JOHN MILLS

- One of the most remarkable actors of our century. His great films are classics. He was also one of the most popular actors in the business because he was so straight down the line. He always said what he felt.

  PEGGY ASHCROFT

- We lived in tents in and around Nairobi while on location, [for *White Mischief*] and Trevor was not well. But it was extraordinary. The moment he appeared in front of the camera, all the energy leapt into him.

  JOSS ACKLAND, 1988

106

WILLIAM K. HOWARD (1899–1954)

- On his death bed, he said: 'Jacques, I've had a very good career, but it would have been better still if I hadn't stupidly refused so many films. Don't do as I did, don't make the same mistakes.' His advice was very sound and I have followed it. Indeed, how is one to know what can be done with a script?

  JACQUES TOURNEUR, 1975

ROCK HUDSON (1925–1985)

- I thought I saw something. So I arranged to meet him, and he seemed to be not too much to the eye, except very handsome. But the camera sees with its own eye . . . I put him into *Has Anybody Seen My Gal?* Within a very few years he became a number one box-office star in America.

  DOUGLAS SIRK

- He had size, good looks, strength and a certain shyness that I thought would make him a star like Gable. He had the kind of personal charm that makes you think you'd enjoy sitting down and spending time with him.

  HENRY WILLSON

- Reams of copy have been written about Hudson to explain his appeal and success, but none of them has touched on the vital point—that he is a traditional romantic hero in an era when such types are exceedingly rare.

  JIMMIE HICKS

- Rock Hudson, of all people, emerged from *The Last Sunset* more creditably than anyone. Most people don't consider him a very accomplished actor, but I found him to be terribly hard-working, dedicated and very serious . . . If everyone on the picture, from producer to writer to other actors, had approached it with the same dedication, it would have been a lot better.

ROBERT ALDRICH

ROSS HUNTER (born 1916)

■ He's a very pleasant man. He may sound like Reader's Digest, but he believes every word he says. He's never lost touch with Disneyland.

PETER FINCH

TAB HUNTER (born 1931)

■ Also talented, but primarily a character actor—yet always used as a leading man because he's so pretty. I've seen him do character parts in which he's really great. But as a leading man he tightens up. Mostly he turned to character work in American television when his Hollywood career started going sour. Then he played the roles of psychotic killers and so forth, and his talent became clear.

SIDNEY LUMET

WILLIAM HURT (born 1950)

■ I hired William Hurt for *Altered States*, and found I was his analyst for six months. . . . It wasn't the part he talked about, never that, but how it was such a terrible thing being a billionaire after being born in abject poverty. I was quite deferential to him, but [my wife] listened to the crap he was talking and said, 'Okay, preppy, let's cut the shit.' He was

stunned and amazed but he was quite human after that.

KEN RUSSELL, 1987

■ A lot of differences emerged between us in our approaches to the script. He's a forceful personality and I was ready to let him go. Fortunately, *he* wasn't ready to let me go. He came back and he *was* the character so completely I had to hire him.

LAWRENCE KASDAN

JOHN HUSTON (1906–1987)

■ On the strength of it [*The Treasure of Sierra Madre*], I have no doubt that Huston, next only to Chaplin, is the most talented man working in American pictures.

JAMES AGEE, 1948

■ John, I think, wrote his life as a script when he was very young, and has played it ever since.

DENNIS MORGAN, 1972

■ I'm told there is a Huston style; if so I'm not aware of it. I just make the film to its own requirements.

HIMSELF

■ But we had a great time on *Prizzi's Honour*. My father is extremely easy to work with. He chooses his actors, places his confidence in them, and lets you get on with it. He is living proof that a director doesn't have to run all over the place.

ANGELICA HUSTON, 1987

■ I kinda loved John. He was like a second father to me in many ways, which I know may sound odd considering I was 45 when I first worked with him, but when

107

you had to say goodbye there was always this feeling of loss, that terrible sadness that you'd be deprived of his company. I've seen more films by him than anybody else on the planet.

ALBERT FINNEY, 1987

■ One is tempted to ask what on earth Griffith, Duvivier, Rene Clair and Lean could have done in life if the profession of film director had not been invented for them. In Huston's case he could have become a preacher, an explorer, even perhaps a great political leader. He had the courage, the gift of leadership, the confidence, the charm and the cheek.

ROBERT MORLEY, 1987

■ He was *about* something.

LAUREN BACALL, 1987

■ John had so much to give, it's significant to remember that, when he was directing, there were no surprises because he had been there . . . He'd done just about everything he ever wanted to attempt, and he did it with grace and some triumph.

ROBERT MITCHUM, 1987

■ He had a tremendous talent for friendship and loyalty. He was the most loyal man in the world, and the one thing he couldn't forgive was disloyalty.

GOTTFRIED REINHARDT, 1987

■ John was my oldest and youngest friend, a startling combination of Puck and King Lear.

RAY STARK, 1987

■ One new development was Huston's acting career. A wise director would exploit his persona of intimidating affability, and Huston was incomparable at playing charming crocodiles.

NEIL SINYARD, 1988

108

■ Yesterday and the day before I saw a new Huston film called *The Kremlin Letter*, and it's a masterpiece. Masterly, the work of a master, and teacher, and *The Kremlin Letter* could serve as a lesson in cinema. I'm delighted to see a man like John Huston, who already has so many great films behind him, return to the front rank . . .

JEAN-PIERRE MELVILLE

■ John Huston, the director, is a genius, and like a lot of geniuses, he can be erratic. But his perception, charm, and warmth are so extraordinary that you want to give the best of you. He has an incredible curiosity about life. While cutting one movie he starts working on another. I think he enjoys the process of work more than the results.

STACEY KEACH

■ He's such an old hack that I nearly walked off the picture [*Myra Breckinridge*] when they told me I was going to be working with him. However, he is such an enormous fan of mine that perhaps it will influence him into giving the only decent performance of his entire career.

MIKE SARNE

WALTER HUSTON (1884–1950)

■ I hate stars. They're not actors. I've been around actors all my life, and I like them, but I never had an actor as a friend. Except Dad. And Dad never thought of himself as an actor. But the best actor I ever worked with was Dad . . . Dad was a man who never tried to sell anybody anything.

JOHN HUSTON

■ I doubt we shall ever see . . . better acting than Walter Huston's beautiful performance [in *The Treasure of the Sierra Madre*] . . . Huston has for a long time been one of the best actors in the world and he is easily the most likeable; on both counts this performance crowns a lifetime. It is an all but incredible submergence in a role, and a transformation; this man who has credibly played Lincoln looks small and stocky here, and is as gaily vivacious as a water bug. The character is beautifully conceived and written, but I think it is chiefly Walter Huston who gives it its almost Shakespearian wonderfulness, charm, and wisdom. In spite of the enormous amount of other talent at large in the picture, Huston carries the whole show as deftly and easily as he handles his comedy lines.

JAMES AGEE

JAMES IVORY (born 1928)

■ There're several things unusual about James Ivory. He has very little ego, he's not a tyrant or very pleased with his status. On the first day you stand there trembling with fear, everyone not involved clears the set, and he just says 'Oh God what are we going to do? Hugh? James?' It's so fab compared to being told to stand there, do this, say that.

HUGH GRANT

■ [His relationship with Ismael Merchant is] more than a marriage.

SHASHI KAPOOR

GLENDA JACKSON (born 1936)

■ Funny things do happen, though. *Harper's* wanted to include me in their gallery of 'Most Beautiful Women'. That was hilarious. It was all a terrible mistake, of course. I wound up on a separate page as 'a stern young beauty bursting upon London.' Stern, you see. Not that I'm really tough.

HERSELF

■ Glenda Jackson I'd never heard of. When she walked into the room I found myself watching her varicose veins more than her face, and only later in the movie of *Marat/Sade* did I realise what a magnificent screen personality she was. I couldn't quite understand it. Sometimes she looked plain ugly, and sometimes just plain and then sometimes the most beautiful creature one had ever seen.

KEN RUSSELL, 1973

■ But I do hope that some of them will stop shedding their clothes at every opportunity. It is so unnecessary for an actress like, say, Glenda Jackson. If she was a ravishing young beauty . . .

GEORGE CUKOR, 1976

109

■ Glenda Jackson is an absolutely superb actress. What is she doing now? She should be making movies. I'd love to make one with her.

MERVYN LEROY

■ Glenda Jackson's thunderous, full-frontal, carpet-clawing caricature [in *The Music Lovers*] is a calamity of mistiming.

MARK WHITMAN

■ Quite aside from her age, Miss Jackson is not appealing in any part—face, body, or limbs . . . yet all this could, perhaps, be overlooked if she were an artist. But nothing she says or does stems from genuine feeling, displays an atom of spontaneity, leaves any room for the unexpected. It is all technique—and not the most intricate technique at that— about as good as computer poetry.

JOHN SIMON

■ I admire Michael Caine in this film [*The Romantic Englishwoman*] and have great respect for Glenda Jackson. She is of a different generation to mine and a different theatrical background. She can be like a bird. I have to run after her. She is so exciting, she gives so much.

HELMUT BERGER

EMIL JANNINGS (1884–1950)

■ Oh, everyone is sick to death of that one [*The Blue Angel*]. And I thought Jannings was just awful in it. Such a ham.

MARLENE DIETRICH

110

HUMPHREY JENNINGS (1907–1950)

■ *Fires Were Started* is one of the most precious possessions of the cinema. It is a constant disillusionment to those of us who, as part of our job, see the great films of the past to discover how many of them have grown weak at the joints with age. One knows instinctively that *Fires Were Started* can never lose its strength. It is without doubt the crowning achievement of the British documentary school.

DENNIS FORMAN

■ What counted for Humphrey was the expression, by certain people, of the ever-growing spirit of man; and, in particular, of the spirit of England. He sought, therefore, for a public imagery, a public poetry. He addressed himself, in much the same spirit as Blake, to 'the British public', not expecting the mass to understand him, but because he was seeking to discover and activate the collective symbols of England.

KATHLEEN RAINE

NORMAN JEWISON (born 1926)

■ A tough, feisty, no-nonsense director.

WILLIAM GOLDMAN

ROLAND JOFFÉ (born 1945)

■ A combination of Zorro, Jesus and Rasputin.

SPALDING GRAY

CELIA JOHNSON (1908–1982)

■ The magic of the film [*Brief Encounter*] is Celia.

DAVID LEAN

■ Celia Johnson was the best actress I've ever worked with. Beneath Celia's Women's Institute gentility there was a most lovable woman, and a real trouper.

TREVOR HOWARD

AL JOLSON (1886–1950)

■ I'm certain that his divorced wife and widow would attest to that—Jolson demanded the adulation of an audience. His ego was such that when he heard applause for another star, he reacted as though he had been robbed. All the applause in the world belonged to him.

HENRY LEVIN

■ He was a no good son of a bitch, but he was the greatest entertainer I've ever seen.

GEORGE JESSEL

■ A great instinctive artist with magic and vitality. He was the most impressive entertainer on the American stage . . . Whatever he sang, he brought you up or down to his level; even his ridiculous song *Mammy* enthralled everyone. Only a shadow of himself appeared in films.

CHARLES CHAPLIN

■ The screen didn't give him enough space to project in. I remember as a kid seeing him on stage, and I think to this day there have been two great performers in the world: one is Jolson and the other is Judy Garland. They had some kind of magic in front of people that no one could surpass—they were sheer, magnificent talent beyond belief.

JOAN BLONDELL

■ When you talk about the world's greatest entertainer you have to say Al Jolson because there was just no one like him. Only Judy Garland and perhaps Frank Sinatra got anywhere near him!

JACK BENNY

NEIL JORDAN (born 1950)

■ I think Neil is a magician. And I believe in magic.

BOB HOSKINS

LOUIS JOUVET (1887–1951)

■ I have known actors with brilliant minds who were lamentable on the stage. This was not the case with Jouvet, who was bursting with both talent and intelligence. Jouvet analysed his parts word by word. He knew how to extract the deepest sense of a text. His rehearsals were a constant series of discoveries. Giraudoux often re-wrote his own lines after Jouvet had found a new meaning in them.

JEAN RENOIR

BORIS KARLOFF (1887–1969)

■ His face fascinated me. I made drawings of his head, adding sharp bony ridges where I imagined the skull might have joined.

JAMES WHALE

■ In *The Mummy* he was billed by surname alone, 'Karloff the Uncanny' a cinematic accolade hitherto confined to Garbo.

DENIS GIFFORD

DANNY KAYE (1913—1987)

■ If you weren't the star yourself, you had to learn to live with the star. And Danny—well, because he was talented you forgive him an awful lot. Yes, he's a hog. He has to be on every moment, and everybody has to watch him. But he is terribly funny and he makes me fall on the floor with laughter sometimes.

ANGELA LANSBURY

■ *Who's Who* which lets nobody seedy in, Lists him as 'actor, comedian'.
But as wife and writer, as critic and fan, I'd list him as Danny Kaye—Renaissance Man.

SYLVIA FINE

ELIA KAZAN (born 1909)

■ As you know, people will give their right arm, literally, and most of their blood to work with him. He's got a kind of incredible instinct with people. He's so in sympathy with all the fears and frights of actors, through having done it himself. And he's got a personal magic that gets within your very being.

DEBORAH KERR

■ Kazan brings to this material the qualities one has now come to expect from him: a brilliant and ultimately boring surface efficiency. He succeeds in some cases in getting remarkable performances from his players, but in a way that makes one feel he is 'good with actors' rather than that he has a real, a direct response to character.

KAREL REISZ

■ Kazan is a great director. He is probably as much a manifestation of auteur theory as you could find. He's a magnificent machine in film-making, regardless of what your feelings might be about him politically. He's a wonderful director and a wonderful film-maker.

WARREN BEATTY

■ I had a wonderful relationship with Kazan. There are gentlemen in the theatre as well as ladies and Kazan was a gentleman. He changed the last act of *Cat* and because of that it was more successful than *Streetcar*. He helped make it a success.

TENNESSEE WILLIAMS

■ His later films like *A Streetcar Named Desire* and *On The Waterfront* are ostentatious displays of shock tactics and technical tricks . . . but each is coldly playing for obvious effects and responses. It is the pretentiousness of the material which make Kazan's films so unacceptable. Only as a melodrama on

the cinema's blowsiest level does *On the Waterfront* really work at all.

TONY RICHARDSON 1954

■ He chose the actors that he wanted, made the film he wanted to make and he made it the way he wanted to make it with absolutely no contribution or interference from the major distributors at that time. That was a major step forward at that time in the film industry. He was a pioneer and he made it possible for other people.

STANLEY BAKER, 1975

BUSTER KEATON (1895–1966)

■ Imperturbably serious, inscrutable and stubborn, who acts under the impulse of an irresistible power unknown to himself, comparable only to the mysterious urge that causes the birds to migrate or the avalanche to come crashing down.

DR ERWIN PANOFSKY

■ An altogether extraordinary emotional effect came from the dreamlike, obsessive, hallucinatory repetition of that strange frozen face. It was almost nightmarish—a phantasmagoria of masks. There is no question that Buster Keaton, among other things, was a surrealist even before surrealism.

ALBERT LEWIN

■ He taught me most of what I know about timing, how to fall and how to handle pros and animals.

LUCILLE BALL

■ He used to put in gags for Harpo when we were at MGM. *A Night at the Opera, A Day at the Races, Go West.* He was washed up by then, but he was good for Harpo. Harpo was always looking for a good piece of business. He didn't talk, he didn't need lines, but he did need good business, and Keaton was a hell of a comic in silent films.

GROUCHO MARX

His face went with the silence. It's motionlessness and the film's soundlessness compounded each other. Its immobility compelled attention, its expression compelled sympathy. Fundamentally bewildered yet completely matter-of-fact, it was a basic human portrait. It stared unblinking and unsurprised as mad mishaps and mad triumphs unfolded like marginal notes by Mark Twain.

RUDI BLESH, 1966

He always put the camera in the right place, and every shot in his films was necessary to the development of the storyline. He was brilliant. You take a film like *The General*, which he made in 1926, and look at it eight or ten times. You can't take a shot away from it. They're all necessary.

RICHARD LESTER

His enduring, unsentimental self-sufficiency has its own intimations of melancholy, in the contrast between his determination and his resources as he marches off down the line in pursuit of his runaway train and, always, in the sad, thoughtful eyes set in the pale poker face. Keaton is the most exact, the most mathematically precise, of comedians . . . yet the quintessential Buster Keaton seems always to retreat a little, behind the enigmatic, impassive mask of the comedian.

PENELOPE HOUSTON

Keaton became what film is. Capable, when he wishes, of turning visible space itself into momentary void. Faceless, he moves through the nameless.

WALTER KERR

Sunset Boulevard: there he was again, superbly glum in the entourage of Gloria Swanson as the forgotten star. The trouble was that with Keaton on the screen other faces, other gestures were apt to fade; even the greatest performers were diminished. In the famous duet in *Limelight* it was Keaton, struggling with the vagabond sheets of music, whom one watched, not Chaplin.

DILYS POWELL

He appeared in many different roles: father and son, millionaire and bum, half-wit and scholar, cowhand and stockbroker, fugitive and man-about-town, ardent lover and oppressed husband. Yet ultimately they all fuse into one figure, a small solitary, solemn animal with a face of other worldly beauty and great melancholy unsmiling eyes that gaze unflinchingly outwards upon a world which must always dwarf him, but cannot diminish him; because behind those eyes, there is a soul.

DAVID ROBINSON

Chaplin clearly considered himself to be the clown for all ages—and that's why the stuff creaks a bit today. Buster Keaton holds up much better—and Keaton had no idea he was playing for posterity.

JOHN CROSBY

The greatest genius ever to work in the American cinema (you heard me, and no arguments).

DAVID DENBY, 1981

113

■ Keaton, for most critics today, is the greatest of the silent film comedians — not only because of his appealing sense of humour and screen persona, but also because he was an outstanding director, an inventive genius the equal of any other great film-maker of the time.

KEN WLASCHIN

■ Rarely sentimental, always innovative, Keaton stands head and shoulders above his peers simply through his cinematic creativity; where others — including Chaplin — remained restricted by the conventions of slapstick and vaudeville, Buster excelled in the presentation of strong characters, dramatically suspenseful plots, and a well-defined world ... The man, without doubt, was a genius. And very, very funny.

GEOFF ANDREW, 1987

114

DIANE KEATON (born 1946)

■ She is the dream actress that every director should have. She is absolutely professional. There's none of that star business about being late or not turning up or staying out all night, or any of those things. She is absolutely dedicated and hardworking, and she gave me the same intensity in take after take.

GILLIAN ARMSTRONG

■ Tony Roberts and I couldn't stop laughing at Diane. It was nothing you could quote later; she couldn't tell a joke if her life depended on it. Tony tried to figure it out one time, what it is she does. He says she has this uncanny ability to project you back into an infantile atmosphere, and you are suddenly a little kid again. There is something utterly guileless about her. She's a natural.

WOODY ALLEN, 1976

■ She's innocent, perverse, vulnerable, vengeful, sad, funny, sexy and sweet — not by turns but in a flashing prism of character that's constantly reflecting light, and darkness, from its different surfaces. It's the most remarkable performance by a young actress in a long time. In that most unbearable final episode she is still looking — for Goodbar, Godot or God. They're not unrelated in this savage, troubled time.

JACK KROLL, 1977

HOWARD KEEL (born 1917)

■ A very special guy. Practically seven feet tall! A virile, manly, western voice. He used to have his voice teacher in at five in the morning when he had an eleven o'clock recording! A frightened guy, but in his way a good performer.

JOHN GREEN

■ A very engaging, very bright fellow who didn't give a fig for the movie industry.

BENNY GREEN

SALLY KELLERMAN (born 1938)

■ Sally drove everyone on the set crazy from the film director right down to the hairdresser — but in the film [*The Last of the Red Hot Lovers*, she was] tremendous.

ALAN ARKIN, 1972

GENE KELLY (born 1912)

■ I noted a player new to me, one Gene Kelly. To this young man I doff my hat and cry bravo. He can act, he has charm, he has personality. He has an arresting smile composite in its ingredients, being made up as to three-quarters of the early Godfrey Tearle and one quarter of our Noel when he is feeling pleased with the world.

JAMES AGATE, 1942

■ You know, that Kelly, he's just terrific. That's all there is to it. He dances like crazy, he directs like crazy . . . I adore this guy. I really am crazy about his work.

FRED ASTAIRE

■ Kelly's career stands as an example for all of us how a performer can produce an unforgettable work of art. There are no dancers like Gene Kelly anymore.

MIKHAIL BARYSHNIKOV

■ [In *On the Town*] Gene Kelly plays—and dances—the ordinary guy, in whom his audiences can recognise themselves, their happiness, sadness, bewilderment made articulate in movement. Unlike Astaire, Kelly does not need to play the role of a dancer to justify his numbers. I believe that in this film they [Kelly and Donen] have consciously attempted to translate into terms of cinema the objects and methods of the modern American Lyric Theatre.

DAVID VAUGHAN

■ From hoofer extraordinaire to a choreographer-dancer of genius.

CLIVE HIRSCHHORN

■ If they ever get around to handing out Oscars for outstanding performances as a human being, you'll know where to find Ol' Blue Eyes—on the nominating committee rooting for his old buddy, Gene.

FRANK SINATRA

■ For me, Gene Kelly has been the single most important influence on the musical cinema, as a conceptualiser, director and, of course, as a musical performer.

FRANCIS COPPOLA

■ He is the long-distance dancer who kept up the pace long after he helped set it.

PETER EVANS

■ It would be hard to express the elation of a man who has won his heart's desire more eloquently than does Kelly in his literal interpretation of the title number *Singing in the Rain* . . . You are left feeling that nothing could be more cheering than the rain.

CATHERINE DE LA ROCHE

■ It was mostly an aura about him. For me he was Hollywood. The way I'd imagined it as a child.

CATHERINE DENEUVE

■ The American film musical at its best, we shall see if we live so long, was a genuine art form with all the necessary qualifications like conviction and originality, durability of appeal and universality and at the heart of the best of the genre was Gene Kelly.

JOHN SANDILANDS

■ Fred could never do the lifts Gene did, and never wanted to. I'd say they were the two greatest dancing personalities who were ever on screen. Each has a distinctive style. Each is a joy to work with. But it's like comparing apples and oranges. They're both delicious.

CYD CHARISSE, 1987

GRACE KELLY (1929–1982)

■ I've dressed thousands of actors, actresses and animals, but whenever I am asked which star is my personal favourite, I answer 'Grace Kelly'. She is a charming lady, a most gifted actress and, to me, a valued friend.

EDITH HEAD

■ Grace Kelly does forty parts on television, and then she gets her first break in films and is an 'overnight success'. Well, she was an overnight success for many months in New York in television.

ALBERT McCLEERY, 1974

■ She's a great lady, with great talent and kind, considerate, friendly with everybody. She was great with the crew and they all loved her.

BING CROSBY

■ Grace Kelly was a Dresden doll, I thought, with a kind of platinum beneath the delicate porcelain, a beautiful girl who I felt was always in control of her world.

MAURICE CHEVALIER

■ She was very serious about her work . . . had her eyes and ears open. She was trying to learn, you could see that. You can tell if a person really wants to be an actress. She was one of those people you could get that feeling about, and she was very pretty. It didn't surprise me when she was a big success.

GARY COOPER

■ I think Grace Kelly was the finest actress I ever worked with. Forgive me, Ingrid, Kate, Audrey and all the others. But Grace had something extraordinary. She was so very, very relaxed in front of the camera. When we did *To Catch a Thief*, you know, she was quite young. Had someone else played it, her role could have been unpleasant—a spoiled, silly

116

girl. But the way Grace played her, you liked her.

CARY GRANT

■ I've never wanted to have the obvious blonde, the one who has sex hanging around her neck like jewellery, the big-bosomed girl. . . . So what did I do in *To Catch a Thief*? I kept deliberately photographing Grace Kelly in profile, coldish, aloof, then right at the door of the room she turns and plunges her mouth onto Cary Grant's. You've made your statement, but you've made the audience wait for it.

ALFRED HITCHCOCK

KAY KENDALL (1926–1959)

■ The honours [in *Les Girls*] go to the delectable Kay Kendall, who commits highway robbery every time she appears.

CLIVE HIRSCHHORN

■ She was without question the greatest female clown we ever had—apart from someone like Bea Lillie, whom your audience won't have heard of. Or Cicely Courtneidge.

DIRK BOGARDE

■ I'd heard stories from other directors of how adorable Kay was on the set. She would be raucous and vital and lovable, and when the day's work was over, everyone would want to take her home . . . She was wonderfully co-operative, lending all her resources to the enterprise, spelling out only one condition: 'Careful how you photograph my Cyrano nose, darling.'

VINCENTE MINNELLI

■ I felt strangely desolated whenever she disappeared. It was frightening that somebody I knew only superficially should have such a violent effect on me. It was like a light going out in the room when she left.

REX HARRISON

DEBORAH KERR (born 1921)

■ She is the only star who genuinely treats each and everybody exactly alike.

JULIA FOSTER

■ Deborah Kerr is enormously sensitive and responds to a director particularly. I think she could have gone on to become a very great actress, but she went on as a contract artist with MGM for just too long.

MICHAEL POWELL

■ I made *King Solomon's Mines* and I became popular because Quatermain was a mysterious man with a leopard skin around his hat. It was Africa romantic. Deborah Kerr and I made love up a tree. I said to Deborah—I had a six-month affair with her—that we should never have come down from that tree.

STEWART GRANGER

HENRY KING (1886–1982)

■ That film [*Tender is the Night*] was very disappointing to me, so I didn't have the greatest time except I loved Henry King, but he was like my father! He kept telling me stories.

JASON ROBARDS, 1978

KLAUS KINSKI (born 1926)

■ I have never met a man like my father. He is so mad, terrible and vehement at the same time. Because of him, I never knew anything other than passion. When I began to meet other people I saw that it wasn't normal.

NASTASSJA KINSKI

■ He's not ageing well. The best thing to happen to his career is for him to die immediately.

WERNER HERZOG

NASTASSJA KINSKI (born 1961)

■ Nastassja Kinski has a habit, at times, of looking like Ingrid Bergman, which may be disconcerting but cannot be bad. She has some other qualities in common, youth, radiance, and sensitivity—and in a changed industry, the intelligence to choose films because of the creative talent involved.

MILOS FORMAN

■ She does not sound like a brainless nymphet jerking to the strings pulled by her Svengali. She has a core of healthy, mittel-European toughness, an adolescent openness that is very attractive.

CLANCY SIGAL

■ She's fragile, yet a hunter . . . I found she requires a lot of care, love and work. She makes great demands—and woe to the director who cannot satisfy them. You have to be strong with Nastassja. Otherwise she will devour you.

JEAN JACQUES BEINEIX

■ She combines the innocent look of an angel with the guilty appeal of a sex kitten.

TERRY WILLOWS

117

HILDEGARD KNEF (born 1925)

- She's the best thing that ever came out of Germany.

  STUART SCHULBERG

- She's Mother Courage.

  MARLENE DIETRICH

ALEXANDER KORDA (1893–1956)

- A director newly appointed to the reconstituted board called on him and actually asked him if he could recommend a successor for his job. Alex, privately amused by the situation, replied solemnly, 'That is a very difficult question for me to answer. You see, sir, I do not grow on trees.'

  SIDNEY GILLIAT

118

- Whenever I met Alex, if only for a moment, he always gave me something. Sometimes it might be a conscious gift— like a little piece of advice, but it was not that so often as something that seemed to be unconscious, an attitude of mind; a gleam of light from the steel of his personality that gave one courage. Alex received little. To receive was not in his nature—he gave always, that was his nature.

  RALPH RICHARDSON

- He has no successor, no one with whom it is possible not to talk about films, the matter in hand, but about painting, poetry, music, anything in the world rather than that 'industry' which always seemed on the point of quietly, out of neglect, becoming an 'art' while he was away, reading Baudelaire somewhere among the islands of Greece.

  GRAHAM GREENE

ERNIE KOVACS (1919–1962)

- There were two great and unexpected pleasures in making that film; one was getting to know Ernie Kovacs, who played the Chief of Police (he was tragically killed in a car accident in Beverly Hills some years ago), and the other was spending an evening with Ernest Hemingway . . . Kovacs was as different as could be; outrageously extrovert, wild, rash, gipsy-like and, in a Goonish way, just about the funniest man I have ever met.

  ALEC GUINNESS

KRIS KRISTOFFERSON (born 1936)

- I somehow feel a great kinship with him. I want him to play the part in the movie I've written for Ann. When I read his cuttings, I find his life and mine have parallels. We started off big, were very productive, highly intelligent people. I damaged a talent because I couldn't come to grips with the disappointments that were laid upon one by producers or the heads of studios.

  RICHARD HARRIS

- I like Kris Kristofferson because he writes poetry, and he's a fucking good man. Working with Kris on *Pat Garrett and Billy the Kid* was one of the great experiences of my life.

  SAM PECKINPAH

STANLEY KUBRICK (born 1928)

- I find his films quite long and boring, but I quite liked *Dr Strangelove*.

  KEN RUSSELL, 1973

■ The toughest part of Stanley's day was finding the right first shot. Once he did that, other shots fell into place. But he agonised over that first one.

RYAN O'NEAL

■ By the time of *Dr Strangelove* he [Kubrick] had become very human— maybe it was the power that came with successes like *Lolita*—for he is now very strong. My first day was torture. I was nervous, scared, did 48 takes. I expected Kubrick to explode but instead he was gentle, calmed me, convinced me that the fear in my eyes would help the character.

STERLING HAYDEN, 1981

■ But Stanley is very meticulous and hates everything that he writes or has anything to do with. He's an incredibly, depressingly serious man, with this wild sense of humour. But paranoid. Every morning, we would all meet and practically rewrite the day's work. He's a perfectionist and he's always unhappy with anything that's set.

GEORGE C. SCOTT

■ I complained that he was the only director to light the sets with no stand- ins. We had to be there even to be lit. Just because you're a perfectionist doesn't mean you're perfect.

JACK NICHOLSON

■ He's kind of a dyspeptic film maker, a Type A film maker, worrying and wanting to edit right up to the end. He's very painstaking, obviously. You know what? I think he wants to hurt people with this movie [*The Shining*]. I think that he really wants to make a movie that will hurt people.

STEPHEN KING

■ By contrast, Kubrick proved anything but, despite his reputation. By comparison with a swine like Otto Preminger he was kindness and considerateness personified. When something went wrong, he wouldn't scream and shout about it. He'd take me to one side, seemingly blaming himself more for the mistake than me. In reality, of course, he was fingering my fault in an adult and sensible way.

KEIR DULLEA, 1985

AKIRA KUROSAWA (born 1910)

■ One of the great creative figures of our times, in any medium.

DAVID ROBINSON, 1978

ALAN LADD (1913–1964)

119

■ He was awfully good in putting across what he had, in looks and in manner; he had something very attractive—a definite film personality which he had worked very hard to perfect.

DEBORAH KERR

■ Alan Ladd was a marvellous person in his simplicity. In so many ways we were kindred spirits. We both were professionally conceived through Hollywood's search for box office and the types to insure the box office. And we were both little people. Alan wasn't as short as most people believe. It was true that in certain films, Alan would climb a small platform or the girl worked in a slit trench. We had no such problems together.

VERONICA LAKE

■ By a curious chemistry of film Alan has a great following, but it has nothing to do with acting. So you are surprised to find, when you play opposite him, that he is a very good actor just the same.

EDMOND O'BRIEN

■ Having been fascinated by the Alan Ladd phenomenon, I now had the opportunity to study it at close quarters. It turned out that he had the exquisite coordination and rhythm of an athlete, which made it a pleasure to watch him when he was being at all physical.

JAMES MASON

■ And I worked with Alan Ladd, who along with Gregory Peck, was my favourite leading man. He was a beautiful man, charming and gentle, and I think of all my leading men he worked best with me.

VIRGINIA MAYO

120 ■ Spencer Tracy was an actor's actor. Everybody thought he was great. Marlon Brando is an actor's actor—or was. Richard Burton also. I don't try to be cruel, but Alan Ladd was not an actor's actor. But he was a very successful film star.

STEWART GRANGER

VERONICA LAKE (1919–1973)

■ Miss Lake is supposed to be a *femme fatale* and to that end it was arranged for her truly splendid bosom to be unconfined and draped ever so slightly in a manner to make the current crop of sweater girls prigs by comparison. Such to do has been made over doing justice to those attributes of Miss Lake that everything else about her has been thrown out of focus.

CECELIA AGER

■ She's one of the little people, like Mary Pickford, Douglas Fairbanks and Freddie Bartholomew when he started, who take hold of an audience immediately. She's nothing much in real life—a quiet, rather timid little thing. But the screen transforms her, electrifies her and brings her to life.

PRESTON STURGES

■ *The Blue Dahlia* wasn't a topnotch film by any means, largely because Veronica Lake couldn't play the love scenes and too much had to be discarded.

RAYMOND CHANDLER

HEDY LAMARR (born 1913)

■ Her beauty made up for whatever she lacked in acting ability. Acting probably didn't come naturally to her but the note of unsureness in what she did seemed to give her a certain childish attractiveness.

KING VIDOR

■ She was a nice girl, or she was then. Hedy didn't make trouble, didn't have an ego problem. The problem was that she couldn't act.

JOHN CROMWELL, 1983

DOROTHY LAMOUR (born 1914)

■ Dorothy Lamour is the most popular person on the Paramount lot, a statement not likely to be disputed by man, boy, or even rival actress.

EILLEEN CREELMAN, 1946

■ Dottie was fearless. She stands there before the cinema and ad libs with Crosby and me, fully knowing, the way the script's written, she'll come up second or third best.

BOB HOPE

■ When they toast your wonderful career, count us in; when they mention your unparalleled contribution to this nation in World War II, we agree whole-heartedly; and when they applaud one of the brightest stars to ever shine in the Hollywood firmament, ours will be the loudest clapping you hear.

RONALD and NANCY REAGAN

BURT LANCASTER (born 1913)

■ John Wayne was a great star. But he always played Wayne. Anything else he didn't regard as manly. Now someone like Burt Lancaster is just the opposite. The living proof that you can be a sensitive actor and macho at the same time.

KIRK DOUGLAS

■ He can walk into a room and there is a change in the heartbeat. If you had some instrument you could measure it. It's like having a wild animal there suddenly. It has to do with aggression and potential violence. I think some politicians have it, but no English actor. [Tony Curtis] could act Burt off the screen, but he will never be a star. He hasn't this granite quality of the ego.

ALEXANDER MACKENDRICK

■ I saw Burt Lancaster in *The Crimson Pirate* on TV the other night, and I enjoyed every minute of it. I'm sure that Burt got to the point where he said 'I'm not gonna do that crap anymore.' ... but when I sat there watching *The Crimson Pirate*, I found myself jumping

up and down and enjoying him 1000 times more than watching him in some of his later films.

BURT REYNOLDS

■ He has matured gracefully, plays men his own age and understands the need not to win the girl. He is much more tolerant of other people's point of view.

ROBERT ALDRICH, 1976

■ When Burt Lancaster showed up we began shooting [*The Train*]. We worked one morning, a perfectly fine morning. After lunch I was called to the phone and I was off the picture. I've no idea to this day as to why ... Lancaster's *The Leopard* had just opened in America to bad reviews for 'trying to be arty' etc. [Perhaps] he was fearful that somehow I was going to make an arty film of *The Train*.

ARTHUR PENN, 1982

■ The Prince [in *The Leopard*] was a very complex character—at times autocratic, rude, strong—at times romantic, good, understanding—and sometimes even stupid, and above all, mysterious. Burt is all these things too. I sometimes think Burt the most perfectly mysterious man I ever met in my life.

LUCHINO VISCONTI

■ You have to give him a reason for everything. Once you do, he's easy to handle.

ROBERT SIODMAK

■ Burt Lancaster is an actor of instinct and sensitivity, whose playing has always had a certain gentleness and sensibility. But his range is limited, and this difficult part [in *Come Back, Little Sheba*] is beyond it.

LINDSAY ANDERSON

121

■ He attacks the part [in *The Rose Tattoo*] with zest and intelligence . . . But one is always aware that he is acting, that he is playing a part that fits him physically but is beyond his emotional depth . . . The earnestness of his effort only serves to highlight Magnani's own complete submergence in her role.

STANLEY KAUFFMAN

■ If I know anything about movie acting, it's from practising my Burt Lancaster sneer—from *Vera Cruz*—at 16 in front of a bedroom mirror.

SAM SHEPARD

HARRY LANGDON (1884–1944)

■ The trouble was, that highbrow critics came around to explain his art to him. Also he developed an interest in dames. It was a pretty high life for such a fellow. He never did really understand what hit him. He died broke. And he died of a broken heart. He was the most tragic figure I ever came across in show business.

FRANK CAPRA

■ He was a quaint artist who had no business in the business.

MACK SENNETT

FRITZ LANG (1890–1976)

■ In *The Return of Frank James* I had a scene where I came into a barn hunting down John Carradine, who has killed Jesse. I had to come in to a point, look around, hear something, and exit. That's all there was to the scene. We were about five hours doing it because Lang decides he wants cobwebs . . . By this time I knew Lang so well I would make bets with guys that we would be three hours, fucking with the cobwebs in a scene where I come in and stand for two seconds, then walk out!

HENRY FONDA, 1973

■ Lang made fewer bad films than any of that handful of directors who truly deserve the adjective 'great'. And Lang was always very clear and honest about those films with which he was not satisfied and the reasons for his having accepted to make them. 'Even a director has to eat' he would joke in his Viennese accented English.

DAVID OVERBY

JESSICA LANGE (born 1950)

■ Jessica Lange, the ex-model who was the only good thing in the *King Kong* remake, uses her dreamy voice and her thin, slightly twisted upper lip, drawn back from her teeth, to suggest an inexhaustible erotic ravenous. Lange might have had a triumph [in *The Postman Always Rings Twice*] if she had been given some better lines and a handsome, vibrant young actor to work with.

DAVID DENBY

■ She is like a delicate fawn, but crossed with a Buick.

JACK NICHOLSON

■ Tall, blonde and athletic, Jessica Lange is one of those natural beauties who seem regularly to be shipped out of the American mid-West along with the cows and the corn.

JOAN GOODMAN

■ Jessica loves the movies so we go to drive-ins together. She grew up on the

122

whole Hollywood thing. She has a knowledge of the history of the cinema and her place in it, and she can pretty much call the shots.

SAM SHEPARD

MARIO LANZA (1921–1959)

■ Mario Lanza had a little problem about being fat. You had to record his songs when he was fat. Then you had to close down the show while he reduced. You would then make the picture. His ability as an actor was somewhat less than zero.

LEONARD SPIGELGLASS

■ He was neurotic and you never knew if he'd turn up on time. I had to keep flattering him, telling him how wonderful he was.

LEW GRADE, 1987

CHARLES LAUGHTON (1899–1962)

■ With Laughton, one has always been uneasily aware that he knows one is watching; the illusion becomes self-conscious. A film actor should never reveal that awareness.

BASIL WRIGHT, 1938

■ He was the first kind of legend I actually had contact with professionally, which was very exciting. I admired him in his movies—I'd never seen him on the stage. I thought he was terrific.

ALBERT FINNEY

■ With him acting was an act of childbirth. What he needed was not so much a director as a midwife.

ALEXANDER KORDA

■ I had great difficulty managing Laughton; so did Korda.

JOSEF VON STERNBERG

■ Charles Laughton was not a method actor but he used to behave like one. In *Jamaica Inn* we couldn't film him below the waist for ten days because he hadn't got the character's walk. One day he said he'd got it—from listening to Von Weber's *Invitation to the Waltz*.

ALFRED HITCHCOCK

■ And then there was Charles Laughton, the most vulgar actor of all. You always thought when you saw him 'What a great performance' or 'What a ridiculous performance.' It was brassy and extraordinary.

ANTHONY HOPKINS, 1976

■ Charm, you see, a terrific man to work with . . . You had to hold him down a bit . . . What a talent!

DAVID LEAN

123

■ The only actor of genius I've ever met.

LAURENCE OLIVIER

■ He was profoundly ill-at-ease in society, in his profession, even, perhaps especially, in his own body. This is common with actors. The usual manner, however, is to change oneself into someone one does like and display that (star acting) or keep escaping into different characters and thus elude oneself. Laughton does something different. He knows what he's like and he painstakingly displays it.

SIMON CALLOW, 1987

■ Charles never once said anything that expressed a worry for others. People don't turn into angels because they are ill, but sometimes there is a glimmer of what another person might be feeling. Yet Charles [during his last illness] was as he had always been all through his

life. If he said, 'How do you do?' I don't
think he even knew the real meaning of
the words.

ELSA LANCHESTER

STAN LAUREL (1890–1965) and OLIVER HARDY (1892–1957)

■ I don't know what would have happened
to the Laurel and Hardy films if it hadn't
been for Stan. He was the one who
usually took an idea that Roach would
have and brought it to life. In a sense,
he is the spirit behind the films.

CHARLES ROGERS

■ A joke of Laurel and Hardy's is no
transient thing. It is sniffed and savoured
before use, then used, squeezed dry and
squeezed again; smoothed out, folded
up with care and put away ready for the
next time.

DAVID ROBINSON

■ Bud Abbott ditches Lou Costello in a
second when the chips are down.
Groucho Marx gleefully cheats Chico
and Harpo—and vice versa. . . . But
between Laurel and Hardy there is a
loyalty that transcends all their trials.
While it often seems that other comedy
teams are together purely out of
convenience, Stan and Ollie are an
organic whole from the first frame of
every picture. You never question their
oneness.

JOHN LANDIS

■ Speaking for myself, I cannot like anyone
who does not like Laurel and Hardy, nor
love anyone who does not love them. In
104 films they never ran out of comic
ideas, insane invention, charming
conceits.

GARSON KANIN

124

■ Their final unhappy attempts at film-
making and their disappearance from the
screen passed almost unnoticed. This is
ingratitude. Laurel and Hardy have made
too many films. They have made bad
films: and they admit it themselves. They
are neither of them geniuses. But they
are very, very, good clowns. And they
have made a real, and characteristically
unassuming, contribution to screen
comedy.

DAVID ROBINSON, 1954

■ They saw little of each other outside the
studio. In their private lives they did not
mingle much socially. Stan Laurel was
the more creative of the two. He was one
of the best gagmen in the business. He
was not very good on story construction
but he was great at creating individual
pieces of business.

HAL ROACH, 1969

DAVID LEAN (born 1908)

■ When you work with David you have to
be prepared to wait. To be patient. *Ryan's
Daughter* took over a year to make and
some people did get bored. Not me.

JOHN MILLS

■ David Lean is at once the most
prestigious and most mysterious British
film director: he is also perhaps the least
understood . . . Lean's films, especially
his later ones, attract huge audiences and
win Academy Awards, yet the majority
of commentators dismiss him as a
brilliant technician without a personality,
squandering needlessly inflated budgets
on calculatedly tasteful spectacles.

ADRIAN TURNER

■ He is both a charmer and a despot . . .
he spoke with fervour and authority . . .

he was frank. No movie [*A Passage to India*] made for mass circulation, he said, could ever be faithful to Forster's novel. What it could do would be to respect the novel. His final words were that Forster's novel was eternal; movies were ephemeral.

LORD ANNAN

JEAN-PIERRE LÉAUD (born 1944)

■ An eternally callow, crushing bore.

JOHN SIMON

■ The most interesting actor of his generation.

FRANÇOIS TRUFFAUT

VIVIEN LEIGH (1913–1967)

■ ... So I offered Vivien the secondary role of Isabella [in *Wuthering Heights*]. She turned it down. I was astounded. I told Vivien she was totally unknown in America and that she wouldn't get anything better than Isabella for her first Hollywood part.

WILLIAM WYLER

■ Scarlett O'Hara was mine at that point. Then Charlie [Chaplin] gave a luncheon party and David O.Selznick brought the Oliviers. And as soon as I saw the way David was looking at Vivien I knew that Scarlett was mine no longer.

PAULETTE GODDARD

■ She is the skittish belle with a whim of iron of Miss Mitchell's packed, *mouvementé* book to the life: amazing in fact, just how much life she imports. The huge, sprawling circus is really her show and she steals it by little fragments of cameo-playing, oeillades, a tightening of

the lips, the petulant truth she brings to a phrase like 'I certainly have turned out disappointing.'

JOHN COLEMAN, 1968

■ Apart from her looks, which were magical, she possessed beautiful poise; her neck looked almost too fragile to support her head and bore it with a sense of surprise, and something of the pride of the master juggler who can make a brilliant manoeuvre appear almost accidental. She also had something else: an attraction of the most perturbing nature I had ever encountered.

LAURENCE OLIVIER

■ I loved Vivien Leigh. She had this *grace*.

TENNESSEE WILLIAMS

■ ... a stunner whose ravishing beauty often tended to obscure her staggering achievements as an actress. Great beauties are infrequently great actresses—simply because they do not need to be. Vivien was different; ambitious, persevering, serious, often inspired.

GARSON KANIN

■ No-one could dispute the fact that she was both a great beauty and a great star; and if Blanche in *Streetcar* was not a great performance I have never set eyes on one. She was also ... just as strikingly effective on the screen as on the stage, and stage stars have often good reason to be wary of film-making. But Vivien was wary of neither, and seldom wary of anything.

ALAN DENT

■ Quite apart from her looks she had something very strong and individual and interesting. She was a consummate

125

actress anyway, hampered by beauty—
and as a person the complete romantic.
. . . when she invited you to dinner the
food and everything were perfect. [Yet]
. . . you felt something tragic even when
she was at her happiest. She was
Rabelaisian, this exquisite creature, and
told outrageous jokes in that voice cool
and pretty enough to make you weep.

GEORGE CUKOR

■ Parts seem to haunt more actresses than
actors. Poor darling Vivien was very
much haunted. *A Streetcar Named Desire*
didn't do her any good at all.

LAURENCE OLIVIER

■ She was very like a cat. She would purr
and she would scratch and she looked
divinely pretty doing either.

REX HARRISON, 1974.

126

■ The casting of the beautiful Vivien Leigh
in [*The Deep Blue Sea*] was absurd. She
was supposed to be an outwardly
ordinary but secretly highly-sexed
woman who meets a young pilot on the
golf course and falls for him. . . . But
when the part is played by a woman
generally held to be one of the most
beautiful in the world, the whole
meaning is lost.

KENNETH MORE, 1978

CLAUDE LELOUCH (born 1937)

■ He asked me like a newcomer to test!
After fifteen years in the business! I said
yes with a certain smile. It was for *Vivre
pour Vivre*. He almost saved my life since
that was the great departure. Producers
were asking to see me who wouldn't
have given me a minute a few months
earlier.

ANNIE GIRARDOT

JACK LEMMON (born 1925)

■ I've worked with some of the major stars,
such as Olivier, Coward, Morley,
Hepburn, Vivien Leigh. As a rule, the
bigger they are, the easier to work with.
Working with Jack is the easiest of all; I
can only call him a marvellous person.

MORTON GOTTLIEB

■ He's like St Francis of Assisi. He's a good
man and likes birds. I wish I could think
of an adjective to show some sign of
depravity but I can't. . . . He has the
greatest rapport with an audience since
Chaplin. Just by looking at him people
can tell what goes on in his heart.

BILLY WILDER

■ He has extraordinary instinct. He's almost
infallible.

LEE REMICK

■ During that time, there was a lot of
animosity towards my father. I guess I
was identifying with him, I was jealous
of his omnipotence. There was a lot of
psychological stuff going on. I was tired
of being identified as his kid and not as
myself and so I became rebellious. But
we glued it back together very nicely,
thank you . . . I think he's the finest actor
alive today. Watching this man's craft,
watching him prepare for a role, how he
sinks his teeth into it—he's a role model
for me.

CHRISTOPHER LEMMON

■ And the plant supervisor in *The China
Syndrome* in his agonising dilemma very
nearly becomes a genuine tragic hero.
Jack Lemmon trenchantly portrays this
unspectacular man's rise to great moral
heights as well as his ultimate collapse:
no one can convey specious cheerfulness

better than Lemmon or make you feel more clammily sweaty under the collar.

JOHN SIMON

■ Jack Lemmon is brilliant in a role [in *The War between Men and Women*] which he handles with the genius of a Chaplin, the tearful laughs of a Stan Laurel and the inadvertent slapstick of Buster Keaton.

ARMY ARCHER

■ A prototypical American ... When he gets in trouble—let's say as an alcoholic in *Days of Wine and Roses*—we're rooting for him to get cured. If he does something crooked in *Save the Tiger*, or something off-colour in *The Apartment* or *The Fortune Cookie*, people are rooting for him to straighten out, because of their tremendous identification with him.

I. A. L. DIAMOND

■ Jack Lemmon is perfect [in *The China Syndrome*] though. He's a very unique guy. I kept thinking of him in *Save The Tiger*. When you keep him straight and simple, he gives some wonderful performances.

MICHAEL DOUGLAS

SERGIO LEONE (born 1921)

■ I spun off Sergio, and he spun off me. I think we worked well together. I like his compositions. He has a very good eye. ... I liked him, I liked his sense of humour, but I feel it was mutual. He liked dealing with the kind of character I was putting together.

CLINT EASTWOOD

MERVYN LEROY (1900–1987)

■ It is perhaps because Mervyn is not glib at high-flown, academic theorising, and simply stresses basics like heart and pace, and—if it's worth anything in the present market—a useful item like good taste.

JOHN LEE MAHIN

■ I have yet to see a dull movie by LeRoy. Whatever his movies fail to do, they always *move*. He knows how to give speed and pace to a film.

DWIGHT MACDONALD, 1933

RICHARD LESTER (born 1932)

■ Lester has no hang ups. He's a very nice man to work with, and his technique is fascinating. He uses four or five cameras at the same time, covering all the possible angles of a scene. I imagine it's a television technique, but it does make it extremely difficult for the lighting cameraman because he never knows which camera-shot will end up in the final film.

MALCOLM MCDOWELL

■ I objected to Lester's methods and to [Michael] Crawford's concern with boosting himself at the expense of the film. But his style of gangling, awkward comedy appealed to Lester. Lester of course became Crawford's mentor, they went on to *How I Won the War* and *A Funny Thing*. He thought Crawford sort of epitomised his style.

RAY BROOKS

HERSCHELL GORDON LEWIS (born 1926)

■ If you detest horror films that show how many shocking ways a creative sadist

127

can do away with young women, then Lewis is the man to blame.

DANNY PEARY

JERRY LEWIS (born 1926)

■ Jerry is my best friend. I know if ever I were in any need, all I'd have to do is make a phone call. Sometimes, on a professional basis, he's exasperating—but anyone who's talented is. He has his high moods and they're very high—and his low moods are very low.

FRANK TASHLIN

■ I'm a multi-faceted, talented, wealthy, internationally famous genius. I have an IQ of 190—that's supposed to be a genius. People don't like that. My answer to all my critics is simple: I like me. I like what I've become. I'm proud of what I've achieved, and I don't really believe I've scratched the surface yet.

HIMSELF

■ Jerry Lewis hasn't made me laugh since he left Dean Martin.

GROUCHO MARX

■ Jerry Lewis, who's very talented, aimed his humour too much for kids.

WOODY ALLEN

■ Lewis used to be one of my heroes. When I was a kid, I did pantomimes to his records. He was an enormously talented, phenomenally energetic man who used vulnerability very well. But through the years, I've seen him turn into this arrogant, sour, ceremonial, piously chauvinistic egomaniac. I'm just amazed at his behaviour.

ELLIOTT GOULD

MARCEL L'HERBIER (1890–1979)

■ He was a well-behaved, rather affected man who changed suits, gloves and shirts every day. He was always impeccably dressed; I think he must have had at least 50 suits. It was very difficult working with him because he kept changing his mind.

MICHEL KELBER, 1981

BEATRICE LILLIE (born 1894)

■ Her first picture, *Exit Smiling*, is a complete personal triumph for the star, whose sense of burlesque is admirably catered for in the story of the love affair of a maid of all work in a 'fit-up' touring company. Not only is the burlesque some of the best I have ever seen, but there is also an underlying sense of pathos and human feeling which is irresistible.

LIONEL COLLIER, 1927

MAX LINDER (1883–1925)

■ Linder was one of the truly great comedians of our time . . . his pantomime and appeal were eloquent. He had an inspired comedy sense, and he also had an analytical, ingenious mind.

DIMITRI TIOMKIN

HAROLD LLOYD (1893–1971)

■ Lloyd depended more on story and situation than any of the other major comedians . . . He had [also] as he has written 'an unusually large comic vocabulary'. More particularly he had an expertly expressive body and even more expressive teeth, and out of this thesaurus of smiles he could at a moment's notice blend prissiness, breeziness and asininity, and still remain tremendously likeable.

JAMES AGEE

■ Lloyd compensates for his meagre stature as a clown by packed invention and meticulous construction.

RICHARD WINNINGTON, 1953

■ He gave us an eager young man whose fortitude and initiative more than made up for any lack of special talent or ability. He simply took off the makeup and put himself on screen. And it worked.

RICHARD KOSZARSKI

MARGARET LOCKWOOD (born 1916)

■ Working with her was an education. She was an out and out 'pro'—no retakes for Maggie, no hint of temperament. She turned out to be a most down-to-earth lady with a delicious sense of irony, mostly directed at herself.

MICHAEL WILDING, 1982

GINA LOLLOBRIGIDA (born 1927)

■ Gina's personality is limited. She is good playing a peasant but is incapable of playing a lady. That said, I don't think she's positively mad about me. Because I'm bigger than she? It's possible. Who knows?

SOPHIA LOREN

■ The only leading lady who displeased me . . . It's wicked to say this now she's a retired old lady, but we had a completely different conception of things: between each shot she called for her hairdresser and make-up man. It was very painful to work under those conditions. And then, she was a little stupid: she understood nothing of what she was doing and completely embarrassed the director.

JEAN-LOUIS TRINTIGNANT

CAROLE LOMBARD (1908–1942)

■ A wonderful girl. Swore like a man. Other women try, but she really did. She was like one of the fellas, yet there she was, this beautiful girl.

FRED MACMURRAY, 1987

■ You could toss a bolt of fabric at Carole Lombard and however it would land on her she would look smart.

TRAVIS BANTON

■ The greatest star in the world. The greatest actress. She could do anything— you could do everything with her . . . It was his idea that she sit in that curiously straddled position in *Nothing Sacred* during the hangover scene. 'A very unladylike position but she did it like a shot. And, you know something? She looked great.

WILLIAM A. WELLMAN

■ She overwhelmed me completely. There was just something about her that I found uncannily wonderful . . . She was the only Hollywood legend I found totally accessible and felt I could shake hands with. The others, like Garbo and Hepburn, were polite and friendly, but somehow in the early 1940s, untouchable.

GENE KELLY

■ I never dreamed that Lombard had such a performance in her. Her work is superb. Her art in this picture is compelling, understanding and convincing.

JOHN BARRYMORE

129

■ I was wild about the dame ... She was the only woman I've ever known who could say four-letter words and make it come out poetry. I can watch *Nothing Sacred* for ever.

WILLIAM A. WELLMAN

■ She was wonderful to work with. She would stay behind till any hour of the night, and if something bothered us we'd get together at night and go over it and get it solved. She was always on time and knew her lines, and was a great, great artist.

WALTER LANG

■ She was one of the most wonderful women who ever lived. I was so much in awe of her when we started shooting *Swing High, Swing Low* that I kept blowing my lines over and over. Then Carole started blowing hers on purpose so I wouldn't feel bad. She really took me under her wing and gave me a lot of encouragement. It didn't matter to her that she was a big star.

DOROTHY LAMOUR

■ She was married to Gable at one time, you know. I met her out on the street one day—I did a whole series of shows with her—and I said,'How are you and Gable getting along?' and she said 'He's the lousiest lay I ever had.' ... Very sexy dame. She was also a hell of an actress.

GROUCHO MARX

■ It is always a pleasure to watch those hollow Garbo features, those neurotic elbows and bewildered hands, and her voice has the same odd beauty a street musician discovers in old iron, scraping out heart-breaking and nostalgic melodies.

GRAHAM GREENE

■ She was breathtakingly beautiful in a day which demanded plastic beauty of its heroes and heroines. What would, I think, have led her on to still greater stardom were the interior qualities, of wit and unaffected worldly wisdom, untrammelled spirits, honest directness, and her apparent awareness that freedom is not necessarily the same thing as being alone and that the truest freedom is within a secure love.

CHARLES CHAMPLIN

■ One of my closest friends, and the Godmother of my son ... and a lovely person, a great person.

WALTER LANG

SHELLEY LONG (born 1950)

■ Then there was the question of Shelley's hair [on *Hello Again*]. We had to re-shoot the first ten days because it was wrong. All I can say about Shelley is that she is a perfectionist.

GABRIEL BYRNE

SOPHIA LOREN (born 1934)

■ I was never in love with any woman as deeply as I was with Sophia.

PETER SELLERS

■ She is as beautiful as an erotic dream ... Tall and extremely large bosomed. Tremendously long legs. They go up to her shoulders, practically. Beautiful brown eyes, set in a marvellously vulpine, almost satanic, face.

RICHARD BURTON

■ That's a real working woman. Not like those teenage tots who think once they've been in a picture, they're too important to be gracious to their colleagues by being on time.

TREVOR HOWARD

■ Sophia is gorgeous, a marvellously put-together machine. But she's a grievous card sharp; in Naples, they're born with a pack of cards . . . give her a nudge and she's the funniest woman in the world. A helluva woman!

PETER O'TOOLE, 1972

■ I consider Sophia a great—a good actress and a great personality. Because she is a Neopolitan. Like me. We are the same people, the same origin. And we feel together the same. Yes, for me, I am very happy when I work with Sophia.

VITTORIO DE SICA

■ She is not the most attractive lady in the world at first glance but, my God, two seconds later you felt you were in a dream world. Just for her to say 'Hello' was enough. You just capitulated. For me she is the most beautiful person I've ever met.

STEPHEN BOYD

■ She gives herself to you as an artist. During shooting, she'd ask me: 'What did I do wrong? What can I do to make it better?' I never knew her to pull an act—the headache, the temperament. Usually with such a beauty, there is worry about the looks. She doesn't bother about looks. She's interested in acting.

CAROL REED

■ My favourite actress? Ah! Sophia without a doubt. She is so warm, so lovely, so . . . Italian! There is a woman who thinks like a woman, talks like a woman, behaves like a woman—never a star.

MARCELLO MASTROIANNI

■ All in all the most trying work time with an actress I can ever recall. Mind you, she's not a bitch. She's a warm lady, truly; she's just more star than pro.

CHARLTON HESTON

■ I do not talk about Sophia. I do not wish to make for her publicity. She has a talent, but it is not such a big talent.

GINA LOLLOBRIGIDA

■ She should have been sculpted in chocolate truffles so that the world could devour her.

NOËL COWARD, 1987

PETER LORRE (1904–1964)

131

■ Smiling at his own occasionally likeable jokes, reacting with coarse relish to the discomfiture of others; chain-smoking; neurotically attached to a woman who rarely leaves his side; given to alarming facial spasms of contempt, fury or disappointment, Lorre presents [in *The Man Who Knew Too Much*] a portrait of suppressed sadism so definitive that one suspects it must have struck a chord somewhere in Hitchcock's own cat-and-mouse heart.

PETER JOHN DYER, 1961

■ Peter Lorre was one of the finest and most subtle actors I have ever worked with. Beneath that air of innocence he used to such effect, one sensed a Faustian worldliness. I'd know he was giving a good performance as we put it on film but I wouldn't know how good until I saw him in the rushes.

JOHN HUSTON, 1980

JOSEPH LOSEY (1909–1984)

■ My wife [Elizabeth Taylor] and Joe Losey are having a professional love affair. He's the only director besides Mike Nichols who she will work overtime for. It must be love.

RICHARD BURTON, 1968

ROB LOWE (born 1964)

■ If Rob Lowe can get somebody to give him $10 million to hire 75 or 100 people to make a picture, he's aces by me. They need the jobs.

BRIAN DENNEHY

MYRNA LOY (born 1905)

■ It's unbelievable that anyone could work as hard as she does, be on her toes always, accomplish things with dispatch and efficiency, buck the exhausting nervous strain of stardom ... Her charm is that she never tries too hard. She is what she is; her freckles are honest, and so is her appraisal of herself. What she possesses, she exploits. What she does not possess, she does not claim. That's the nicest thing I can say about anyone.

WILLIAM POWELL

■ Myrna Loy, what a joy!

LILLIAN GISH

■ I am an irrationally devoted fan.

LAUREN BACALL

■ Acting is like playing ball. You toss the ball and some people don't toss it back; some people don't even catch it. When you get somebody who catches it and tosses it back, that's really what acting is all about. Myrna kept that spontaneity in her acting, a supreme naturalness that

had the effect of distilled dynamite. She really became the perfect wife. Melvyn Douglas and I used to talk about it on *Blandings*. All the leading men agreed— Myrna was the wife everybody wanted. The only problem we had was her photographic memory. She seemed to look at a page and know her lines and mine. It was harder for me.

CARY GRANT

■ I wish I had been born earlier. I don't know if I am a good enough actor, but I would love to have acted opposite her.

BURT REYNOLDS

■ I asked her, 'How can you stand the heat?' She said, 'There's nothing I can do about it, is there? Would you have me be unattractive?'

ROBERT MITCHUM

■ A great star and a woman of accomplishment who is angry about all the right things.

LENA HORNE

■ A real peach. You can sit down and talk with her about something more than who's doing what and to whom and what's going on in the studio; you can talk politics.

SHEILA O'BRIEN

■ When for instance, you work with people like Freddy March or Myrna Loy, a director might improve their work, but he certainly can't make a performance, because they are too knowing. After Myrna gets Freddy to bed in his drunk scene, I thought she should have an exit line, but there was none in the script. It worked perfectly. How many actresses would cut their own line to improve a scene? But she always considered the

132

good of the picture and the impact of her fellow actors.

WILLIAM WYLER

ERNST LUBITSCH (1892–1947)

- Working mainly on the Maurice Chevalier—Jeanette MacDonald musicals, Lubitsch quicky established himself as one of the most inventive directors of the period. With his strong feeling for the relationship between music and visuals, he brought back some of the rhythm that had been present in the silent films.

ARTHUR KNIGHT

- Lubitsch, I think, shows himself a greater artist here [*Design for Living*] than Coward. He adds his own mellow comment to Coward's criticisms of life, giving them a broader, but not less shrewd, application. Coward laughs at life, but Lubitsch laughs at life and Coward too.

C. A. LEJEUNE

- In a world of gardenias, ultra-modern flats, globe-trotting and champagne, we can chase the flying witticisms of a man [Lubitsch] who can use satire, who is daring, and who has a command second to none over every trick and subtlety possible to cinema.

BASIL WRIGHT

- He was the only director in Hollywood who had his own signature.

S. N. BEHRMAN

- Ernst Lubitsch was a great director, worthy of his enormous reputation, but I found working under him in *Design for Living* cramped my style a bit. He left one no leeway at all, telling you when

to light a cigarette, when to put your hands in your pockets, regulating every movement and gesture, every expression. I felt like a robot after a few days.

FREDRIC MARCH

- A giant. His talent and originality were stupifying.

ORSON WELLES, 1965

- After his funeral, William Wyler and I were walking away and I said 'My God! Lubitsch is gone' and he said 'Worse than that, not only no more Lubitsch, but no more Lubitsch pictures!' It was a kind of lost art, like Chinese glass-blowing, you know; he took the secret with him to the grave. . . . when we came to some comical aspect in a picture . . . always thought 'How would Lubitsch have done it?

BILLY WILDER, 1979

133

GEORGE LUCAS (born 1945)

- I really like my contemporaries and can get more out of George Lucas, who's a good friend of mine, than I can by sitting in a screening room and screening eight Preston Sturges films.

STEVEN SPIELBERG

- But you know, I would probably have turned down *Star Wars*—which just goes to show what an ass-hole I am! There was nothing in that picture I could relate to. I mean the dialogue, if you'll excuse me for saying so, was simply *terrible*! The genius of the picture was George Lucas. I mean *what* a concept! Absolutely breathtaking when you consider what Lucas did and he deserves everything he's ever gotten.

JOHN FRANKENHEIMER

- I hate to sound idealistic and George Lucas and I, who are very good friends, we always fight over this. George is very money-oriented, George thinks the reason he's in the movie business is just to make money, but that's not my feeling because I enjoy it *as a hobby*.

  STEVEN SPIELBERG

BELA LUGOSI (1882–1956)

- His voice was laced with melodic menace; a natural aid was his native accent which, like his acting, was strictly from Hungary.

  DENIS GIFFORD

SIDNEY LUMET (born 1924)

- Lumet never keeps anybody waiting— no director has earned a larger reputation for efficiency and organisation.

  WILLIAM GOLDMAN

- I chose Sidney to direct *Twelve Angry Men* because I knew we would have two weeks to rehearse and he could get performances out of actors. What I got was a bonus I didn't count on: his incredible use of the camera which he had learned in television.

  HENRY FONDA, 1973

- All I want to do is get better, and quantity can help me to solve my problems. I'm thrilled by the idea that I'm not even sure how many films I've done. If I don't have a script I adore, I do one I like. If I don't have one I like, I do one that has an actor I like or that presents some technical challenge.

  HIMSELF, 1973

- I've done three films with Sidney Lumet and I would do anything to work with him again.

  HENRY FONDA

- Sidney Lumet works by being part camp councillor, part psychiatrist and part technical director. You simply walk into a world in which he is a benevolent dictator and you trust yourself completely—like those exercises where people stand backwards on a table and fall off trusting the group will catch them. Well you do that with Sidney and he catches you.

  CHRISTOPHER REEVE, 1987

DAVID LYNCH (born 1947)

- I'm doing it because of David, because I think that man is one of the last great eccentrics in the world of film. He's a maniac. And if anybody can pull *Dune* off, it's David. They just handed him fifty million dollars and told him to do what he liked.

  STING

JEANETTE MACDONALD (1901–1965)

- That silly horse, Jeanette MacDonald, yakking away at wooden-peg Eddy with all that glycerine running down her Max Factor.

  JUDY GARLAND

- I later heard her referred to as the Iron Butterfly, although I was surprised to hear that she found that amusing. I never thought she had much of a sense of humour. When we worked together she always objected to anyone telling a risque story.

  MAURICE CHEVALIER

134

■ *The Merry Widow* marked the end of what many consider the most interesting part of Jeanette MacDonald's career, when she was the only singer in pictures who could sing with her tongue in the cheek.

CLIVE HIRSCHHORN

■ Jeanette MacDonald and Nelson Eddy were my fellow musicians as well as my close friends. They had certain personal characteristics in common, which involved almost story-book qualities; unremitting fealty to their profession, loyalty to their associates, and 'no compromise' in the matter of doing justice to their talents. Unflaggingly did they accept the virtually unlimited demands their careers constantly made upon them.

MEREDITH WILLSON

ALEXANDER MACKENDRICK
(born 1912)

■ The trouble for Mackendrick ... was that he outgrew Sir Michael Balcon's marvellous stable of writers, technicians, directors and actors, and yet since the end of that era he and other talents have not had the opportunity to work systematically or frequently. As artists they were inhibited by the very thing that originally helped them.

BRIAN BAXTER

SHIRLEY MACLAINE (born 1934)

■ We always had lots of laughs, and we've shared a few sorrows, too. But I'd never worked with her. I heard she was a tough nut. *Terms of Endearment* was an important movie, and the work was

tough. But tough and interesting. And playing with Shirl—like in the love scenes, which are funny but also touching—was great.

JACK NICHOLSON

■ She hated rehearsals and had a bad habit of adlibbing, which didn't set well with Billy Wilder. But we got used to each other, because mainly she's a helluva girl.

JACK LEMMON

■ She just behaved badly—like she was competing with me [on the set of *Terms of Endearment*]. I understand that Shirley grew up in a different era, when women had flesh under their fingernails from competing with one another, but I'm not like that. I was actually forever grateful when she won [the Oscar] because I thought that would shut her up for a while. Imagine my dismay when she just kept having 50th birthdays and doing interviews. Jack Nicholson called me up for her second 50th and said, 'Didn't we celebrate her 50th birthday in Texas?'.

DEBRA WINGER

■ We discovered we each needed a wife to take care of us. That role is not for me, and it is certainly not for Shirley. She is a very strong woman. She is Warren Beatty's older brother, not his sister. We were a very combustible combination, her and I. She is one of the jewels in American culture, a rare person. We just couldn't live together.

ANDREI KONCHALOVSKY, 1987

■ Shirley—I love her, but her oars aren't touching the water these days.

DEAN MARTIN

■ She's an extraordinary woman, a little round the bend I think, but she's been

135

doing what she does for a long time, and she does it very well. Where Meryl is intellectual, Shirley follows her gut. I like that better.

CHARLES DANCE, 1987

altogether. He faces work in such a free way: I've never seen anybody else work like that. He doesn't prepare it, he just does it.

SALLY FIELD

MADONNA (born 1959)

■ *Who's that Girl* is a vehicle for material womanhood, but Madonna, harshly photographed, [armed with a] wiggle and a Minnie Mouse squawk, is coarse and charmless: a performer to be kept tightly reined.

SHEILA JOHNSTON, 1987

■ Who's that girl? Who cares?

ALAN FRANK

ANNA MAGNANI (1908–1973)

■ I would like to see Anna Magnani playing beside the most popular pin-up of the year. It is my belief that beside Anna Magnani she would seem devoid of content, as an empty shell. For Anna Magnani proves anew the old axiom that beauty is truth.

JILL CRAIGIE, 1956

■ A force of nature.

MARLENE DIETRICH

■ She conforms only to the law of nature at its most primitive . . . She is a wild animal with its grace, health and vitality.

CECIL BEATON

JOHN MALKOVICH (born 1954)

■ A very strange fellow—but, again, so loveable that I felt a great comfort in being with him. His humour is so off the wall that you think maybe he's lost it

LOUIS MALLE (born 1932)

■ Malle seemed to me like a bad child. There were these two amazing women. [on *Viva Maria!*] Each of them had been in love with him for some time and each had her separate camp within the location. Malle liked to milk that tension. I think I was just an eleventh-hour replacement for Alain Delon. It was only a memorable experience for me in that I met Jeanne Moreau, whom I subsequently lived with.

GEORGE HAMILTON, 1982

HERMAN J. MANKIEWICZ (1897–1953)

■ I knew that no-one as witty and spontaneous as Herman would ever put himself on paper. A man whose genius is on tap like free beer seldom makes literature out of it.

BEN HECHT

■ *Citizen Kane* is an absolutely perfect marriage of writer and material, as it combined the political and the sociological aspects that Herman knew better than almost anybody I know.

JOSEPH L. MANKIEWICZ

■ Sure, Mank was witty, but his wit took a much more elaborate form than wisecracks. He could improvise in a way that just held you spellbound.

NUNNALLY JOHNSON

JOSEPH L. MANKIEWICZ (born 1909)

■ *Letter to Three Wives* and *All About Eve* were marvellous films. I thought that the last good film that he made was *Five Fingers,* because I personally have not seen a Mankiewicz film that appeared to be well directed since then. For instance, *Cleopatra* was a hideous film but nevertheless you could see that it had some good, well-written script ideas, and the director . . . had not served the writer well.

JAMES MASON, 1970

■ For Joe Mankiewicz—
Always at my back I hear,
Winged release dates hurrying near.
I'm glad my producer's literate,
Gentle, kindly and considerate.

OGDEN NASH, 1940

■ Joe Mankiewicz ruins you for anyone else. He never let me down in all the pictures we made together. When he didn't think it was working, he'd ask for more time to change and polish it. When I ran into a problem on other pictures, I could always reach Joe on the phone, and he'd come over. He'd say 'Give me 20 or 30 minutes—I know how to fix it.' And he would.

NORMAN TAUROG

JAYNE MANSFIELD (1933–1967)

■ Dramatic art in her opinion is knowing how to fill a sweater.

BETTE DAVIS

■ Jayne surrendered all her privacy and considerable dignity to the daily job of getting her name and picture in the papers. Her home, whether it was a house, apartment, or hotel suite, was always open to reporters, and photographers were constantly running in and out, stumbling over her dogs and cats or her little daughter Jayne Marie.

EARL WILSON

JEAN MARAIS (born 1913)

■ [On the cast of *Les Parents Terribles*] If I keep Jean Marais for the last, it's because his performance escapes analysis. Not only is it prodigious: he played what he used to execute, instinctively, and tripled his effects by a fusion of passion and style.

JEAN COCTEAU

FREDRIC MARCH (1897–1975)

■ Fredric March's laborious stylishness— which always made up in persistence what it lacked in persuasiveness.

ANDREW SARRIS

137

■ He was able to do a very emotional scene with tears in his eyes and pinch my fanny at the same time.

SHELLEY WINTERS

DEAN MARTIN (born 1917)

■ After the break-up, I asked Patti why she'd never said anything against Dean, and she told me that Dean was like a second wife to me and that she had no right to speak against him. Isn't that something? . . . I still love Dean, but I don't like him anymore.

JERRY LEWIS

■ He believed in the value of time a lot less than I did. In his happy-go-lucky way, he paid little attention to the shooting schedule. Instead of the ordinary one-hour lunch break, he would stretch his into two or three.

LANA TURNER, 1982

STEVE MARTIN (born 1945)

■ I couldn't get to really know Steve because he had the whole thing [*The Man with Two Brains*] on his shoulder; he didn't have time to be just a human being.

KATHLEEN TURNER, 1985

■ After *Roxanne,* one imagines he could play anything in movies—a lover, a warrior, an athlete, a poet. He has heroic skills, which is perhaps a strange thing to say, since his modern-man's streamlining doesn't seem, at first, to support heroism. The lean, square-shouldered body looks right in a business suit; the short, prematurely gray hair has a lawyer or stockbroker's cut (not for him the conventional show-business hip of sweaters and fluffy locks). The powerful forehead and wide smile are so . . . *presentable*.

DAVID DENBY

LEE MARVIN (1924–1987)

■ Lee Marvin is a superb physical actor (and a much more interesting action hero than Clint Eastwood). That long face with its great, heavy, warlord's brow, sardonic eyes, and huge snout is a movie all in itself, both funny and threatening, and the voice is a rich actor's bass, gravelly and black yet with a surprising lilt that makes the simplest line vibrate with insinuation.

DAVID DENBY

■ Stimulation? Thursdays. Motivation? Thursdays. Pay-days. That's it. It's important not to think too much about what you do . . . You see, with my way of thinking there are always Thursdays—no matter how the picture works out.

HIMSELF

■ I'm not his psychiatrist. I don't know whether he has one or needs one. I'm only saying that to understand him, one needs help.

STANLEY KRAMER

■ I am prepared to talk about, say, Burt Reynolds, Robert Redford, Walter Matthau or any other pleasurable subject. But not about Lee Marvin. He said some wicked things about me and I am not disposed to reply in kind. Nor, on the other hand, am I disposed to say anything favourable either.

MICHAEL RITCHIE

■ I learnt more from Lee about film-making than from anyone. He has this incredible economy and brilliant camera technique. Most actors are completely spastic when it comes to moving properly, but Lee has the economy and quickness of a dancer.

JOHN BOORMAN

■ He was everything I hoped and feared he would be—as unpredictable, honest, intimidating and inflammable as I had imagined. He is unusually interesting in the way that was more interesting than peace. I thought if I got out of there merely disfigured I'd be lucky.

CANDICE BERGEN

■ Look, this feller is a pretty good boozer, he's got a short fuse, but he can be handled okay.

ROBERT ALDRICH

138

■ Lee Marvin is more male than anyone I have ever acted with. He is the greatest man's man I have ever met and that includes a lot of European stars I have worked with.

JEANNE MOREAU

■ Not since Attila the Hun swept across Europe leaving 500 years of total blackness has there been a man like Lee Marvin.

JOSHUA LOGAN

■ Once Lee Marvin said to me, 'You know, as character actors we play all kinds of sex psychos, nuts, creeps, perverts, and weirdos. And we laugh it off saying what the hell, it's just a character. But deep down inside, it's you, baby.'

STROTHER MARTIN

■ This giant among actors who has become one of my greatest friends. He can appear complicated, eccentric, but he does his work with a rare professional conscience. Of all the actors with whom I've worked he is certainly the most impressive. More, he has a particularly wide range, from odious gangsters to tender, naive men.

JEAN SEBERG

THE MARX BROTHERS,
CHICO (1886–1961)
HARPO (1888–1964)
GROUCHO (1890–1977)

■ Groucho, you're the greatest comedian of them all.

CHARLES CHAPLIN, 1954

■ Largely speaking Harpo and Chico were only interested in their specialities. Groucho was concerned with the whole picture . . . But the Marxes were boorish, they were ungrateful. It was a very uneasy combination. Harpo was the nicest brother.

S. J. PERELMAN

■ If you ever eat at the Hillcrest Country Club and Groucho is there you'll find he'll make you laugh in the same way he does on screen. Chico, I would say, loved women and gambling, period. Harpo was probably the sweetest man you would ever want to meet.

JACK BENNY

■ It was I who introduced my wife to the Marx Brothers films and she is now as keen a fan as I am.

T. S. ELLIOT

■ Watching these films you may learn no more than . . . that left-handed moths ate the stolen painting. But you can also relish anew the invigorating independence and agility of three superb clowns with completely contrasting but interlocking styles and marvel at the epic resilience displayed by their untiring target, Margaret Dumont.

ALLEN EYLES

■ These men were not motivated by greed, ambition, or lechery. Their zaniness sprang from pure hearts: . . . Clipping ties off stuffed shirts at a banquet, setting an orchestra adrift on a large raft, confounding everyone with Groucho's cloudy logic—the Marx Brothers scampered through their films like a horde of impetuous children. The strictures of society and the unwritten law to behave by conforming had no meaning for the Marx Brothers except as targets.

WILLIAM KAHNS

■ The Marxes were so confidently unreasonable as to awaken in the

139

spectator bitter doubts as to the worthwhileness of not being a fool.

CLIFTON FADIMAN

- Cedric Hardwicke is my fifth favourite actor, the first four being the Marx Brothers.

BERNARD SHAW

MARCELLO MASTROIANNI
(born 1929)

- Marcello is a man who thinks like a man, talks like a man—is a man! He has so much magnetism, he brings out the very soul in a woman.

SOPHIA LOREN

- I could fall in love with Marcello even though he is older than my father.

NASTASSJA KINSKI

140

- He's very human and easily identifies with the man in the street. He's never a hero. Rather, he's an anti-hero, and that's why in turn the public adore him. That's his great merit and his appeal.

LUCHINO VISCONTI

- God, he's a good actor, one of the best I ever worked with.

JACK LEMMON, 1986

- Mastroianni fascinates me . . . there are few people who are more intelligent than they wish to appear. That's Marcello exactly!

JEAN-LOUIS TRINTIGNANT

JAMES MASON (1909–1984)

- That Mason is the greatest actor.

D. W. GRIFFITH

- James Mason has already proved that he can play just about anything; in this kind of elegant high comedy role [in *The Last of Sheila*] he is unsurpassable— wonderfully, subtly, sardonic.

STEPHEN FARBER

- Everyone was so used to seeing him as a villain. I wanted them to see the side of him I knew—the cute, adorable side. People thought he was cold and aloof, but he was really just terribly shy.

PAMELA MASON

- He was a punctilious man, beautifully mannered, quiet, generous and amusing. I never heard him say a vicious or bitter thing about anything or anyone.

JOHN GIELGUD

- By creating characters that command attention, he gives the other characters in the films importance they do not deserve under the circumstances. Having recently reseen *Lolita, North by Northwest,* and *Georgy Girl* it now occurs to me that he has always been superb. He is, in fact, one of the few actors worth taking trouble to see, even when the film that encases him is so much cement.

VINCENT CANBY

- He was one of the closest friends I ever had. A wonderful actor, and a humble and wonderful man.

STEWART GRANGER

- It was in the open air, bitter cold, and I was amazed at the patience and the good humour and the thoughtfulness showed. I was delighted to see him in the part of Dr Fischer. For me, in future, Dr Fischer will have the face of James Mason. His eyes conveyed simultaneously enormous pride and a profound sadness which is exactly what I wanted.

GRAHAM GREENE

WALTER MATTHAU (born 1920)

- Walter is a helluvan actor. The best I've ever worked with.

  JACK LEMMON

- One of the funniest men I've ever worked with and didn't understand anything about the movie [*Charley Varrick*] at all. When I showed him the first cut all he said was 'Well, I got to admit it's a picture but can anyone tell me what the hell it's all about?'

  DON SIEGEL, 1973

- A lot of parts I want they give to Robert Redford.

  HIMSELF, 1983

- There are two Matthaus. One minute he can be Saint Francis of Assisi, and the next, very, very cantankerous and tough to work with. But he's an economical actor; he knows the power of close-ups, how to get the maximum out of everything. I wish I had him for my next fifty pictures. Walter can play *Richard III*, *Fiddler on the Roof, Charley's Aunt*, and *The Elephant Man* all in one afternoon. And in between he can squeeze in a few poker games.

  BILLY WILDER

- Conceivably the best character actor in America.

  KENNETH TYNAN

- He has talent that still hasn't been tapped. Films haven't yet touched on his depth.

  JACK LEMMON

- He was an absolute delight and a professional in every sense of the word.

  CAROL BURNETT

JESSIE MATTHEWS (1907–1981)

- Jessie could dance like an angel, sing with point and significance, and she could act. . . . but her taut nerves, combined with her passionate involvement with her work, kept her at a dangerous point of strain. Often her nerve-strings were on the point of snapping, and indeed they did at one stage at the peak of her career. 'Good Trouper' is a glib and hackneyed phrase, but it precisely describes Jessie Matthews.

  MICHAEL BALCON

- Part of the appeal of Jessie Matthews is, of course, the appeal of the 1930's; the blend of insouciance, sauciness and sentimentality that lies in all her characterisations, the exaggerated ballet mannerisms, the plummy, quaintly affected voice. But the major part is her own talent.

  JOHN GILLETT

- A beauty with a name more fitted to someone who might come in to clean the brass, and a face even more amazingly circular than those of all other primrose stars of her day. She sings with the clear boy-soprano voice that one associates with the original English cast of Sandy Wilson's *The Boy Friend* and a life of sleeping with the windows open without central heating in a larynx-bathing-mist.

  PENELOPE GILLIATT, 1973

- She was a much greater dancer than Ginger Rogers and I thought a better actress.

  DIRK BOGARDE, 1987

- Sustaining a long personal relationship was just not within her power. She wanted to be a star. She was a star and I think she was quite happy with it . . . She was too selfish to want anything

141

else ... When she ceased to be a big star she was a very lonely lady.

VINCENT SHAW

■ Basically, you see, Jessie had a generous, openhearted disposition. She was plagued all her life by a set of nervous disorders which nearly wrecked her career and resulted in the loss of friends.

CHARLES SIMON

VICTOR MATURE (born 1915)

■ The very name Victor Mature captures the brawny, if somewhat seedy, appeal of this performer.

KINGSLEY CANHAM

CARL MAYER (1894–1944)

142

■ The film was the first and only medium in which he created, and the cinema was the first artistic instrument he used. It was not that he merely 'understood' the film medium. A script by Carl Mayer was already a film—a detailed recording of every shot that he had formed in his imagination. ... He was persistent in learning more, always more about the camera's possibilities.

KARL FREUD

LOUIS B. MAYER (1885–1957)

■ MGM's no great shakes now, but it was a damned sight better when the old man was around. I never liked him much but at least you knew where you stood.

AVA GARDNER

■ For seventeen years it was Mr Mayer who guided me, and I never turned down a picture that he personally asked me to

do. He was kind, fatherly, understanding and protective. He was always there when I had problems.

ROBERT TAYLOR

■ He has the memory of an elephant and the hide of an elephant. The only difference is that elephants are vegetarians and Mayer's diet is his fellow man.

HERMAN J. MANKIEWICZ

■ I never expected 100-percent sainthood from men like Louis B. Mayer or Harry Cohn, but they had a great sense of the romance of this business. I never had an agent or a lawyer, and I always found Louis B. Mayer scrupulously honest.

KATHARINE HEPBURN

PAUL MAZURSKY (born 1930)

■ *Greenwich Village* was the story of a young, successful Hollywood film–maker who can't decide what his next film is going to be, it is 'personal' but ... it is so profoundly superficial (is that possible?) that it has the air of something based not on life but on things other people have published, filmed, or put on television during the last 10 or 15 years. It's second-hand.

VINCENT CANBY

LEO McCAREY (1898–1969)

■ The most gifted director [I ever worked with].

DELMER DAVES

- I had faith in Leo McCarey. I knew he was a brilliant director and knew what he was doing.

  IRENE DUNNE

- I did try to get out of the movie [*The Awful Truth*] rather stupidly because I didn't understand Leo McCarey. He had some brilliant ideas, but unfortunately he was very inarticulate about them. When Irene and I finally caught on to him, it was a joy. We finally realised where he was trying to go. But for one thing, his permitting us to adlib was so unusual in those days.

  CARY GRANT

MARIE McDONALD (1923–1965)

- A triple threat who can't sing, dance, nor act.

  GENE KELLY

KELLY McGILLIS (born 1957)

- I needed the sense of vulnerability she projects onscreen. The late 40s and early 50s were a much more innocent time in America, and the mystery element called for an actress who could really portray that quality rather than simply rush, Nancy Drew–like, through the action. It didn't hurt that Kelly looks good in a hat and gloves.

  PETER YATES

STEVE McQUEEN (1930–1980)

- I am a limited actor. My range isn't that great and I don't have that much scope. I'm pretty much myself most of the time in my movies, and I have accepted that.

  HIMSELF

- Once I asked him why do you ride those motorcycles like that and maybe kill yourself, and he said 'So I won't forget I'm a man and not just an actor'. You know in back of this is a very strong truth. Rather odd people become actors and they are vain, they are much vainer than women.

  BETTE DAVIS

- A Steve McQueen performance just naturally lends itself to monotony: Steve doesn't bring much to the party.

  ROBERT MITCHUM

- One thing about Steve, he didn't like the women in his life to have balls.

  ALI MCGRAW

- I can honestly say he's the most difficult actor I've ever worked with.

  NORMAN JEWISON

- The story [*Bullit*] on reflection is jaded: good policeman against power-hungry politicians, gangsters, even the girlfriend. McQueen's trim movements and vulnerable, sub-heroic face somehow, make it all matter.

  JOHN COLEMAN

- More versatile than Caan or Newman, but lacking their coat-hanger appeal; rangier than Hackman, but without his coiled-wire urban intensity; no personality to match Marvin's; lacking the urbanity of Coburn; of far greater range than Eastwood but without his immediate screen impact. Looked at closely, McQueen was the thorough outsider . . .

  DEREK ELLEY

- So, these modern stars—it's crazy, how little they have in common with the ancient archetypes of seduction.

143

Nowadays, people fantasise over Steve McQueen and Dustin Hoffman. They're really excellent fellows but can one, honestly, compare them to Rudolf Valentino or Clark Gable?

WILLIAM WYLER

■ He walked around with the attitude that the burden of preserving the integrity of the picture was on his shoulders and all the rest of us were company men ready to sell out, grind out an inferior picture for a few bucks and the bosses. . . . Eventually, we grew to like each other.

DON SIEGEL

■ The independent buoyance with which he carried himself, the sharp way his icy blue eyes would watch for an opening, the way he carried the only authority he ever needed within him marked him as a 1950s hep cat who aged better than most because he was smarter than most.

SCOTT RYMAN

■ Early in his life he developed a toughness and a calculated determination, first perhaps for survival, later for his professional ambitions . . . And the arrogance which motivates some of his actions is mitigated by the charm of that quick half-smile which assures us that, at bottom, he is a 'good guy'.

HOWARD KOCH

■ Steve McQueen is a very difficult man. He's not very bright, but he's very shrewd and very talented. He's a very gifted guy, but he's very strong-willed. Working with him on *The Reivers* was difficult because he wanted to be the boss, and I wouldn't let him.

MARK RYDELL, 1979

JEAN-PIERRE MELVILLE (1917–1973)

■ He begged us to turn our backs on what he considered to be misguided works like *Johnny Guitar* and to look instead to the American classics for inspiration. Biased as he was, he contended that only two—at that time, disdained— directors counted for anything at all; William Wyler and Robert Wise.

VOLKER SCHLÖNDORFF

BETTE MIDLER (born 1945)

■ In one scene [of *Jinxed*] I have to hit her in the face, and I thought we could save some money on sound effects here.

KEN WAHL, 1982

■ I loved working with Bette. I rarely get to have a good leading lady, and Bette and Marsha Mason are the best. I'd work with them again anytime.

RICHARD DREYFUSS, 1987

SARAH MILES (born 1941)

■ She's a monster. If you think she's not strong, you'd better pay attention.

ROBERT MITCHUM

■ Every actor has certain ways of expressing their nerves and with Sarah it was always terribly difficult to actually get her on the set. There was always a problem, usually with her clothes. . . . I found myself shouting at her. Then she'd burst into tears and her eyes would go all red so we wouldn't be able to shoot the scene.

JOHN BOORMAN, 1986

LEWIS MILESTONE (1895–1980)

■ From Lewis Milestone I learned diplomacy in dealing with actors.

ROBERT ALDRICH, 1956

144

JOHN MILIUS (born 1944)

■ He's out there hammering and sawing, building a Milius legend.

GARY BUSEY

■ John Milius is a very good writer, especially of heroic stuff. But he is so *busy* with being butch and Hemingway and samurai and all that, it gets in the way of his direction nowadays. But his invention as a writer is wonderful.

SEAN CONNERY

RAY MILLAND (1905–1986)

■ This enormously famous star is so self-effacingly modest, he's an object lesson for the rest of us in show business.

FRANKIE HOWERD

■ A nice old bloke.

MICHAEL CAINE

ANN MILLER (born 1919)

■ On the table in her hotel room is a book titled 'Remarkable Women of Ancient Egypt.' Miss Miller firmly believes she lived in Egypt in another life.

MOIRA HODGSON

LIZA MINNELLI (born 1946)

■ I think she decided to go into show business when she was an embryo, she kicked so much.

JUDY GARLAND

■ She's a great trouper, Liza, I wish I had her talent. If anybody's going to take over from me, it's her. She's got a mind like a trip hammer and huge vitality. She's great.

LUCILLE BALL, 1973

■ I'm annoyed when people keep comparing her to her mother. She's nothing to do with her mother. She's a completely different woman. The film [*Cabaret*] is a great hit for her and that's all one wants.

MARLENE DIETRICH, 1972

■ America has a habit of seizing upon new faces and new talents and burning them up. Right now they've put Liza, who is a joy to work with, Miss One Hundred Per Cent, a real professional, up on a pedestal and any minute now they're going to start shaking it just to prove that she's only flesh and blood really.

MICHAEL YORK, 1972

■ After 15 minutes I realised that not only could she sing she could be one hell of an actress . . . She's so malleable and inventive. And fun, even when things are hard.

MARTIN SCORSESE

■ What she has is presence, and that's a gift like perfect pitch. She has something to make your eyes follow her, yet she's not pretty and far from a beauty. But she has only to move, to loosen into a dance or hit a badminton shuttlecock a winning smash, and she becomes as supple as a scarf. You see then the precise articulate dancer's body: you see what she wants you to see.

MARCELLE BERNSTEIN

■ I love Liza. She is so original. People speak of her in terms of her mother, but she is herself, very definitely. A good, strong, unique person.

MYRNA LOY

145

■ Liza was always show business. The basic quality has been there since she first said 'goo'.

KAY THOMPSON

■ She's the greatest musical actress and performer we have.

CY FEUER

■ One of the happiest times in my life was during *The Sterile Cuckoo*, mostly because of Liza. I've never seen anybody get more joy out of working and it's contagious.

ALAN PAKULA

■ She is one part memory of her mother, one part unsubtle appeal to the homosexual flock by campy travestying of what little femininity she has; one part brash infantilism angled at teenyboppers of all ages; and one part jokes about her ridiculous looks and freakish success.

ELIN SCHOEN

146

VINCENTE MINNELLI (1910–1986)

■ No other director had Minnelli's taste for colour and design. A good collaborator is very important. Minnelli's contribution was just immense.

GENE KELLY

■ Vincente Minnelli's a beautiful director, but I don't think he understood this show [*Bells are Ringing*] the way that we who wrote it did—he understood it the way *he* understood it. But it's a motion picture director's world today, he runs the whole show. In the theatre it's a collaboration.

JULE STYNE

CARMEN MIRANDA (1909–1955)

■ A wonderfully funny gal to work with.

HERMES PAN

ROBERT MITCHUM (born 1917)

■ I only read the reviews of my films if they're amusing. Six books have been written about me but I've only ever met two of the authors. They get my name and birthplace wrong in the first paragraph. From there it's all downhill.

HIMSELF

■ Far from being like his image of a lazy kind of character who didn't seem to care about anything, he was in fact extremely intelligent, and cared about so many things. He was such a suprise. Whenever we've worked together we have never had any trouble. He's a natural, with perfect timing, and if you're playing with that, then it's just wonderful.

DEBORAH KERR

■ He has what many of the great 1930s and 1940s actors who are today's cult heroes had: a capacity to retain and even expand their dignity, their image, their self-possession, even in the midst of the worst possible material. . . . you see Mitchum in bad movies, but you can never spot him being bad.

ROGER EBERT

■ You're the biggest fraud I ever met. You pretend you don't care a damn thing about a scene, and you're the hardest working so-and-so I've ever known.

HOWARD HAWKS

■ All his hip talk is a blind. He's a very fine man with wonderful manners and he speaks beautifully when he wants to. He won't thank you for destroying the tough image he's built up as a defence. In fact he's a very tender man and very great gentleman.

CHARLES LAUGHTON

■ I think that Bob is one of the very great actors and that his resources as an actor have never been fully tapped. He could be a Shakespearean actor. In fact, I think that he could play King Lear.

JOHN HUSTON

■ The beauty of that man. He's so still. He's moving and yet he's not moving.

LEE MARVIN

KENJI MIZOGUCHI (1898–1956)

■ I've been making films for thirty years. If I look back on all I've done in that time I see nothing but a series of compromises with the capitalists, whom we nowadays call producers, in order to make a film in which I could take pleasure.

HIMSELF

■ The highly individual compound of sensuality, elegance, bitterness and vigour is very marked. Through a series of assignments, he was able to create a consistent world, a place of brief pleasures and enduring sadness where moments of tenderness and repose break the action with a suddenness that is itself close to violence.

V. F. PERKINS, 1972

■ Mizoguchi's haunting images created an atmosphere in which the film comes perhaps as close as it can to the pity and terror of the classic Greek tragedy. The Japanese cinema in general emphasises the landscape and phenomena of nature . . . Mizoguchi goes even further and uses the environment as the chief actor in his film.

EILEEN BOWSER, 1964

MARILYN MONROE (1926–1962)

■ Difficult? Yes . . . But she was a wonderful comedienne and she had a charisma like no one before or since.

JACK LEMMON, 1987

■ I found myself in the privileged position of photographing somebody who I had first thought had a gift for the camera, but who turned out had a genius for it.

EVE ARNOLD

■ I have just come from the Actor's Studio where I saw Marilyn Monroe. She had no girdle on, her ass was hanging out. She is a disgrace to the industry.

JOAN CRAWFORD, 1955

■ They treated her as a bubblehead—but she was very bright, very sharp.

JOHN SPRINGER, 1987

■ She seemed like a lost child.

ROBERT MITCHUM

147

■ What she wanted most was not to judge but to win recognition from a sentimentally cruel profession, and from men blinded to her humanity by her perfect beauty. She was part queen, part waif, sometimes on her knees before her own body and sometimes despairing because of it.

ARTHUR MILLER, 1987

■ Absolutely unafraid . . . she would take on anybody if there was something she wanted. She was intelligent, highly articulate but she could be imposed on and was.

GEORGE CUKOR, 1972

■ You don't have to hold an inquest to find out who killed Marilyn Monroe. Those bastards in the big executive chairs killed her.

HENRY HATHAWAY

- Marilyn was a girl who I just knew would go a very, very long way. The men on *All About Eve* disagreed. I'm glad I was right.

  BETTE DAVIS

- The only gal who came near to me in the sex–appeal department was pretty little Marilyn Monroe. All the others had were big boobs.

  MAE WEST

- All the people who were on the film were misfits—Marilyn, Monty, Huston, all a little connected to catastrophe, Gable not saying much, just himself being Gable. It showed how some stars are like stars in heaven that are burnt out.

  ERNEST HAAS

- Marilyn was an incredible person to act with . . . the most marvellous I ever worked with, and I have been working for 29 years.

  MONTGOMERY CLIFT

- There were two entirely unrelated sides to Marilyn. You would not be far out if you described her as schizoid; the two people that she was could hardly have been more different . . . she was so adorable, so witty, such incredible fun and more physically attractive than anyone I could have imagined, apart from herself on the screen.

  LAURENCE OLIVIER

- The moment that face comes on the screen, people drop the popcorn bags, believe me. You can't take your eyes away from her. You can't watch any other performer when she's playing a scene with somebody else.

  BILLY WILDER

- She has a daffodil beauty, but in repose her face is strangely tragic. I said to Arthur Miller that she should play Ophelia and he agreed.

  EDITH SITWELL

- Directing her was like directing Lassie. You needed fourteen takes to get each one of them right.

  OTTO PREMINGER

- Near genius as any actress I ever knew. She is an artist beyond artistry. She has the mysterious unfathomable mysteriousness of a Garbo.

  JOSHUA LOGAN

- Anyone can remember lines, but it takes a real artist to come on the set and not know her lines and give the performance she did.

  BILLY WILDER

- It's like kissing Hitler.

  TONY CURTIS

- I knew her from the time she was 15 years old and I liked her. She was really a sweet, marvellous, funny girl. She thought the dumb sexpot role she played was ridiculous. She was bothered by all the attention, and she got upset everytime anyone so much as opened a door for her. Everytime a director yelled 'Action!' she'd break out in a sweat . . . I mean it. She was scared.

  ROBERT MITCHUM

- Wonderfully funny, and she looked absolutely luscious—like a ripe bowl of peaches. She was really wide-eyed about *everything*, and as a result was naturally funny. You know she *really* did want to be a great actress; to learn and make up for lost time.

  ANNE BAXTER

- I thought she was a genius. The trouble was, she loved being a film star, but she

148

couldn't act. She was a natural with no technique.

GEORGE AXELROD

■ As a director Marilyn's bent for turning up late, or not at all, would have driven me nuts. But I was only *acting* in it, and to act with Marilyn was a joy.

JACK LEMMON

■ For what you finally got on the screen she was worth every hour you had to wait for her. I wish she was around today. How often do you have a face like hers that lights up a screen? Even with the difficulties, I'd work with her again in a second if she were here.

BILLY WILDER

■ There is a broad with a future behind her.

CONSTANCE BENNETT

■ Marilyn Monroe was never on time, never knew her lines. I have an old aunt in Vienna. She would be on the set every morning at six and would know her lines backwards. But who would go to see her?

BILLY WILDER

■ Marilyn Monroe's delivery seemed so very strange and I couldn't hear what she was saying. It seemed dreadful and I thought, 'Well, if this is the American idea of acting and glamour I'll just have to put up with it for the rest of the film [*The Prince and the Showgirl*].' Then Larry [Olivier] let me see the rushes, and Marilyn's manner and timing were delicious . . .

SYBIL THORNDIKE

■ Marilyn? Surely you are referring to Hollywood's Joan of Arc, aren't you? The Myth? The Legend? Our Ultimate Sacrificial Lamb? She was the meanest woman I have ever met around this town. I am appalled by this cult. It's getting to be an act of courage to say anything but saintly things about her. . . . I have never met anyone as utterly mean as Marilyn Monroe. Nor as utterly fabulous on the screen, and that includes Garbo.

BILLY WILDER

■ It is a sad comment on contemporary values that a beautiful, famous and wealthy young woman of thirty-six should capriciously kill herself for want of a little self-discipline and horse-sense. Judy [Garland] and Vivien [Leigh] in their different ways are in the same plight. Too much too soon and too little often.

NOËL COWARD

149

YVES MONTAND (born 1921)

■ Yves wasn't happy [in *Sanctuary*]. His English wasn't very good and he had to learn his lines phonetically. . . . It was a great shame, because in his own language he's one of the best film actors in the world.

LEE REMICK

■ I wanted to have someone who was very much a star [for *Z*], because the relationship between the public and a star is a sympathetic one and immediately positive, so the public wants to follow him. . . . Another reason why I chose Montand is because I simply like to work with him. He is a friend and we have good relations. He understands what I want.

COSTA GAVRAS

COLLEEN MOORE (1900–1987)

■ I was the spark that lit up flaming youth. Colleen Moore was the torch. What little things we are to have caused all that trouble.

F. SCOTT FITZGERALD

ROGER MOORE (born 1928)

■ I suppose I was just window-dressing at MGM. You might call me Taylor's dummy. I wore Walter Plunkett's costumes beautifully though. I was the last of the Englishmen, after Edmund Purdom and Stewart Granger, both of whom had been giving them trouble in Hollywood. I very quickly learned that I had to be highly humble and obsequious and grovel a lot.

HIMSELF

150

■ He really *enjoys* making those Bond movies. The result is that, in *The Spy Who Loved Me*, he gives a performance that communicates that enjoyment.

PETER YATES

AGNES MOOREHEAD (1906–1974)

■ One of those rare actresses whose voice, eloquent face and incisive attack can suggest not just a character but an entire lifetime.

PETER JOHN DYER

KENNETH MORE (1914–1982)

■ A lovely, deft comedian in the proper Hawtrey, Du Maurier, Coward tradition! In fact he doesn't apparently make any effort to get his effects and manages to get every one. No asking for laughs or begging for attention.

NOËL COWARD

JEANNE MOREAU (born 1928)

■ To act with her [in *Le Tiroir Secret,* for television, 1986] has been an enchantment. More than that, we can speak of complicity. This is a charming, generous woman. When she plays a scene, she doesn't want to draw attention to herself alone.

MICHÈLE MORGAN.

ROBERT MORLEY (born 1908)

■ Actors live in a cocoon of praise. They never meet the people who don't like them.

HIMSELF

IVAN MOSJOUKINE (1889–1939)

■ . . . a combination of Rudolph Valentino, Errol Flynn and George Arliss. He is rather too slimly elegant to be believable when he throws bailiffs out of the door two at a time or holds off a company of soldiers with his sword, but at the first scent of an assignation, he smoulders until smoke comes out of his nostrils and his eyeballs cloud over.

WALTER GOODMAN, 1986

PAUL MUNI (1895–1967)

■ He was very difficult to work with . . . He said he didn't want to hear how I did it, he had no interest in how I portrayed it, he had his own conception of Chopin and he told me he'd worked on his role in relation to that conception, and he didn't care how I played it. And that was the approach to teamwork on that film.

CORNEL WILDE, 1970

■ Paul Muni was a fascinating, exciting, attractive man—Jesus, was he attractive!—and it was sad to see him slowly disappear behind his elaborate make-up, his putty noses, his false lips, his beards. One of the few funny things Jack Warner ever said was, 'Why are we paying him so much money when we can't find him?'

BETTE DAVIS

EDDIE MURPHY (born 1962)

■ Words fall from him in flashing torrents, more words than we can take in, . . . with his incredible gift of gab Murphy's mouth can take him anywhere. That he's young, black, obscure and dressed in a high school phys-ed department sweatshirt doesn't hurt him one bit: he's so aware of the way he fits into the society that he can turn his low status to his own advantage.

DAVID DENBY

■ He grabs his occasions—and most of the movie [*48 Hours*]—as the beautifully tailored, street-honed young fast talker, whether patronising big Nolte rotten, yuk-yukking away in mock-coon mirth, or (his set-piece) riotously humiliating a country and western bar crowded with menacing rednecks.

JOHN COLEMAN

■ His effect was dazzling. There was a ding! when he walked on, almost like Marilyn Monroe.

JOHN LANDIS

■ Despite all his success, Eddie acts like he's 22 years old. His life is cars and girls, girls and cars. More cars. More girls.

JAMIE LEE CURTIS

■ Eddie can hear the rustle of nylon stockings at 50 yards.

WALTER HILL

■ His infectious grin, the manners of a foot-in-the-door salesman and the exuberance of a bouncing ball, . . . turns an ordinary police thriller *Beverly Hills Cop* into something special.

MILTON SHULMAN

ANNA NEAGLE (1904–1986)

■ I have just finished an autobiography by Herbert Wilcox called *Twenty-five Thousand Sunsets*. It is curiously endearing. His unquestioning adoration of Anna shines through every page. You would think, from reading it, that dear Anna is the greatest actress, singer and dancer and glamorous star who ever graced the stage and screen. The fact that this is not strictly accurate never for a split second occurs to him.

NOËL COWARD

151

■ And then there is this film star's accent, overlaid by layer after layer of the best suburban refinement. At any moment we expect Miss Neagle [as Queen Victoria] to toss her pretty head and say: 'I hope it keeps fine for you, Albert!' Instead of which she tosses her pretty head and flounces hither and thither.

JAMES AGATE

■ Anna has little else to do [in *I Live in Grosvenor Square*] but to be sweet, and sweet she duly is. If in the one scene where she could do a bit of real acting, she doesn't do it—well there is probably an excellent reason for it.

JAMES AGATE

PATRICIA NEAL (born 1926)

■ It [*Three Secrets*] was one of the three films I made with Patricia Neal. Marvellous lady.

ROBERT WISE, 1972

PAUL NEWMAN (born 1925)

■ Paul Newman is full of innovation. He has wonderful immediate ideas. Very often supplements mine, or has something better than my notions. Some action perhaps.

JOHN HUSTON

152

■ Part of the reason movies from the 1920s through the 1950s had such a grab on the American psyche was because of the force of personality stars managed to sustain despite mediocre roles and forgettable pictures. There was a lot to identify with, fantasise about, or even look up to ... Paul Newman, is practically the only actor of his generation to achieve that elusive dual quality of maturing while somehow remaining the same.

LARRY McMURTRY

■ Sex may be more rampant when younger men are around. But there are some fabulous exceptions like Paul Newman, who looks better than ever.

HELEN GURLEY BROWN

■ Paul is the most generous man with whom I've ever worked. We had a fantastic rapport shooting *Butch*

Cassidy. It was one of the happiest experiences of my life.

ROBERT REDFORD, 1972

■ Paul and Joanne Newman are old friends—ten years ago my first play was his second play, and I was his little brother for a year . . . I never think of him as being a movie star, probably because he's still the same nice guy.

GEORGE GRIZZARD

■ I still remember the first day of my first trip to Hollywood: I met with some representatives of Paul Newman. We were talking about the scheduling of *Harper,* and I was worried whether Newman would be ready when Warner Bros wanted to go with the picture. One of the men in the meeting said this after I voiced my concern: 'Someday Paul will be Glenn Ford, but right now they'll wait for him.'

WILLIAM GOLDMAN

■ He's so easy that you keep thinking he's not doing anything. You know, 'When is this guy going to act?

SALLY FIELD

■ My assessment of an actor is based on two levels. One is his quality as copy. I mean, I may like an actor very much, like Paul Newman, but there's no way that I'd cross the street to interview him because he's a very dull man. But someone like Lee Marvin I love on the 'great interview' level.

RODERICK MANN

■ He has always been tough, quiet, not insensitive, with that mannerism originated by Brando of seeming constantly, casually aware of his mouth, as though he were speaking with tobacco or a Lifesaver in it.

RENATA ADLER

■ I've never thought that Paul was a particularly good actor. He's one of the sweet people of the world, an excellent producer. But I've never been a Paul Newman fan as far as acting goes. The only thing Paul's ever done I really thought was first class was *Hud*.

GEORGE C. SCOTT

■ A cool sexuality that is unique in the American cinema—an amused quality and a high promise of sex and danger.

MARTIN RITT

■ Paul's always been one of the best actors we've got, but there was that great stone face and those gorgeous blue eyes and a lot of people assumed he couldn't act. He got relegated to leading-man parts and he wasn't using a quarter of his talent. Now he's able to cut loose and do sensational work.

SIDNEY LUMET

■ There's stillness in his acting now that is quite magnetic. You can feel his intelligence, you can see him thinking. He has the depth of a clear pool of water.

SYDNEY POLLACK

■ I remember *Pocket Money* . . . At the beginning, it was understood that Newman and I would earn the same amount and have roles of equal importance . . . Well, I've never seen a situation so much reversed. It was Newman's company who produced the film and when they came to show it, Newman had become the sole star and I was nowhere.

LEE MARVIN

ROBERT NEWTON (1905–1956)

■ [In *Treasure Island*] though hardly one's exact idea of Long John Silver, more like a gipsy brought in to help with the hay making and frightening the wits out of the children, he at least put on a display of 'acting' which no one could fail to notice. But how expressive was it? . . . Mr Newton rolled his eyes and leered and moved but one often did not understand very clearly what was being expressed.

PHILIP HOPE WALLACE, 1951

■ Anyway actors are awful at playing drunks. Robert Newton was good at it but then it was usually for real.

JEFFREY BERNARD

MIKE NICHOLS (born 1931)   153

■ Mike has a funny blind eye when he works. He thinks everyone is having a grand time. Everything may look rosy but inside the command post the subtext is going on: an actor is on the verge of being fired: the lighting director isn't speaking to the director; someone's trying to negotiate with Orson Welles in Spain from the only phone on the base.

BUCK HENRY, 1970

■ Nichols' work is frivolous—charming, light and titanically inconsequential . . . What Nichols is is brilliant. Brilliant and trivial and self-serving and frigid.

WILLIAM GOLDMAN

■ He makes you feel kind of like a kite. He lets you go ahead, and you do your thing. And then when you've finished he pulls you in by the string. But at least you've had the enjoyment of the wind.

DUSTIN HOFFMAN

JACK NICHOLSON (born 1937)

■ He's the only person I know who gives you the feeling of what movie stars were like years ago ... He has a great personal flair and a great sense of life. He's also very smart. Mike Nichols once told me that the only actor he could remember in a very long time from whom he'd learned anything was Jack.

RICHARD SYLVESTER

■ What you see is what you get. What you don't see are the mechanisms, the thousands of tiny little id, ego and superego particles that hold their moment-by-moment board meetings and always vote 12 to 0 that the truth and only the truth is going to come out of that head.

NORMAN DICKENS

154

■ Jack had a great sense of humour. ... He still does. He's crazy and a beautiful guy. I always think it's nice when somebody who's paid his dues, like Jack, makes it. But he hasn't really changed much.

QUINCY JONES

■ Nicholson performances provided little oases of reason in deserts of pretension. When the films were good the virtues of the films tended to overshadow the contributions of the actor. There's a deceptive lightness, almost a blandness about Nicholson's approach to acting that, even though it is self-assertive, defers to the role to such an extent that audiences remember the role as much as, if not more than, the actor who played it.

VINCENT CANBY

■ That smile of his is simply a killer. Jack must know it's devastating, because he uses it very rarely.

DIANA VREELAND

■ A very levelling influence on *Chinatown*. He doesn't feel threatened and so can be generous. After all, why not? Talent is a very big mountain top.

FAYE DUNAWAY

■ [On seeing him play Eugene O'Neill in *Reds*:] Dear Jack, I don't know how to thank you enough, you have accomplished the impossible. After all these years you have made me fall in love with my father. And even more important you have given him a sense of humour.

OONA CHAPLIN

■ I have great respect for him. Not only as an artist but as an individual. He has a fine eye for good paintings and a good ear for fine music. And he's a lovely man to drink with. A boon companion! I'd like to make more pictures with Jack Nicholson.

JOHN HUSTON, 1986

■ Jack is the sort of guy who takes parts others have turned down, might turn down, and explodes them into something nobody could have conceived of ... All his brilliance of character and gesture is consumed and made invisible by the expanse of his nature.

MIKE NICHOLS, 1987

■ Jack had abandoned his career as an actor ... and we wrote and produced this picture together. Jack would act out all the parts, as would I, and my eyes were just glued to the expressions on his face and the intensity he brought to the performance in a script conference. I told

him that the next time I made a picture
he had to be in it.

BOB RAFELSON, 1976

■ The best performance in *Easy Rider*—
funny, utterly winning and quite
moving—is by Jack Nicholson, as a
cynical, hard-drinking young lawyer.
There is a crazy pathos in Nicholson that
is pathetic without ever asking for
pathos.

STANLEY KAUFFMAN

■ Jack! You see how angry he gets in a
scene? Unbelievably scary! He cannot
stop, he goes into a kind of it, you dunno
whether he is acting any more!

ROMAN POLANSKI

■ . . . The most eloquent smiler on the
screen.

JACK KROLL

■ He's eccentric but very interesting. A
unique kind of approach. He shines
because he's himself a rather interesting
eccentric. A very fascinating actor.

GEORGE C. SCOTT

■ The moment he begins to work, he
becomes a servant: he knows the story,
he knows the film, he arrives each day
prepared to perfection, he is interested
in an excellent ambience and he helps to
create it.

MILOS FORMAN

ASTA NIELSEN (1883–1972)

■ She is all. She is the vision of the
drunkard and the dream of the hermit.

GUILLAUME APOLLINAIRE

DAVID NIVEN (1909–1983)

■ Now if I could be David Niven, I'd be
content. He knows how to live life. He's

charming, he's amusing, he's so up. An
up man! I'm sure he's also complicated,
but he never lays it on you.

JOHN HURT

■ He was a model of how people who are
famous and who enjoy the terrific
privilege of stardom or public acclaim
should behave.

JOHN MORTIMER

KIM NOVAK (born 1933)

■ I worked one day with her and I quit.
HENRY HATHAWAY, 1970

■ Is Kim Novak a joke in her own time?
ROBERT ALDRICH, 1974

■ Frank [Sinatra] was so patient [doing 40
takes on *The Man with the Golden Arm*].
She was doing her best.

OTTO PREMINGER

155

■ I don't usually get into battles, but
dressing Kim Novak for her role in Mr
Hitchcock's *Vertigo* put to the test all my
training in psychology.

EDITH HEAD

■ I was warned about Kim Novak before I
started to work with her. They said she
was difficult, . . . in fact working with
her has been a most pleasant surprise.
She has the quality of Monroe and
Dietrich and that is remarkable because
she was a studio-created star—a nylon
artificial thing to be scraped off—
something created as a threat to Rita
Hayworth.

BILLY WILDER

RAMON NOVARRO (1899–1968)

■ Ramon Novarro was a man of another
generation, very courteous, very

charming, who spoke French with a delightful accent. He had great discretion. It was whispered that he was homosexual, which was without doubt true.

MICHELINE PRESLE

JACK OAKIE (1903–1978)

■ He was the sap who spoke in malapropisms, the ingenuous country bumpkin always taken for a ride by the society girl. He found out just in time that she was wrong for him [*The Social Lion, June Moon*] and wound up with the more plain and virtuous girl—Mary Brian or the equivalent.

JOSEPH L. MANKIEWICZ

156   ## WARREN OATES (1928–1987)

■ His most successful films are probably those in which the morality is as cockeyed as his grin.

NEIL SINYARD

MERLE OBERON (1911–1979)

■ She's still so beautiful. She says she's 52. That would make her 12 years old when we made *The Private Life of Henry VIII* together.

BINNIE BARNES, 1973

■ She is a dream hostess. She leaves you alone when you want to be left alone and entertains you when you want to be entertained. At all times she is gay, considerate and kind. Nor has she the faintest inclination to show you off as a visiting lion. We had a truly lovely time with them both.

NOEL COWARD

■ In spite of her stardom, the former typist was always somewhat in awe of her fellow movie stars. When she was having an affair with Jimmy Cagney during a bond-selling tour in World War Two, se interrupted the proceedings saying, 'Just imagine, I'm in bed with Jimmy Cagney!' As he told the male friend who told me, it somewhat diminished his ardour.

SHEILAH GRAHAM

MARGARET O'BRIEN (born 1937)

■ If that child had been born in the Middle Ages, she'd have been burned as a witch.

LIONEL BARRYMORE, 1945

■ She was a very happy little girl. The stories you're talking about are probably about when she was very little and had to do a crying scene. You can't just say to a little kid 'Cry', you have to make them cry, so they would take her off to the side and someone would tell her a terrible story about what they were going to do to her dog or cat, something really graphic, and she'd get hysterical. It was great on the screen, but I don't think it was good for her nervous system. But she's an extremely sane lady, very down to earth, practical and intelligent—we were recently in South America with her and she was fabulous.

JUNE ALLYSON

■ I found her performance—and the lengths one had to go to achieve it— engrossing but enervating.

She'd played a war ophan desperately in need of psychiatric help in her first starring film, *Journey for Margaret,* and the roles in her next four pictures were equally neurotic. Now she was playing a child. A seven-year-old Bernhardt or Réjane was no longer needed. It took some doing to capture a more natural performance, though she was exceptional in the emotionally charged scenes in the picture.

VINCENTE MINNELLI

MAUREEN O'HARA (born 1920)

■ She looked as though butter wouldn't melt in her mouth—or anywhere else.

ELSA LANCHESTER

LAURENCE OLIVIER (born 1907)

■ Olivier's performance is the only one in the film [*Pride and Prejudice*] that remains true to the original novel.

CHRISTOPHER ISHERWOOD

■ He's like a blank page and he'll be whatever you want him to be. He'll wait for you to give him a cue, and then he'll try to be that sort of person.

KENNETH TYNAN

■ Larry Olivier is not an actor. He's a chameleon. He wears all that make-up and all those costumes and just disguises himself. Half the time you don't even know its him.

BETTE DAVIS

■ When the actor of the century asked me would I mind if he switched six words around—is the most memorable incident of my movie career. Olivier. Calling me 'Bill'. Olivier. Asking *me* would I mind.

WILLIAM GOLDMAN

■ I think that when Sir Laurence went into the theatre, motion pictures lost one of the great romantic stars of our time.

ALFRED HITCHCOCK

■ Sir Laurence Olivier is one of the most disciplined, prepared, able and intelligent and cooperative actors I have ever worked with. This may well be because he is also a director, and a very good one.

WILLIAM WYLER

■ Laurence Olivier has everything. He has enormous imagination and talent. He is so constructed, physically, that he is neither tall nor short, neither handsome or unhandsome, neither fat nor thin, so that he can be fat or thin. handsome or unhandsome, tall or short, or whatever the part calls for. He has a wonderful voice, which he has worked on. He has stamina. He can play a heroic character, and he's one of the few actors who can.

ALEXANDER DAVION

■ If you had to worship something mortal on earth I would go and bow twice a day to wherever Olivier was standing.

SAMMY DAVIS Jr

■ There have been times when I've been ashamed to take the money. But then I think of some of the movies that have given Olivier cash for his old age, and I don't feel so bad.

STEWART GRANGER, 1987

■ Like most English actors, Olivier had little patience with acting systems—although he prepared himself for his roles not really very differently from Stanislavksy actors. But to him such preparation was simple common sense, the imitation of life, and something that did not bear all this portentous introspective palavering.

ARTHUR MILLER, 1987

■ I'm flattered out of my trousers at being the next Olivier.

PETER O'TOOLE

- He came up to me and said 'Bravo'. One word from an actor like Olivier is worth a thousand more from others.

  DIANA DORS

- Between good and great acting is fixed an inexorable gulf, which may be crossed only by the elect, . . . Gielgud, seizing a parasol, crosses by tightrope; Redgrave, with lunatic obstinacy, plunges into the torrent, usually sinking within yards of the opposite shore; Laurence Olivier pole vaults over, hair-raisingly, in a single animal leap. Great acting comes more easily to him than to any of his colleagues: he need do no more than lift his head, neigh, and extend a gauntleted hand to usher us into the presence of tragic matters.

  KENNETH TYNAN, 1954

158

- He'll put himself out on a limb, totally out on a limb. In fact he'll put himself out on a twig of a tree; if it snaps off and falls, then the fall is very big. He'll risk being appalling. He'll risk being very bad. His portrayal in *The Entertainer* is an example of how far he will go. He dares.

  ANTHONY HOPKINS, 1972

ERMANNO OLMI (born 1931)

- Olmi's films, and the director himself represent a phenomenon that is not only rare but, one is tempted to assert, unique in the western world. . . . whether in terms of Italian film, general Italian culture, Italian politics/ideology/religion, or in terms of world film production and marketing patterns.

  MARCUS GERVAIS

TATUM O'NEAL (born 1963)

- I loathe the whole nostalgia kick, the Peter Bogdanovich trip. I think it's so damned unhealthy. In *Paper Moon*, all Tatum O'Neal did was remind me what a brilliant artist Shirley Temple was.

  LINDSAY ANDERSON, 1975

- If ever things get real bad, I can live off her.

  RYAN O'NEAL

MAX OPHULS (1902–1957)

- I loved Max Ophuls because he had a very unsuccessful career as far as America was concerned, but he had an irrepressible spirit. He was a brave, resilient man and a great man of the theatre and he loved his work, he had an undying enthusiasm. He was a lovely man.

  JAMES MASON, 1970

- Max often improvised on the set, but these improvisations were in the nature of refinements, not basic changes in the storyline or characterisations.

  HOWARD KOCH, 1979

- Max Ophuls was for some among us together with Jean Renoir the greatest French cineaste. Immense is the loss of an artist of Balzacian stature, who made himself the advocate of his heroines, and the ally of women; that's the cineaste we have under the pillow at night.

  FRANC OISRUFFAUT

- A man with an ingrained perversity, the kind who would make the smallest wristwatch in the world and then hang it from a church spire as a time-piece. I liked him but I didn't feel comfortable, I felt like a cog in his machine. His methods were far from mine. I agreed with him on nothing, but he had a marvellous humour and we got along delightfully.

PETER USTINOV

■ He didn't look upon film narcissistically as a public mirror to display his virtuosity. He has a deep respect for what other talents contributed and, particularly, for ... the screenplay, a quality understandably endearing to a writer. This may come as a surprise to some critics who praise Max, and justly, as a superb stylist: but from my observation, his style was invariably related to content, never to expense.

HOWARD KOCH

■ Ophuls' vision hugs the spectator like a warm bath, pours over him like a stream of consciousness, gently submerges him in a seamless flood of real and imagined memories and unrequited feelings.

DEREK ELLEY, 1980

MAUREEN O'SULLIVAN (born 1911)

■ I didn't know my parents very well, but they represent a great deal to me. My mother was a terrific mother, full of fairytales, with a soft voice and a soothing manner. She wasn't that involved in the more physical aspects, such as feeding us and dressing us. And we lived in a separate part of the house and always had a couple of nannies. But the time I shared with my mother was of the top quality. She was a mystical figure, and I sort of romanticised her, and my father, too.

MIA FARROW

PETER O'TOOLE (born 1932)

■ He can do anything. A bit cuckoo, but sweet and terribly funny.

KATHARINE HEPBURN, 1981

■ If you had been any prettier, it would have been Florence of Arabia.

NOËL COWARD

YAZUJIRO OZU (1903–1963)

■ But let's face it—there is an inescapable tedium in Ozu's films. I believe that most moviegoers either consciously or unconsciously avoid Ozu even as they feel obligated to verbally acknowledge his genius.

LARRY MILLER

159

G. W. PABST (1885–1967)

■ To work with Pabst was certainly extraordinary luck. He was a man of great intelligence and great sensibility. Immediately contact was established between us he put me perfectly at ease.

MICHELINE PRESLE

AL PACINO (born 1940)

■ Cold-eyed, slightly built, impassive. None of the emotion of his Sicilian ancestry in view, no Hollywood flamboyance on parade.

MIKE LITCHFIELD

■ Al dreads the thought of being in the bad man bag forever, but he does the ne'er-do-well so well that critics are comparing him to early Brando and George C. Scott. His two favourite actors they are not. Those honours go to John Gielgud and Christopher Plummer.

JUDY KLEMESRUD

■ He's always asking questions . . . he's very hard on a director. In a nightclub scene he wanted to know, 'Is this the first time or the second time we've been here?' He wants to know what day of the week it is for a scene. He wants to know the entire background to the relationship with the character played by Anny Duperey. 'Did I pick her up? Did she pick me up'. . .

SYDNEY POLLACK

ALAN PAKULA (born 1928)

■ Alan is a gentleman. We had mutual acquaintances in the business and they said nothing but good things about him as a human being. Neither can I. He is well educated and serious about his work.

WILLIAM GOLDMAN

160

JACK PALANCE (born 1919)

■ I must say Jack Palance was a drag. We were together in *The Silver Chalice*. The way he did his work was strange. He was a weird actor, and I didn't like working with him at all.

VIRGINIA MAYO

LILLI PALMER (1914–1986)

■ The only one I never got on with was Lilli Palmer. Always late. A brilliant artist, but no sense of humour, of course. That was on *English Without Tears*.

HAROLD FRENCH, 1983

■ The week has been hell made so entirely by Lilli who has contrived to make a bitch of herself with untiring energy . . . I have made a truce with [her] because I have to play with her. But I have never— with the possible exception of Claudette Colbert—worked with such a stupid bitch.

NOËL COWARD

■ I soon found Lilli to be a steadfast, reliable, stalwart person. She was not overburdened with our particular English sense of humour, but she had other sterling qualities.

REX HARRISON, 1974

■ The last close-up we shot had also been in the south of France, thirty–eight years ago. She was, I thought, looking younger and more attractive than she did in 1935, and even then she was somewhat more than an eyeful. Several times during that early epic I remember wishing I'd been single.

JOHN MILLS, 1980

ALAN PARKER (born 1944)

■ I love Alan Parker because he's like an inventor—they're ready to close the patent office and he comes along with something new and they have to open it again.

MATTHEW MODINE

■ Yes, I *did* say Alan Parker has no sense of humour, and this comment will haunt me for the rest of my days. But he doesn't does he? Have I missed something?

OLIVER STONE

ELEANOR PARKER (born 1922)

■ The best actress I ever worked with.

ROGER MOORE

■ She was sweet [on *Eye of the Cat*] but obviously of a different era. A bit grand. She expected things to be done—and she got them done. She was a star. I admired her. But now we're more flexible and it's better. Actors today don't have to live up to such expectations.

GAYLE HUNNICUTT

PIER PAOLO PASOLINI (1922–1975)

■ A remarkable director . . . a great loss to Italian culture. It was as if he was discovering cinema from scratch.

BERNARDO BERTOLUCCI

GREGORY PECK (born 1916)

■ One of my favourite actors is in that [*Yellow Sky*]—Greg Peck. I say that sarcastically. We made a good picture with him, despite him.

WILLIAM A. WELLMAN

■ I had asked him what he thought of the film [*Beloved Infidel*] and this was his answer: 'I thought I was splendid!'

SHEILAH GRAHAM

■ Of all the actors who have been on the screen since movies began I think the three whose faces most express the American ethos are Gary Cooper, Henry Fonda and Gregory Peck.

JEANNE STEIN

■ But to become a star and to maintain that status over many years are two different things; and to appraise his assets that have made the latter possible is to take a look at the man himself. Solid, kindly, dignified, likable, and somewhat self-effacing, he is at his best in roles

that match these qualities. When miscast, he has gone down with a dull thud.

CASEY ROBINSON

■ One of the most charming men I've ever met.

SOPHIA LOREN

■ You write to your star. For instance, in *World in His Arms*, when I went there originally to do it, John Wayne was the character. . . . But Gregory Peck, although he is a fine actor, isn't Wayne. In a scene where Wayne would just kick a door down, pick up a few fellows and throw them through the window, . . . this [sidekick] fellow does the physical work while Peck directs it. . . . So you write to the lead.

BORDEN CHASE

■ It [*Moby Dick*] misses because Peck couldn't bring madness to it. A dear sweet gentleman, but he's not mad. Olivier [whom Bradbury wanted] is a madman to begin with. There's always been that quality of madness there in many things he did. He can call on that madness. Well, Greg Peck is never going to be a paranoid killer or a maniac devourer of whales. He can play in *To Kill a Mockingbird* and make a beautiful film. That's a different quality there.

RAY BRADBURY

161

SAM PECKINPAH (1925–1984)

■ I think Peckinpah is a fine director. I don't think he's as good as I am, but I think he's a sensational director.

ROBERT ALDRICH

■ Sam is, I think, a great film-maker. Of course, he's his own worst enemy. Sam is an unusual human being, and he needs to be treated like an unusual human being. He can create an atmosphere, whether he's drunk, sober, pissed off or in a rage, or whatever. I mean, for about three or four hours a day, he's a fucking genius. But the rest of the time he spends wallowing in a kind of emotional reaction to either good or bad memories.

JAMES COBURN

■ I didn't care for Peckinpah at all. He was one of those little guys who tries to bully big guys and he almost got his ass whipped for trying to do it to me. Every time I was going to throttle Peckinpah, McQueen would come over and calm me down like a brother would.

JOE DON BAKER, 1987

■ Sam has always believed, and I believe rightly, that he is there to make the film and that anyone who stands in his way is dead. They're in deep, deep trouble. And anyone who doesn't come up to snuff and do their job absolutely perfectly is in deep trouble with Sam.

WARREN OATES

■ Sam was dangerous for me. He had my number and I had his, and that can be bad between an actor and a director. Cos he was a little guy.

LEE MARVIN, 1986

ARTHUR PENN (born 1922)

■ I learned a lot about writing from it [*Bonnie and Clyde*: he wasn't credited] because Arthur was treating me like an actor. He kept saying, do this, do that. Arthur was really razor-sharp during that movie; he was really at the top of his game. He taught me more than anyone I've ever worked with.

ROBERT TOWNE

GEORGE PEPPARD (born 1928)

■ He's arrogant—the sort of man who expects women to fall at his feet at the slightest command; who throws his weight around. He gives the impression that he's the star, what he says goes and that nobody else is very important.

JOAN COLLINS

ANTHONY PERKINS (born 1932)

■ For the past six years, Tony has lived in a three-story red brick house on a leafy Chelsea street, which he owns and shares with a friend who is a director and choreographer. Weekends are spent at his roommate's country home a couple of hours out of the city. When I ask Tony about his private life style, for a moment he looks stunned. Then he quickly dismisses the enquiry, saying, 'Movie stars in the fifties never had to discuss their personal lives and I see no reason why I should now.'

BERNARD CARRAGHER

VALERIE PERRINE (born 1944)

■ Quite simply, she is the best actress I have ever directed.

BOB FOSSE

FRANK PERRY (born 1930)

■ I've been in so many bad movies and worked with so many bad directors that I go into a film expecting nothing. That's why I respect and admire Frank Perry so much. He's a rare man and I've worked with enough stiffs to know the difference pal . . . but [he] knows the problems of actors and I know the problems of a director. . . . Frank is as far away from Otto Preminger as you can get.

CLIFF ROBERTSON

GERARD PHILIPE (1922–1959)

■ Like everyone who came near him, I had much admiration, esteem and friendship. He was a generous and unselfish man with an extraordinary moral force—of the sort to lead you into artistic ventures which appeared completely mad.

FRANÇOISE FABIAN

■ The word 'actor' has no meaning as applied to him, and in his playing there is no trace whatever of a 'role'. His performance flows across the screen in flawless perfection. . . . In *Le Diable Au Corps* youth, love, the egoism of childhood, suffering, are realities and emotions which Philipe finds within himself, which are part of his own life, revealing themselves in an adventure in which laughter is mixed with tears, with love and with death.

LO DUCA, 1948

■ He always seemed to me an elusive being, betraying very little of his real feelings to others. He maintained a certain distance from everyone, not out of vanity, but as a result, it seemed to me, of some old trauma, very carefully hidden—an impression which was reinforced by the bare ghost of a smile which would pass across his face . . . the romantic spirit which he emanated . . . often accompanied by melancholy and unrealised dreams.

MARCEL CARNÉ, 1979

■ Gerard Philipe, who is a settled married man, has a flair for reproducing on the stage and screen the most touching transports of adolescence. This he did to perfection in *Le Diable Au Corps*; . . . At the moment he has more power than Jean Marais, more poetry than Daniel Gelin, and more youth than Jean Desailly: he is, in short, the best *jeune premier* in France.

KENNETH TYNAN, 1954

■ I decided that he would be my co-star [in *Le Diable Au Corps*]. He wasn't yet a great star but everyone was talking about him . . . Autant-Lara and the writers were thinking about two other actors. I said 'I see Gerard Philipe, no one else. So, I will make the film with him or I won't do it.'

MICHELINE PRESLE

■ He was an angel searching avidly, wildly, to become a man.

MARIA CASARES

■ A very shy guy in life, very discreet in his private life, but very clever, a good actor.

DANIELLE DARRIEUX

163

MICHEL PICCOLI (born 1925)

■ Such an elusive Machiavelli could only be played by Michel Piccoli. The actor's seductive ambiguity, his far reaching talents, the way he's both reassuring and disturbing at the same time made him perfect for the the part of Malair [in *Une Etrange Affaire*].

PIERRE GRANIER-DEFERRE, 1987

MARY PICKFORD (1893–1979)

■ It took longer to make one of Mary's contracts than it did to make one of Mary's pictures.

SAM GOLDWYN

- It was always Mary herself that shone through. Her personality was the thing that made her movies memorable and the pictures that showed her personality were the best.

  LILLIAN GISH

- Mary Pickford is the only member of her sex who ever became the focal point of an entire industry. Her position is unique; probably no man or woman will ever again win so extensive a following.

  BENJAMIN B. HAMPTON

- Hardly have we written the next essential for stardom, personality, when the magnetic name and presence of Mary Pickford flashes before you.

  MARSHALL NEILAN

164

- The composite Pickford character was considerably less simple than she is generally supposed to have been . . . She was 'America's sweetheart', America's darling child, America's problem child, and at times the Madonna.

  EDGAR WAGENKNECHT

- She was the girl every young man wanted to have—as his sister.

  ALISTAIR COOKE

- Say anything you like, but don't say I love to work. That sounds like Mary Pickford, that prissy bitch.

  MABEL NORMAND

- The two greatest names in the cinema are, I beg to reiterate, Mary Pickford and Charlie Chaplin. Even our witty judges do not pretend ignorance about them. Theirs are the greatest names in the cinema and from an historical point of view they always will be great, as pioneers and patron saints.

  IRIS BARRY, 1926

- Mary's art stays wonderfully alive; the kids still giggle and squeal over her antics. It is not unusual to hear women now and then engulfed in sobs when Mary's tears begin to glisten. For Mary still charms and always will. The poet, too, was right—there is something heavenly about Mary Pickford. It is a quality, we must admit, most uncommon in motion pictures.

  JAMES CARD

SIDNEY POITIER (born 1924)

- White superstars like Burt Lancaster and Paul Newman . . . have done movies every bit as poor as the poorest Sidney has made. Where are all the articles about their failures, the disappointing moments in their careers? Laurence Olivier has been in some of the most dreadful movies ever made—where are the articles decrying this? And Laurence Olivier had more choices than Sidney ever had. An awful lot is expected of that man, and for no reason except that he is black. The microbes of racism run deep.

  HARRY BELAFONTE, 1973

- Sidney has a greatness and professionalism and a deep, deep sensitivity . . . He's an absolutely beautiful man inside and out.

  STANLEY KRAMER

- He is big, black, and beautiful. His talented presence lends dignity and power, not only to the screen but wherever he is to be observed.

  ROY NEWQUIST

ROMAN POLANSKI (born 1933)

- With Roman, it was the most difficult working experience I've ever had. My nerves were very much on end at the time, and it was a tough time for him, too. Maybe I should have talked to Jack [Nicholson] about it because he wasn't under pressure and was wonderful. But I don't think what Roman said was well-founded at all. Because it always takes two to tango, and he was *insufferable.* From what we all know now about his life he's obviously got trouble with women. So it was a clash.

FAYE DUNAWAY

■ I guess there was a conflict of personalities. Polanski and I just don't like each other, but I think he's a fine director and I'd work for him any time.

JOHN CASSAVETES

■ I did get to pick locations, and I think Polanski is very talented, but we had an argument a week before shooting, and after that we just couldn't work together . . . I don't think it's healthy. I think it's healthier to include the writer in the process.

ROBERT TOWNE

SYDNEY POLLACK (born 1934)

■ Sydney Pollack earned $14m from his share in the profits in that picture [*Tootsie*]. He said to me that if he could get back the 18 months of his life which were total misery making it, he would gladly give back the money. He said it was the worst experience of his life. He once formed a company with Mark Rydell and it was called MJ Inc. I asked him what MJ stood for. He said, 'It stands for Melancholy Jew.'

JOHN BOORMAN

ELEANOR POWELL (1912–1982)

■ Eleanor was an out and out dancer. She danced like a man. She slammed the floor and did it great and that's fine and suddenly she's on her toes in the ballet sequence—it did look kinda funny.

FRED ASTAIRE

MICHAEL POWELL (born 1905)

■ His power of invention [in his autobiography] masquerading as fact seems limitless.

MOIRA SHEARER, 1987

■ Powell is one of the major influences in my life . . . His influence is so close to me now that I can't gauge it. His use of colour in *The Red Shoes* and *Black Narcissus* is just . . . amazing. But *Peeping Tom* is the greatest intellectual influence on me. The whole idea that voyeurism is simply an extension of film-making.

MARTIN SCORSESE, 1982

165

WILLIAM POWELL (1892–1984)

■ The later ones [The Thin Man pictures] were very bad indeed, but it was always a joy to work with Bill Powell. He was and is my dear friend, and in the early Thin Man films with Woody Van Dyke, we managed to achieve what for those days was an almost pioneering sense of spontaneity.

MYRNA LOY, 1967

■ Powell and Loy . . . were the quintessential thirties couple. . . . [They] were definitive: they embodied the romantic couple itself with an authority—

and implied monogamy—that belonged only to them.

JAMES HARVEY

■ . . . but to say Tyrone was homosexual is like saying that tonight I'm going to sing *Tosca* at the opera.

ANNABELLA

TYRONE POWER (1913–1958)

■ He was the best looking thing I've ever seen in my life. Kissing him was like dying and going to heaven.

ALICE FAYE, 1987

■ Ty Power was the handsomest man I ever saw! He was very popular. Tragically, he died . . . in his 40s. Beauty is a great curse. It distorts lives, making the wrong things important. Do you know what it means to be that adored? These people may have luxurious lives, but somewhere along the line it becomes very difficult to live with. It was that way with Ty.

ANNE BAXTER

■ Tyrone Power was my ideal man.

SOPHIA LOREN

■ Ty was really a handsome man without being pretty, a fine actor to boot and one of the most considerate in his relations with me. In 1959, as we were filming *Solomon And Sheba* I felt he was giving his best performance; I also thought that the completed picture would have been his best. He died when it was only half-finished.

KING VIDOR

■ A lovely gentleman with a great quality of imagination.

MYRNA LOY

■ I want to do very deep and mystical roles, like Tyrone Power in *The Razor's Edge*.

TONY CURTIS

OTTO PREMINGER (1906–1986)

■ I was warned about him—but could anybody really be *that* bad? Yeah, they could. Elaine May wrote a great screenplay. He took a piece of beauty and screwed it up. It was an incredible part. . . . and he destroyed it. I have been the victim of some killers in my time. He's one of the biggest. He's a *horrible* man. *Phew!* But who ever hears of him anymore? Is he still alive?

DYAN CANNON

■ Otto Preminger started in on him [Groucho Marx], giving him a hard time. And Groucho was old and feeble. . . . Preminger also started berating Frankie Avalon, and, Christ, it was just terrible to see. So when that was over, I said, 'Otto, come here. If you ever talk to me like that, I will hit you over the head with a fuckin' chair!' From then on, he was as gentle as rain with me.

JACKIE GLEASON

■ I thank God that neither I nor any member of my family will ever be so hard up that we have to work for Otto Preminger!

LANA TURNER

■ A great showman who has never bothered to learn anything about making a movie . . . no one is more skilled at giving the appearance of dealing with large controversial themes in a bold way, without making the tactical error of doing so.

DWIGHT MACDONALD

166

He's really Martin Bormann in elevator shoes with a face-lift by a blindfolded plastic surgeon in Luxembourg.

BILLY WILDER

He gives some people a very bad time on the set. He doesn't have much patience with inefficiency. If an actor's got a job acting, he should be able to act, he shouldn't have to teach him how to act. He will go into these tirades and I'm sure that he has bawled out very competent actors but I have seen him—as I have seen many directors—go into tirades against incompetents.

DANA ANDREWS, 1974

O.P. is only happy if everybody else is miserable. Still, if you can keep his paranoia from beating you down, you can learn a lot from the guy.

MICHAEL CAINE

ELVIS PRESLEY (1935–1977)

Before Elvis, there was nothing.

JOHN LENNON

I decided that this guy had the same animal magnetism as Brando. I couldn't care less about his singing.

HAL B. WALLIS

He never contributed a damn thing to music . . . He was successful—hard to account for. Oh, he sings well enough, I suppose.

BING CROSBY

Colonel Parker couldn't have cared less about the quality of the movie [*Jailhouse Rock*]. When Berman asked the Colonel if he should send the script to Elvis, the Colonel said no. 'Do you want to read it?' persisted the surprised producer.

Again, the Colonel said no. Suspecting a trap, Berman insisted: 'What *do* you want?' The Colonel, no less surprised, replied: 'I don't want nothin', except to get all the music I want in the picture and have it done by my boys.' Even if the movie profits were small, the Colonel would reap his profits from the record sales and publishing royalties. No wonder he was so indifferent to the picture's quality. As for Elvis, he could always console himself with a fleet of new Cadillacs. . . .

ALBERT GOODMAN

He's an animal. Definitely an animal. A very interesting animal.

ANN-MARGARET, 1976

Elvis was my idol from the beginning, and even today when I'm alone, I'll often put on the King Creole album. He's produced the most exciting pop music sounds of all time.

CLIFF RICHARD

He was a very sexual man, but I truly believe in the beginning it wasn't meant to be sexual, it just *was* because that was the way he felt when he played. I think later it became more of a performance, but at the beginning he just wanted to play that guitar and to *feel* it. It was natural.

BARBARA EDEN

He was a symbol to the people the world over of the vitality, rebelliousness and good humour of this country.

JIMMY CARTER

It was Scotty Moore's guitar riff when he was doing the Steve Allen Show that got me into rock music. I've been an Elvis fan since I was a kid.

ELTON JOHN

167

- I was so young and naive at the time, there was just no way I could have made a success of that marriage. I realised I couldn't give him the kind of adulation he got from his fans, and he *needed* that adulation desperately. Without it he was nothing.

  PRISCILLA PRESLEY

ROBERT PRESTON (1918–1987)

- Watch him as night after night he gives you an opening-night performance in the most glittering polish a role could ever hope to achieve. You have to watch closely to see those flashing feet—yes the same *Northwest Passage* ones—as they seem to touch the Majestic stage not more than twice in the nearly two hours that Harold Hill is on view.

  MEREDITH WILLSON, 1959

168

RICHARD PRYOR (born 1940)

- Bill Cosby I love. About 1980, Richard Pryor was the funniest man I'd ever heard in my life.

  PAUL HOGAN

V. I. PUDOVKIN (1893–1953)

- With his immensely ranging and complex genius Eisenstein could flash lightning around us until we became almost blind to the furnaces which Pudovkin was quietly stoking from time to time.
  Pudovkin was not complex. He was, to quote the title of one of his films, a simple case. Deceptively simple. For his simplicity was that of a great artist.

  BASIL WRIGHT

EDMUND PURDOM (born 1924)

- I didn't enjoy this film [*The Egyptian*] one little bit. I was supposed to do it with Marlon Brando but by the time I was in the air between London and Los Angeles they had changed it to Edmund Purdom. Charming as that was, it was not quite the same thing.

  PETER USTINOV

DAVID PUTTNAM (born 1941)

- He's the best producer I've ever worked for. You can't buy the enthusiasm he brings to a film. Sometimes he's so enthusiastic he's blind to weaknesses or faults in a project which could be corrected. Whenever you work with David, you have a fairly aggressive and bloody time. You could never do two films in a row with him. You have to go and bathe your wounds in between. He's not modest or shy about his work and all of us have had terrific rows with him; but in the end he does respect that you can do a job he can't do.

  MICHAEL APTED

- He was an inspiring executive to work with and he barely got a chance to get started. I think it was a good thing for our industry to have a studio head who is a great film-maker with strong opinions and a personal vision.

  JANE FONDA, 1987

ANTHONY QUINN (born 1915)

- At his best he's a marvellous actor, and he's a very instinctive actor. He has a sort of animal quality, although I think he's got a bit stuck with it . . . with that aspect of himself. . . . He's a larger than life character. He's that without trying before he starts. He's not the easiest man to work with by any means. He's quite temperamental.

ALAN BATES, 1973

■ I personally like big acting like that of Anthony Quinn. He is the quintessence, if you'll pardon the pun, of the actor who is able to control big emotion for the screen. A lot of lightweight performances on the screen don't work for me because I can't see anything behind them. With Quinn it's difficult not to see everything behind it.

STANLEY BAKER, 1975

■ Although there was no Oscar for his biggest picture—the larger than life Zorba—it's the Quinn perfomance that's brain-burned in most people's memory-banks. Critics are forever flinging it back at him, neither fairly nor flatteringly, reviewing 'Zorba the Pope' [*The Shoes of the Fisherman*]) 'the hill-billy Zorba' [*A Walk in the Spring Rain*] 'Zorba from 9 to 5' [*A Dream of Kings*] et cetera, et cetera.

HARRY HAUN, 1983

■ I found out with Tony Quinn who's inclined to be dreadfully flamboyant and overdo things terribly if you let him, the way to get a good performance is to goad him to the point of tears, be nasty to him. If you let him take over, you're dead.

EDWARD DMYTRYK, 1972

GEORGE RAFT (1903–1980)

■ George Raft and Gary Cooper once played a scene in front of a cigar store,

and it looked like a wooden Indian was overacting.

GEORGE BURNS

RAIMU (1883–1946)

■ But above all, the irreplaceable Raimu— Raimu, the bar-keeper, kind, easy-going, argumentative, and wholly magnificent: cheating at cards in so blatant a fashion that even the despised 'northerner' from Lyons tumbles to it; insulting, and insulted by, his friends with the grandiose gestures and epithets of the Marseillais.

MARGARET HINXMAN, 1949

■ He was very bad-tempered, especially with certain people. Raimu was a bit of a coward. He was disagreeable with people who could not really answer back. He grumbled but nobody really knew why. Sometimes, he was really mean.

MICHEL KELBER, 1981

169

CLAUDE RAINS (1889–1967)

■ My favourite person to work with was Claude Rains.

BETTE DAVIS, 1987

■ Spencer Tracy and Claude Rains are for me two of the finest actors that have ever worked in films. But I am convinced that we are all at the mercy of the story that we are presenting.

JEAN GABIN, 1978

■ Film buffs 'collect' Claude Rains performances much as other people collect fine porcelain, vintage port or antique silver, relishing the delicate detail, the infinite variety and the polished professionalism of his acting. He was arguably Hollywood's greatest character actor. But although he was nominated for the Academy Award no less than four times—for *Mr Smith Goes to Washington, Casablanca, Mr Skeffington* and *Notorious*—it is an abiding scandal that he never won his profession's greatest accolade.

JEFFREY RICHARDS

■ I purposely would not go and see the old version [*Here Comes Mr Jordan*]. They told me my part was played by Claude Rains, for whom I have an infinite admiration, and I knew I would never be as good as him.

JAMES MASON

BASIL RATHBONE (1892–1967)

■ Two profiles pasted together.

DOROTHY PARKER

170

■ The shade of Basil Rathbone must be eyeing with disdain the contemporary villains who are neurotic and misguided rather than just . . . bad.

MARKKU SALMI, 1979

NICHOLAS RAY (1911–1979)

■ 'You're a famous director,' I said to Ray. 'Why not try an experiment? You've just finished a picture that cost five million dollars. Why not try one for four hundred thousand dollars and see for yourself how much freer you are?' 'But you don't understand!' he cried 'If I did that in Hollywood, everyone would think I was going to pieces. They'd say I was on the skids, and I'd never make another movie!'

LUIS BUÑUEL

■ Orson Welles, a very funny man, once said to me, 'You know, the French ruin

everything. They come up to you and say, "You are one of the three great directors of the cinema." I nod, I nod. "There is D. W. Griffith. There is Orson Welles. And there is Nicholas Ray." There is always that third name that crushes you'.

GORE VIDAL

SATYAJIT RAY (born 1921)

■ Satyajit I found to be *more* than I'd imagined him to be. He's a man of such wide sympathies, such a gentle, shy person with so many levels—artist, musician, scholar and all the rest—that it's almost frightening. If [John] Huston is a great master of the *sweep,* the great man of the West with touches of Hemingway and Captain Ahab and little bits of Tagore thrown in . . . in his latter years there is a kind of mystical quality about him . . . Ray is very much a man of nuance. Everything he does is toned by a musician's ear.

SAEED JAFFREY

RONALD REAGAN (born 1911)

■ Reagan is by no means a bad actor but he would hardly be convincing, I said, as a presidential candidate [in *The Best Man*]. If I had cast Reagan in the role, it would have sated his appetite for the Presidency, and we'd be much better off.

GORE VIDAL

■ [On his 'stainless reputation':] It must mean that he's as dull as his first wife, Jane Wyman said he was.

BETTE DAVIS, 1987

■ Ronnie is really the only man I've ever known who loved dancing.

DORIS DAY

- Mr Reagan. He was then sort of an unimportant, pleasant, typical, healthy American guy. You couldn't go wrong with him in that kind of part. I don't like those films, and not only because of Mr Reagan.

  CURTIS BERNHARDT, 1969

ROBERT REDFORD (born 1937)

- We don't of course, expect Robert Redford to swagger, but it would be nice if he let *something* spill over. His acting is as close to neutral as any I remember— he holds the camera for an eternity with his level gaze and then doesn't deliver anything.

  DAVID DENBY

- I mean, Robert Redford is a smart man. I have the greatest respect for him. He does not say anything about anybody or anything. He goes to the mountain and he saves trees, and he makes movies, and he makes good movies, and he picks good scripts.

  BURT REYNOLDS

- Robert Redford has always been a natural, intuitive, unemphatic movie actor who draws us close with his good looks and his sweet candour and then shuts us out by never revealing much of himself. Redford has considerably less identity than, say, Burt Reynolds or Jack Nicholson.

  DAVID DENBY

- Redford does not want to be an actor, he wants to be a movie star.

  ARTHUR LAURENTS

- He is known as a fine upstanding man with a strong social conscience which is great for playing the part of an assistant district attorney, but I did wonder where the comedy would come from. In time he started telling me stories about himself, about his bemusement of what's going on around him, and about the fact that when he gets really busy he starts bumping into things.

  IVAN REITMAN, 1986

- Bob will one day get the proper appreciation for his playing of Jay Gatsby because it is such a difficult role to play and he is totally right for it of course.

  JACK CLAYTON

- Redford is adorable, but when they enriched that handsome hunk of white bread they somehow left out the mythic minerals.

  RICHARD SCHICKEL, 1978

- I can't stand around like Redford. I'm not that narcissistic. Not that photogenic either.

  WILLIAM DEVANE

- As a director, I wouldn't like me as an actor; as an actor, I wouldn't like me as a director.

  HIMSELF

- Redford is a dangerous man to let loose on the streets. He has holes in his head, he should be arrested.

  GEORGE ROY HILL

- The minute I meet someone new I'm immediately asked about Bob, as if I have no personality of my own. I get the feeling sometimes that nobody talks to me any more. All they ever want to do is talk about Bob. I can't stand it. I learned long ago that you have to pay for success.

  LOLA REDFORD

MICHAEL REDGRAVE (1908–1985)

■ Redgrave was enchanting to work with. Then later I did a play with him, he phoned me one day, said the rest of the cast were treating him with 'dumb insolence'. Strange expression.

HAROLD FRENCH, 1983

VANESSA REDGRAVE (born 1937)

■ When I worked on *The Seven Percent Solution*, Vanessa Redgrave tried to convert me to a form of communism, Trotskyism, whatever the hell it is. Talented broad, but everyone ducked behind a camera when she came around. I asked her 'Vanessa can you shoot a pistol?' 'Why?' 'Well, when the revolution comes ...' 'No, no,' she interrupted. 'Someone else will do that.' Some Trotskyite. She travels by Rolls Royce.

ROBERT DUVALL, 1983

■ It's been a terrific experience working with somebody as good as she is. An incredible actress. I'm in there [in *Yanks*] with a really high-powered dame, you know. You cut back and forth and Vanessa is incredible. Incredible! She'd survive with Brando and no woman ever has, except maybe Eve Marie Saint at the beginning.

WILLIAM DEVANE

■ I think she is a born proselytiser. I sometimes think that any position you take up she'll make you change your mind even if she holds an opposite view.

MICHAEL REDGRAVE

■ Then, I thought to myself, 'Darn it, maybe I can't do what Vanessa Redgrave can, but can Vanessa Redgrave do what I can do? Who's kidding who here?

RAQUEL WELCH

172

CAROL REED (1906–1976)

■ He was always a director who got as much out of actors as could possibly be gotten ... And he could stage individual scenes as well as they could possibly be staged. If he had a weakness (which I admit he has) it was that he didn't have a sufficiently keen story sense ...

JAMES MASON, 1970

■ Carol doesn't only make films, he lives, breathes eats and drinks them.

TREVOR HOWARD

■ Reed is one of those dedicated beings, the artist who is completely absorbed by his dream. He eats, drinks and sleeps cinema.

MICHAEL REDGRAVE

■ Reed said: 'When in doubt, get involved in a comedy thriller very rapidly. For God's sake don't make the picture you want to make, because you haven't got enough skills. Make a comedy thriller. You will miss some of the thrills, you will miss some of the laughs, but with luck there will be enough left and with luck you will be asked to make another picture.'

GUY HAMILTON

OLIVER REED (born 1938)

■ Do you know what I am? I'm successful. Destroy me and you destroy your British film industry. Keep me going and I'm the biggest star you've got. I'm Mr England.

HIMSELF, 1973

■ Reed is a complex character who doesn't easily give of himself. When you do win his trust, though, he's loyal, protective and a dear, dear friend. And he possesses an extraordinary sensitivity that manifests itself at the most unlikely moments. In discovering Reed's different aspects, I began to understand him, and therefore to like him—not for what he thinks he is, but for what he really is.

AMANDA DONOHOE, 1986

■ Oliver Reed is a maze of stylish contradiction who tells you he adores women but adds, some hours and several drinks later, that he prefers the company of men. He can be elegant, charming and witty. Or the kind of man you would expect to find at the centre of a bar-room brawl.

STUART KNOWLES

CHRISTOPHER REEVE (born 1952)

■ What seemed such a nice, simple, artless performance in *Superman* was the finest kind of acting. Reeve's timing—and humour—has to be just about perfect to make the character come off.

SIDNEY LUMET

■ Chris is good-looking in the pre-war mould when movie stars looked like movie stars and not like the local wine shop manager.

WILLIAM MARSHALL

■ Christopher Reeve's entire performance [as Superman] is a delight. Ridiculously good-looking with a face as sharp and strong as an ax blade, his bumbling, fumbling Clark Kent and omnipotent Superman are simply two styles of gallantry and innocence.

JACK KROLL

STEVE REEVES (born 1926)

■ It was my father who told me I should develop my body seeing as how I wasn't

born with much of a brain an' it was the only thing I had to fall back on. Then I saw Steve Reeves an' I thought, 'Jesus, anybody can go to school an' become a lawyer but I wanna be able to pull down a temple, shift a bridge, take on the whole Roman army. . . . That's a man to me.'

SYLVESTER STALLONE, 1977

KAREL REISZ (born 1926)

■ I think Karel is very good with actors; he's very interested in the actors creating a character and not just relying on personality, he's good at encouraging actors to explore the characterisation, and I think that's the kind of acting I'm interested in.

ALBERT FINNEY, 1967

173

JEAN RENOIR (1894–1979)

■ He's my style. Renoir's good for actors. Renoir obviously loves actors and understands actors, and *La Grande Illusion* which I saw recently, is so modern that it could have been made this year—the acting and the staging of it is absolutely modern and true.

JAMES MASON, 1970

■ Jean Renoir is the greatest film-maker in the world. This is not the result of an opinion poll, but a personal feeling. This personal feeling is shared by other film makers, and in any case aren't Jean Renoir's films about personal feelings?

FRANÇOIS TRUFFAUT

■ By the end of the second week the actors are doing exactly what he wants. But he wasn't very maleable. As a man I enjoyed him, but as a director he wasn't a very pleasant experience. You learn as much not what to do as what to do while working with him.

ROBERT ALDRICH, 1966

■ The creative lives of the Renoirs, Auguste and Jean, father and son, together stretch back practically a century. Working in very different media, they have expressed, in many ways, a common view of life. Together with a phenomenal responsiveness to the plastic image, they share the same large humanity and tolerance, the same joyous faith in life and pleasure and people.

DAVID ROBINSON, 1960

■ To say that Renoir is the most intelligent of directors comes down to the same thing as saying that he is French to his very fingertips. And if *Elena et les Hommes* is the French film par excellence, it is because it is the most intelligent of films.

JEAN–LUC GODARD

■ Jean Renoir is as much a master of his art as was his distinguished father and in criticising *La Grande Illusion* it is necessary to stress the fact that it can only be judged by the very highest standards. Its values, both human and technical, are unquestionably in the first rank, and it holds one in a tension of suspense and sympathy which is a rare experience in cinema.

BASIL WRIGHT

■ A film is the work of a group. Clearly there is one man who influences this group, who in practice leads and animates it, the equivalent to what artisans used to call their master. In the early days of American films, this was often a star player. Sometimes a writer

174

provides the most significant contribution. But most frequently it is a film director. In Europe today a film is still primarily the work of its director; in America it is apt to be the producer's creation.

HIMSELF

■ After all, I have been happy. I have made the films that I wanted to make. I have made them with people who are more than collaborators; they were my accomplices. This, I believe, is one recipe for happiness; to work with people you love and who love you. The advantage of being 80 years old is that one has had many people to love.

HIMSELF

ALAIN RESNAIS (born 1922)

■ Resnais is one of the genius directors too, however difficult it is to work in his way on a script as complex as *Providence*. He's the only poet director I'm aware of.

DIRK BOGARDE

■ I never try to imitate reality. When I make a film, I never know how it will turn out. I want it to develop like nature, emerge the way a plant grows . . . I feel as though I'm tapping away at pieces of stone to bring out what lies within . . . I'm always surprised at the result.

HIMSELF

BURT REYNOLDS (born 1935)

■ It's the man's tremendous wit that just keeps coming across. Listen, there is no acting style. Most people just play themselves. Spencer Tracy used to say to me after a scene, 'Did I ham that one up?' If I said yes, he'd say 'Okay let's do it again.' There's that same honesty in Burt Reynolds. He's a throwback to the old school.

MYRNA LOY

■ He can be a true leading man and still play comedy, and the reason he can do it is that he is a very intelligent guy. There are few actors who do comedy who aren't intelligent. The S.O.B knows what he is doing.

JACK LEMMON

■ He turned out to be the thinking man's actor, working his tail off to make it look simple. Just like the old guys. Sure, he plays himself, but there's a technique to that. He's got it. And he's got that comic timing that really sparkles in drama—the deadpan reaction.

ALAN PAKULA

■ Playing a passive, put-upon man, Reynolds performs comic miracles in *Starting Over* with his deadpan mug and semaphore-like eyebrows.

DAVID DENBY

■ What I look for mostly in a man is humour, honesty and a moustache. Burt has all three.

SALLY FIELD

■ He is the one the ladies like to dance with and their husbands like to drink with. He is the larger-than-life actor of our times. He is gifted, talented, naughty—but nice.

FRANK SINATRA, 1987

■ Burt has a quality that nobody else has. He's funny, sexy, glib, likeable and still very macho. But Burt tries to be all things to all people . . . He thinks that unless

he's doing . . . intense, dramatic work— then he's not an actor. But I don't think he's comfortable with that kind of intense emotional revealing. He doesn't like to reveal himself that way in life, yet he's mad at himself because he can't do that on the screen.

SALLY FIELD, 1985

■ Burt's a very private person. And he has the capacity for loyalty and caring. Here's a man who has made it okay and he forgets no one he's ever cared for—men or women. He certainly has tried to keep me from breaking my neck in all the years I've been doubling him.

HAL NEEDHAM

■ Behind that false humour and false modesty is a bright man who's paid his dues. People think he's Charlie Charm, but that's only part of it. Burt is a strong-willed, self-centered businessman: he does what serves Burt, and he should.

ROBERT ALDRICH, 1978

■ At that time [while making *Nickelodeon*] Burt was suffering from a series of chest pains. He's a dreadful hypochondriac and was convinced he was having heart attacks. In fact, it was just chronic indigestion. Anyone who stacks away as much junk food as that man does, can only be suffering from terminal gas . . . Minions and sycophants appeared out of the walls and a doctor was called. I had the hardest time trying not to laugh, because it was all really so absurd.

LAMONT JOHNSON

■ If Reynolds wanted to, he could spend the rest of his life playing nice guys in trivial movies. He is the best light leading man around, and as long as he plays it safe, he can pull in the big bucks. But

175

Reynolds is restless: he tries to stretch himself. . . . Not all of these experiments have paid off, but . . . Reynolds is still capable of suprising his fans.

FRANK RICH, 1978

■ . . . the director feels that if he signs Burt Reynolds, he's selling out because he's signing the most commercial actor in town. If he wants to be known as an auteur . . . he'll instead hire one of the darlings—Robert De Niro, Al Pacino or Dustin Hoffman. A lot of directors in this town don't realise that the hardest thing to do in movies is to make chicken salad out of chickenshit, and I've done that a lot.

HIMSELF

176   RALPH RICHARDSON (1902–1983)

■ Ralph is a remarkable man, shrewd, observant, warm and generous-hearted, once you get to know him. He is also reserved and cautious, never making a swift decision about anything.

JOHN GIELGUD

■ There's no secret about the fact that Ralph is terrified of the camera. But at the same time he is unquestionably a great actor. Yet he looks to a director, too.

SIDNEY LUMET

■ Of all the actors of our time he has been the most interesting as a man; original, shrewd, down-to-earth and yet visionary, generous to a fault, with a great love of animals, a respect for inanimate objects, an interest in science and a passion for books.

ALEC GUINNESS

TONY RICHARDSON (born 1928)

■ He brutalises actors . . . How the hell is he going to direct a film if one day all the actors walk off the set? He has no respect for actors at all. Now, how is he going to direct with no actors to work with? If they actually refuse to work, he's powerless. . . . So what is this myth about a director's power?

ANTHONY HOPKINS

LENI RIEFENSTAHL (born 1902)

■ During the Labour Service Parade [of the Nuremberg Rally] the sun disappeared behind the clouds. But the moment the Fuehrer arrives, its rays break through the clouds: Hitler weather! . . . in the will of the Fuehrer his people triumph.

HERSELF, 1936

■ You know I have gone to court over 50 times since the end of the war often to get an apology from a newspaper that called me a Nazi—which I never was—but also to stop the pirate prints of my films.

HERSELF, 1976

ARTHUR RIPLEY (1895–1961)

■ To me Ripley was a real movie man. He had written and cut for Mack Sennett. He had a beagle's nose for film. He knew everything there was to know. An inspired man, almost a clairvoyant, it took careful knowing to appreciate him. When he grew enthusiastic, he would shout crazily, truculently, as if all listeners, including unseen demons, were fighting his idea.

JOSHUA LOGAN, 1976

ERIC ROBERTS (born 1956)

- Coca Cola ... was the only common ground between Eric Roberts—who like all Hollywood actors is obsessed with power—the Australians, Greta Scacchi and myself. Roberts was so well-prepared he knew what cufflinks and underpants he was going to wear. It was all part of his great image. His attitude was totally different from the Australians who were relaxed and laid back and waited to see what you were going to do next. It was unbelievable.

  DUSAN MAKAVEJEV

PAUL ROBESON (1898–1976)

- We hadn't met before, but he hugged me, almost crushed me. He was like a bear. It was charming. It was lovely. ... He was so full of laughs and so full of fun. ... We were close as friends, because I'll listen to anyone with a sense of humour ... I admired him and I still miss him.

  ELIZABETH WELCH

- If ever a man was born at the wrong time in the wrong place it was Paul Robeson ... probably the greatest singing actor of his time. ... Paul was never noted for his modesty, and it galled him that so few doors were open to him. He blamed, usually rightly, the white establishment, for the fact that he could never appear in an opera in his native land.

  BILL ZAKARIASEN, 1976

- Paul Robeson went early, if naively, into battle for black freedom. He could have sat back on the 50–yard line, rich and famous. But he chose to stand up and be counted—risking everything.

Robeson was a genuine tragic hero—'one that loved not wisely but well.'

HUBERT SAAL, 1976

EDWARD G. ROBINSON (1893–1973)

- Each part he plays, he enriches with deep and warm understanding of human frailties and compels us to pity rather than condemnation, always adding vivid colour to the intricate mosaic of motion picture reality.

  FRITZ LANG

- An immensely effective actor.

  ORSON WELLES

- I had the pleasure of directing Mr Robinson in *Little Caesar* and we have been great friends for many years. He is one of the finest actors living, and one of the finest gentlemen it has been my good fortune to know. I cannot say enough about him as an actor or as a person.

  MERVYN LEROY

- I will never forget the pleasure and instruction I derived from working with a true master of his art, such as Edward G. Robinson was—and is. Surely his record for versatility, studied characterisation—ranging from the modern colloquial to the classics—and artistic integrity is unsurpassed. Furthermore, everyone who has worked with him recalls with pleasure his considerable personal charm.

  DOUGLAS FAIRBANKS JR

- It is, in no small way, a measure of the man that he chose to come to England in the middle of the war at his own expense, and for no salary whatsoever, to play this part in order to pay his own

177

private tribute to this country's effort during those frightening years. . . . For me he is a great liberal and a really exciting human being to be with. As an actor, of course, he is supreme.

RICHARD ATTENBOROUGH

■ Talking of *Soylent Green*, it was nice working with Eddie Robinson. He was a sweet man. I don't think he was very well making the movie, and I don't think somehow he'd had a very happy life. But he was nice.

JOSEPH COTTEN

NICHOLAS ROEG (born 1928)

■ Nothing in Roeg's style appears to be spontaneous; it's all artifice and technique . . . like an entertainment for bomb victims. Nobody expects any real pleasure from it.

PAULINE KAEL

■ Unlike Bergman, Nicholas Roeg, who made the horrible *Performance*, does not arouse expectations . . . [*Walkabout*] is based, apparently, on a nice straightforward novel. Roeg has gimmicked it up with every kind of photographic and scenaristic pretentiousness, irrelevance, and puzzling opacity.

JOHN SIMON, 1971

■ This harsh criticism is not to deny the wayward enterprise of *Performance*, simply to wonder at grown men complaining about an entertainment corporation's bewilderment at such strident mystification.

DAVID THOMSON, 1975

■ With Nic and Dennis Potter what are you going to get? Either something exciting or a load of rubbish.

THERESA RUSSELL, 1987

■ [*The Man Who Fell to Earth*] is, like all of Roeg's films, the blowing up of something simple or simple-minded to arrogantly bloated dimensions and purporting to be chock-full of hermetic truths merely awaiting their interpreters. But a plague of Roeg mystagogues is worse than a plague of locusts.

JOHN SIMON, 1976

GINGER ROGERS (born 1911)

■ She may have faked a little, but we knew we had a good thing going.

FRED ASTAIRE

■ She has a little love for a lot of people, but not a lot for anybody.

GEORGE GERSHWIN

■ Ginger was wonderful in that she came to rehearsals, and was agreeable, and she would work hard. She'd do anything you would tell her—until it came time for her to put on the dress. She used to wear dresses that were full of bugle beads that would whip around and smack Astaire in the face.

HERMES PAN

■ When Ginger Rogers danced with Astaire, it was the only time in the movies when you looked at the man, not the woman.

GENE KELLY

■ She is a great advocate of wholesomeness. She does not smoke or drink but has been married five times. She is a Christian Scientist and her

political sympathies are right-wing. . . .
Ginger has supported Richard Nixon ever
since his first California campaign. She
says his family 'represents all that is best
in America', a statement with which I
could not agree less.

HELEN LAWRENSON, 1969

■ Ginger Rogers is a very lovely person,
but she was a Star with a capital S. By
that time [*Lady in the Dark*], she had
already reached her zenith, and there was
not too much I could do to help her. I
was more of a stage manager on that
picture than a dialogue coach.

PHYLLIS LOUGHTON

■ She's one of the reasons I left show
business. . . . We'd give her a new scene,
and she couldn't remember the lines. She
couldn't sing and, surprisingly, she
couldn't do the dances. And all through
the horror of it all she was smiling and
grinning and unreal. There's no denying
her appeal to the public. That's what
makes her so dangerous. She almost
smiled me into bankruptcy.

PAUL GREGORY

■ Ginger Rogers was one of the worst,
red-baiting, terrifying reactionaries in
Hollywood.

JOSEPH LOSEY

WILL ROGERS (1879–1935)

■ [He has] his own ability to make
audiences forget that he was a comedian.
This quality of his was very apparent in
the scenes where Rogers was called
upon to portray the simple, human
emotions that touch the very soul of
mankind. The sincerity and conviction
with which he did them is what might

be expected of a great tragedian.
Audiences forget Rogers the wisecracker
and think of him as a human being torn
with emotion.

FRANK BORZAGE

ERIC ROHMER (born 1920)

■ The doyen and oddest man out of that
group of French film-makers which
emerged from the pages of *Cahiers du
Cinéma*, Eric Rohmer, gradually acquired
a delighted, devoted audience with a
series of six movies—his *'Contes
Moraux'*. What was so remarkable about
these tales is that they were 'talkies' in
the best sense of the word. If the action
was minimal, languid, superficially
undramatic, the verbal encounters of his
men and women were anything but:
rueful scruples, small points of
conscience, humorous deflations had
rarely had such an authentic airing on
the screen.

JOHN COLEMAN

MICKEY ROONEY (born 1920)

■ I've been thinking about Mickey Rooney,
because he goes back to everybody's
childhood. Even if you didn't have a
childhood, Mickey Rooney goes back
there. He and Judy Garland doing those
shows in the barns where it was always
summer, he and Judge Hardy having
those man-to-midget chats designed to
help a boy live right.

CHRIS CHASE

FRANÇOISE ROSAY (1891–1974)

■ Another advantage of America. It made
me discover Françoise Rosay as an

actress. Up until then, she had appeared in each of my films in a little cameo part, and really only for superstitious reasons. Strange as it may seem, it was the Americans who discovered her, photographed her, sought after her. The French cameramen had decided that she was not photogenic.

JACQUES FEYDER

DIANA ROSS (born 1944)

■ . . . she remains an uneasy actress [in *Mahogany*] who pushes everything past endurance—including the audience. Ross laughs eagerly but never with a semblance of spontaneity, weeps without sorrow and rages without passion.

JAY COCKS, 1975

180

HERBERT ROSS (born 1927)

■ I think Herb Ross is the best director I've worked with in films. The others just didn't understand my material as well.

NEIL SIMON

ROBERTO ROSSELLINI (1906–1977)

■ Roberto and I were just too different. Being Italian, he was a jealous husband. And I was a bad influence on him. All the films we made together were flops.

INGRID BERGMAN

■ RAI had asked me to do *La Voix Humaine* with Monica [Vitti]. It didn't seem right for me to put myself in posthumous competition with the Maestro. Yes, I mean it, I'm not being ironical. Rossellini really was a maestro for us all. The same

applies to Monica in regard to Magnani's memory.

MICHELANGELO ANTONIONI

■ Rossellini was a stubborn, opinionated genius who had total autonomy over all his productions.

JOAN COLLINS, 1984

MICKEY ROURKE (born 1956)

■ He has a great deal of pride in what he does, and he is somebody who's prepared to work with the same dedication as a Brando or a De Niro. And there's a great generosity towards the rest of the cast. Like De Niro, he'll come to every casting session and read with the people. There's no pettiness, no ego trips.

MICHAEL CIMINO

■ He fascinates me. I can't take my eyes off him because he's never doing nothing.

ADRIAN LYNE

■ A fine actor with an unerring knack for choosing the wrong movies.

PETER TRAVERS

MIKLOS ROZSA (born 1907)

■ Who needs chestnuts from the nineteenth century, when Rozsa's beautiful works of the twentieth have all the attributes of warmth, melodiousness and colour for which so many have been hungering?

CLARK WARD BARENT, 1975

JANE RUSSELL (born 1921)

■ Miss Russell was a very strong character. Very good-humoured when she wasn't being cranky.

ROBERT MITCHUM

■ Don't let her fool you. Tangle with her and she'll shingle your attic.

BOB HOPE

KEN RUSSELL (born 1927)

■ An arrogant, self-centered, petulant individual. I don't say this in any demeaning way.

BOB GUCCIONE

■ I haven't seen the picture and I intend to go on not seeing the picture so that when people ask what I think about it I can tell them I haven't seen it. [After taking his name off the credits of *Altered States*].

PADDY CHAYEVSKY, 1981

■ Humility has never been Russell's strongpoint; along with subtlety and easy wit, it is one of those things that just seems to get in the way. He is articulate— perhaps not as articulate as he'd like us to believe, but well, he is articulate.

PETER BUCKLEY

ROSALIND RUSSELL (1908–1976)

■ Rosalind Russell plays the mother [in *Gypsy*] as another of her electric, dazzling, tender-hearted impossible harridans: middle age has given [her] . . . all kinds of new styles and dimensions and chances to do things that never suited her when she was young. . . . she has the knack of making quite middling lines sound sizzlingly witty.

ISABEL QUIGLEY, 1964

MARGARET RUTHERFORD (1892–1972)

■ I've always admired Margaret Rutherford. Like her, I'd like to play Miss Marple when I'm eighty.

SIGOURNEY WEAVER

CARLOS SAURA (born 1932)

■ I love Carlos Saura's films. There are no Carlos Sauras in America because they can't get the financing.

ROBERT ALTMAN, 1978

JOHN SAYLES (born 1950)

■ A Renaissance man—Woody Allen with a social conscience, Herzog or Fassbinder with a sense of humour—just when we need one.

JOHN LEONARD, 1986

MAXIMILIAN SCHELL (born 1920)

■ Max reminds me a lot of myself. He's full of energy, very carefree and amateurish in that he doesn't do things by the book. I think he's much better than I would be as a director.

JON VOIGHT

JOHN SCHLESINGER (born 1926)

■ He is sensitive, he has a great eye for detail, and he's fascinated by this communication thing. . . . He's always questioning his work; he never seems satisfied, which is a good thing. He asks you whether you like an idea and you say yes, but he's not convinced. If you say no, he's worried. he has great respect for his actors and listens to their opinions.

GLENDA JACKSON

PAUL SCHRADER (born 1946)

■ I really admire Paul Schrader. He's just terrible when he's trying to be commercial. I don't think *Yakuza's* very good. There's a whole flock of his scripts that are just awful. But . . . no one writes like *Taxi Driver*, *Rolling Thunder* or *Hardcore*. Wonderful style and depth to his material. It's really strong stuff. Visceral. It stinks of him. It's just terrific.

JOHN MILIUS, 1976

■ A sort of junk–food Dostoevski.

NEIL SINYARD

182

ARNOLD SCHWARZENEGGER (born 1947)

■ After Arnold Schwarzenegger, Dolph Lundgren is a bit of a disappointment. At least Arnold looks as if he comes supplied with batteries.

ADAM MARS-JONES, 1987

■ I have always been rather worried about Arnold. Having been elected Mr Universe on no less than four occasions, Mr Schwarzenegger can out-ripple a lot of bodybuilders, but all that pumping iron seems to have given him an ethereal gaze and the toneless voice of an automaton. And it makes me wonder: is he really one of us?

IAIN JOHNSTONE

■ Arnold has done a fantastic job—and real progress in this art of acting: but as he has an accent I've been obliged to work him twice as hard.

RICHARD FLEISCHER

■ Of course, if Arnold hadn't existed we would have had to build him.

JOHN MILIUS

ROMY SCHNEIDER (born 1938)

■ As far as I'm concerned she's not much. She isn't bad but no more. She's made a great career thanks to the Sissi films.

CLAUDE AUTANT-LARA

PAUL SCOFIELD (born 1922)

■ I blame a lot of it [the More cult] on the actor Paul Scofield. He was such a better man than More, we all wanted to believe in him.

PROFESSOR RICHARD MARIUS

■ Scofield's performance [in *A Man for All Seasons*] is a masterpiece of eloquent economy, his splendidly restrained stage performance now scrutinised by the camera and revealing level after level of character.

CHRISTOPHER HUDSON

■ I've been a big fan of his for a long time. He has a keen eye but he's not as noisy as I am. I'm insubordinate.

KATHARINE HEPBURN, 1972

MARTIN SCORSESE (born 1942)

■ Each anecdote that he tells, each film incident he recalls, seems to be prefaced by the memory of disease. His asthma is well enough known, but as his memory unfurls it becomes punctuated by 'Oh, yeah, I'd just got up from double pneumonia', or 'that was when I had flu', as if illness was the pre-requisite rather than the neurotic result of any artistic endeavour.

CHRIS PEACHMENT, 1982

■ It's true, I spatter bits of myself all over the screen. I've got to admit that all of my films, with the exception of *Boxcar Bertha*, which was hack work for Corman, are in some sense autobiographical in that they draw on my own experience. I go to shrinks. But they might as well look at the movies.

HIMSELF

GEORGE C. SCOTT (born 1926)

■ [Consoling Maureen Stapleton:] my dear, the whole world is frightened of George.

MIKE NICHOLS

■ . . . One of the best actors alive. But my opinion of him as an actor is much higher than my opinion of him as a man.

JOHN HUSTON

■ He's difficult to deal with, but always for a purpose. I wish I had a picture with Scott starting tomorrow.

FRANK McCARTHY

■ It's a concentrated fury, a sense of inner rage, a kind of controlled madness.

JOSÉ FERRER

■ Intelligent, constructive, decent, professional. If there was a difference of opinion between us, we worked it out in five or ten minutes.

RICHARD LESTER

■ It was amazing just to stand by him and see him at work on *Taps*—a real experience to see such discipline and concentration.

TIMOTHY HUTTON

■ I'm still paying the price for turning down *Patton*. I thought it was pro-war. So Mr George Scott did it. And now Mr Scott is the hot actor and I have to wait for the scripts he turns down. On days when I wake up feeling good I know I was right to turn it down. But when I wake up feeling lousy I think it was a terrible mistake.

ROD STEIGER, 1972

■ He's all things to me: husband, lover, daddy, child. He's not a violent person at all; he's the farthest thing from a harsh person. And he drinks much less now than he used to. We are so different in many ways, but yet, it's uncanny how alike we are. We have very similar emotional needs.

TRISH VAN DEVERE

■ George just likes to block a scene out in a routine way. And then he does it and we shoot. He starts really acting when the camera goes. And throughout a film, 90% of the 'takes' I've printed with George Scott in them have been first or second takes. And if I have to use the second 'take', it's because in the first one something mechanical went wrong or some other actor blew a line.

RICHARD FLEISCHER

■ It is easy to work with him in the sense that he is a consummate actor. They're the most satisfying to work with. You just touch a button and a whole change can come about. It's very easy to mould an actor who's like that. . . . they come in so prepared and knowledgeable that you feel as if you personally are not doing very much. [But] there are all sorts of situations where they need help too.

ARTHUR HILLER

183

RANDOLPH SCOTT (1898–1987)

■ To a whole generation of boys he was quite simply 'the cinema'. In a Randolph Scott Western you knew what to expect to be delivered to you and, by goodness, Randy stood and delivered.

JAMES MORTON

■ ... Randy Scott is a complete anachronism. He's a gentleman. And so far he's the only one I've met in this business full of self-promoting sons-of-bitches.

MICHAEL CURTIZ

■ But everything [on *High Wide and Handsome*] became a little brighter when I got to know Randolph Scott, one of the finest men in Hollywood ... Now a retired millionaire, he's still as handsome as he was in 1937, totally charming and loads of fun.

DOROTHY LAMOUR

184

RIDLEY SCOTT (born 1939)

■ English directors [are] the coldest, most heartless moviemakers I've ever seen. Or at least most of them are. They're wonderfully proficient. The technical skill is out of this world—no one working in films, for instance, has as good an eye as Ridley Scott. But there's a coldness of temperament I can't get along with.

JOHN MILIUS, 1982

JEAN SEBERG (1938–1979)

■ To understand Jean, you have to understand the mid-West. She emerged from it intelligent, talented, beautiful but with the naivety of a child. She has the kind of goodwill that to me is infuriating—persistent, totally unrealistic idealism. It has made her totally defenceless. In the end it came between us.

ROMAIN GARY, 1974

GEORGE SEGAL (born 1934)

■ I think George, in a way, is the eternal college schoolboy. He's always living in a world where he's slightly missing it, where bewilderment is all. Actually he's tremendous fun to work with.

GLENDA JACKSON

■ George would say [on *A Touch of Class*] 'Let me try it this way' and I would look at Glenda and she'd shrug okay, then immediately judge her moods and adapt her timing to fit in with whatever George threw at her. ... And there he was deliriously happy, with almost complete freedom from the director to do whatever he wanted to try, playing against and experimenting with the best actress he has ever worked with.

MELVIN FRANK

■ The only screen star laying claim to the mantle of Cary Grant, that of the true ladies' man. Not a rotter or a rake, you understand. The modern knight in shining armour is courteous, slightly bemused, well dressed and wholesome looking. He is puppyish rather than passionate and probably in the care of a psychiatrist, or at least wondering whether he should be.

ANTHEA DISNEY

■ [On seeming to enjoy himself on chat shows:] I tell myself I'm playing a character who's enjoying himself.

HIMSELF

TOM SELLECK (born 1945)

■ He is gorgeous, and he has some real power now, but he doesn't use that, or his charm, to exploit women. He genuinely seems to *like* women. For an actor, that's rare.

BESS ARMSTRONG

■ The biggest boy scout in America.

JOHN HILLERMAN

PETER SELLERS (1925–1980)

■ I think his mother had gained such an incredible influence over him that he virtually abdicated his own rights to any individual personality. . . . Finally, he had to invade other bodies to register at all. He had to inhabit, he was like a ghoul, he had to feast off somebody else! But he did it so well, it became an art. He was not a genius, Sellers, he was a freak.

SPIKE MILLIGAN

■ When Charlie Chaplin looked in the mirror he saw a comic genius who was mercenary to the nth degree . . . Peter could stare at a mirror all day and at the end he'd find somebody else's face, another personality to portray, to use. That was both his achievement and his failure as a human being.

ROBERT PARRISH

■ Pete had an extraordinary sense of not being there. He genuinely felt that when he went into a room no one could see him.

PETER O'TOOLE

■ As a man he was abject, probably his own worst enemy, although there was plenty of competition.

ROY BOULTING

■ Nobody here believes that there's a man alive who can control that asshole.

MIKE J. FRANKOVICH

■ The only way to make a film with him is to let him direct, write and produce as well as star in it.

CHARLES K. FELDMAN

■ Talk about unprofessional rat finks.

BILLY WILDER

■ Sellers became a monster. He just got bored with the part [Inspector Clouseau] and became angry, sullen and unprofessional. He wouldn't show up for work and he began looking for anyone and everyone to blame, never for a moment stopping to see whether or not he should blame himself for his own madness, his own craziness.

BLAKE EDWARDS

■ He was ruthless, absolutely ruthless, as all great artists are ruthless. Behind that soft exterior he had an obsessional impulse to get his way. He was a child in that sense.

ROY BOULTING

■ The problem with Peter was that he could never like a girl who liked him. It was the old Groucho Marx routine about not wanting to join any club that was willing to accept him as a member.

HARVEY ORKIN

NORMA SHEARER (1900–1983)

■ Norma, who I have always liked and got along with, was at notorious loggerheads with Joan [Crawford]. You see, she was treated as the Queen of the Lot because of her marriage to the boss, Irving Thalberg. Joan had made a lot of

185

money for the company, and I imagine that's what annoyed both of them; it was a competition of who was really the Queen of the Lot.

ROSALIND RUSSELL

■ A face unclouded by thought.

LILLIAN HELLMAN

■ Oh, Mr Thalberg, I've just met that extraordinary wife of yours with the teensy-weansy little eyes!

MRS PATRICK CAMPBELL, 1974

■ And you can tell Miss Shearer that I didn't get where I am on my ass.

JOAN CRAWFORD

MARTIN SHEEN (born 1940)

■ And Martin Sheen was extraordinary... He's a very gifted man. He's from a working-class family, so he had all the moods down for the film. And when he wasn't before the cameras, he was helping in the background, wrapping cables, packing up light reflectors. One day I found him going around a gas station and picking up aluminium snap-back lids from soda cans. He knew they didn't exist in 1959.

TERRENCE MALICK

CYBILL SHEPHERD (born 1950)

■ I like very much Cybill Shepherd and Peter Bogdanovich. The problems grew when Peter wished to prove that he was right and the critics wrong when he pushed Cybill. All I hope now is that he won't use his next three films to prove that she's the equal of Anne Bancroft. That might perhaps be a mistake.

BURT REYNOLDS

ANN SHERIDAN (1915–1967)

■ Ann Sheridan, Oomph girl supreme, was also a whoppingly good comedienne, a frequently fine actress and a terrific personality.

RAY HAGEN

■ The leading lady of *Angels with Dirty Faces* was that lovely, talented gal, Ann Sheridan. So much to offer—and a three-pack-a-day smoker ... Years later when the lung cancer hit, she didn't have much of a chance, and what a powerful shame that was. A mighty nice gal, Annie.

JAMES CAGNEY

■ Great ... And she outlived some of the worst pictures you've ever known and became good. People liked her. They made her a star in spite of the bad pictures ... Oh, she was quick and good and everything.

HOWARD HAWKS

DON SIEGEL (born 1912)

■ I think that in America I'm looked upon as the equivalent of a European director—which is quite laughable. I've never had a personal publicity man working for me. So all this came out of the blue—all this publicity. The cult was not engineered. It festered, in a sense. And erupted. And it did me a lot of good.

DON SIEGEL, 1973

SIMONE SIGNORET (1921–1985)

■ I suppose it is fair to say that I fell hopelessly in love with Simone Signoret the very first time I clapped eyes on her in a modest Ealing film called *Against the Wind* ... I placed her then on the

186

very peak of her profession, and as far as I am concerned she has never budged from it and I still love her dearly.

DIRK BOGARDE

■ This [*Casque d'Or*] is surely Becker's finest film, which is saying a great deal. It also has my absolute favourite among screen actresses, the magnificent Signoret in perhaps her most magnificent appearance: I can think of no other actress capable of lending Golden Marie such fantastic, heart-stopping allure.

JOHN COLEMAN, 1964

■ Her hair grayish-white now, her voice hoarse, Simone Signoret has crossed 60 and grown rather stout, yet she's more of a movie star than ever. What the American audience—particularly older moviegoers—responds to in Signoret is not so much her talent but her moral authority as a woman. This is one ageing actress who will never ask an audience to mourn her ruined beauty. She will not yield to easy pathos.

DAVID DENBY

■ I got old the way that women who aren't actresses grow old.

HERSELF

■ Signoret posed her fair share of problems, however, because she was obviously reluctant to do the film [*Le Mort en ce Jardin*] . . . so she slipped some Communist documents into her passport, hoping to be turned away by American Immigration, but they let her through without a murmur. Once here and on the set, her behaviour was at best unruly, at worst very destructive to the rest of the cast.

LUIS BUÑUEL

■ Some actors have their qualms and doubts but love this confrontation with an audience. . . . Simone is unconcerned with that direct engagement. Once she has defined her characterisation for a film or television and once the take is printed, she knows that she has done her best at the time of doing it. Whereas in the theatre one always has the feeling that if not to-night then tomorrow one could do better.

FRANÇOIS PERIER, 1986

ALISTAIR SIM (1900–1976)

■ There lives and breathes a comic genius of gargantuan proportions.

PATRICIA ROUTLEDGE, 1977

JEAN SIMMONS (born 1929)

■ The first thing you look for is talent and this girl is full of it. She can play comedy and drama with equal facility.

WILLIAM WYLER

■ She was one of the most undemanding, professional actresses I've ever worked with, but I could imagine what it must have been like to be married to tigresses like Crawford or Davis.

STEWART GRANGER

■ A dream . . . a fantastically talented and enormously underestimated girl. In terms of talent she is so many head and shoulders above most of her contemporaries, one wonders why she didn't become the great star she could have been . . . It's true, it's not that important to her. It doesn't matter to her much.

JOSEPH L. MANKIEWICZ

■ She is surprisingly appealing in a part [in *Guys and Dolls*] with almost no potential, and her Havana dance is a high point of the picture.

STEVEN SONDHEIM

FRANK SINATRA (born 1915)

■ I'm just one of those who thought they could *direct* Sinatra. It's like being one of the girls who thought they'd get Howard Hughes to marry them.

ROBERT ALDRICH

■ Burt Lancaster is impossible and Kirk [Douglas] a pain in the neck, but when they argue their aim is to make a better picture, and I'm for that. Sinatra, on the other hand, only argues about how to shoot the scene quicker so he can get away.

ROBERT ALDRICH

■ Ohhh, he is quite a guy! Frank is a remarkable human being. Very colourful. He is several people, all interesting. He is a man with concern for people—not only his friends, but people he doesn't know. I guess there is just reams that could be written about the things he has done for people which no one knows other than the recipients. He likes it that way.

ROSALIND RUSSELL

■ ... Sinatra's behaviour was unbelievable. There was an old lady playing the slot machines nearby, and this annoyed him. ... he kicked a couple of bottles of champagne towards her and said 'Get away, you're bothering me.' ... We weren't given any choice. He chose wieners and sauerkraut for everyone. And there was more trouble. Sinatra decided

188

he didn't like the pianist. So he tossed a handful of coins at him and told him to take off. That did it. My friend and I got up and left.

VALERIE PERRINE, 1974

■ He has this tense Sicilian quality while I don't have any tenseness at all and I just hang in there with what I call a dead ass ... But Frank gets picked on by people who want to see how tough he is and he usually obliges them with a demonstration. Like all Sicilians, if he is a friend he will always be a friend—and if he is an enemy, go on hating.

BING CROSBY, 1976

■ Unpleasant man. No one has yet worked out what really makes him tick. But he sings well.

ROBERT ALDRICH

■ Undeniably the title-holder in the soft-touch department.

GREGORY PECK

■ He's the kind of guy that, when he dies, he's going up to heaven and give God a bad time for making him bald.

MARLON BRANDO

■ So much has been written about Sinatra, of his talent, his generosity, his ruthlessness, his kindness, his gregariousness, his loneliness and his rumoured links with the Mob that I can contribute nothing except to say that he is one of the few people in the world I would instinctively think of if I needed help of any sort. I thought of him once when I was in a bad spot: help was provided instantly.

DAVID NIVEN

■ Frank is very nice but moody, and if you want to work with him it's up to you to understand *him*, he's not going to put himself out to understand *you*. If he likes you he'll see your point of view. But he's temperamental; and if you line up twelve people who know him, you'll get twelve different versions of his character and behaviour.

LEWIS MILESTONE

■ Ava and Frank bear a great affection for each other, and when in trouble she always turns to him. I don't know Frank well, but I admire him. He sticks by his guns and stands by his friends, ex-wives included. I respect his kind of loyalty very much.

JOHN HUSTON

■ Once a director lets an actor interfere, he is lost. That's why I could never work with Sinatra or Marlon Brando. It would be out of the question because these guys assume rights and attitudes which properly belong to the director. Let them direct themselves, if they know how.

CURTIS BERNHARDT

■ I ran the gamut with Sinatra from where pictures were concerned he wouldn't work without me, to where I got dumped. A hundred per cent pro, but he is so mecurial that even a great pro can have trouble with him.

JOHN GREEN

ROBERT SIODMAK (1900–1973)

■ Siodmak was the master of this style which emerged with the postwar feeling of pessimism in various genres, the style of the Film Noir.

STUART M. KAMINSKY, 1974

VICTOR SJÖSTRÖM (1879–1960)

■ The Swedish people are closer to what our Pilgrims were, or what we consider them to have been, then our present-day Americans. [Victor Sjöström] got the spirit of [*The Scarlet Letter*] exactly, and was himself a fine actor, the finest that ever directed me. I never worked with anyone I liked better than Sjöström.

LILLIAN GISH

■ His films have meant a tremendous lot to me . . .

INGMAR BERGMAN

EVERETT SLOANE (1909–1965)

■ You know how he was so ugly there was a certain beauty about him. But he had his nose altered, wore contact lenses instead of his thick glasses, had his hair straightened and no one wanted him. He became so morose that he walked out into the middle of the road and killed himself.

JOSEPH COTTEN

MAGGIE SMITH (born 1934)

■ She is resourceful, inventive and she has mystery and power. Mystery in a woman is terribly important.

GEORGE CUKOR, 1972

■ I enjoyed the film [*Travels With My Aunt*]. I think Maggie is a brilliant actress and was marvellous in parts. And if they had left in the footage that was needed to cover the eccentricity of the performance . . . she would have been great. She can act and she can overdo. It is becoming the style, you know, to attack the overdoers; so we overdoers have to stick

189

together. But she hadn't the script she needed to protect her.

KATHARINE HEPBURN, 1973

■ Yes, *that* was lovely. Working with Maggie—well, it's like eating a meal in the best restaurant in the world. She's the top. Marvellous.

MICHAEL PALIN, 1985

DOUGLAS SIRK (1900–1987)

■ He was delightful and ambitious and so well-informed.

EDWARD EVERETT HORTON, 1970

GALE SONDERGAARD (1899–1985)

■ Breathtakingly sinister . . . I was so lucky she was cast in the part [In *The Letter*].

BETTE DAVIS

190

SISSY SPACEK (born 1949)

■ Sissy's a phantom. She has this mysterious way of slipping into a part, letting it take over her. She's got a wider range than any young actress I know.

BRIAN DA PALMA

■ She's remarkable, one of the top actresses I've worked with. Her resources are like a deep well.

ROBERT ALTMAN

■ She has an enormous career ahead of her.

BETTE DAVIS, 1987

SAM SPIEGEL (1903–1985)

■ I would rather have him as a friend than as an employer.

JANET SUZMAN

■ One of the most cultivated and enlightened people one could ever hope to meet.

EDWARD HEATH

■ Sam was a weird contradiction, always wanting to take risks and discover new talent, yet cutting you down to size by reminding you how little you knew about making films. The minute we started shooting he was very supportive. He always stuck by the people he liked.

DAVID JONES, 1987

STEVEN SPIELBERG (born 1947)

■ The poet of junk–food and pop culture.

SHEILA JOHNSTON

■ Well, I know that Steven really likes his movies. He thinks of himself as the owner of a huge silver mine. So he'll make sequels to *Raiders* and *ET* because the silver is still down there and someone has to bring it up.

JOHN MILIUS

■ The movies have changed: there's now this wonderful story-teller Spielberg, making benign movies that are enormously successful, while I'm known mainly for making movies about people shooting and cutting each other up. I love his work, but I could never make stuff like that.

ARTHUR PENN, 1972

■ He's the Bjorn Borg of movies. When his mojo is working, there's nobody better. Steve's in touch with a childlike wonder at the way things work—it's the key to his uniqueness.

LAWRENCE KASDAN, 1981

■ But American films will address children as children, and the reason so many adults enjoy Steven Spielberg's films, for instance, is that they appeal to what remains of a child in every adult. I love everything childish in these films. But it's only a film-maker of Spielberg's standing and intellectual independence who can carry it off.

ANDRZEJ WAJDA, 1982

■ Steve's life is his work. It's fascinating to listen to him, and he's a dear friend, not to mention a genius. We do want to work together.

GOLDIE HAWN

■ Spielberg isn't a film-maker; he's a confectioner.

ALEX COX

■ The rule is: no one ever lost money underestimating the intelligence of the audience. Spielberg doesn't need to do this because in a sense he is there already, uncynically. As an artist, Spielberg is a mirror not a lamp. His line to the common heart is so direct that he unmans you with the frailty of your own defences and the transparency of your more intimate fears and hopes.

MARTIN AMIS

■ Steven Spielberg is the only person I've come across who fits my criteria of genius. And I don't throw that word around. Genius is imagination and attention to detail. The ability to achieve to the minutest detail what you perceive in your imagination. . . . I don't think there's another person on earth who's as great a plot structurist, or better storyteller.

RICHARD DREYFUSS

■ Not that he would pay me that to write a script.

[On learning that Spielberg had paid $50,000 for the sled Rosebud, used in *Citizen Kane*]

ORSON WELLES

JOHN M. STAHL (1886–1950)

■ Stahl was a real son of a bitch. He was the kind of director who would do it over and over again without any reason, just as to say, 'Well, I have to do it again because they gave me lousy actors.' We were all downbeat, and everybody hated him. I finally chewed his ass out on the set and my co-workers gave me a silver cigarette box with all their initials engraved on it.

HENRY FONDA

SYLVESTER STALLONE (born 1946)

191

■ *Rocky II* is the most solemn example of self-deification by a movie star since Barbra Streisand's *A Star is Born*.

FRANK RICH

■ Sounds like a Mafia pallbearer, they said. Looks like a bouncer. Has the vocabulary of Mike Hammer, the class of a smack in the mouth. Downright ugly, others said: today, the same people are standing in line to shake his hand.

COLIN DANGAARD

■ Sly is a kisser—the best. I had to go home and lie to my husband and tell him that it's really hard to kiss people in the movies, that it was really embarrassing and uncomfortable. Sly is a great kisser.

DOLLY PARTON

■ Apparently neither Stallone nor anyone else who worked on this picture could bear to part with the lumpish likeability that all tried so hard to establish at the beginning. In the end they sacrifice everything—insight, morality, a dramatic arc—to preserve intact their star's only known quality, best described as a sort of vulgar affability.

RICHARD SCHICKEL, 1978

■ And what is his reward for this career in which he has demonstrated four times in his last five outings that there are no multitudes waiting out there to receive him? Ten-million-dollars. For that is the amount Stallone is being paid to write, direct, and star in *Rocky III*. . . . Probably the largest amount of money ever paid a performer in the entire history of the civilised world. Isn't that insanity?

WILLIAM GOLDMAN

■ His big asset: a face that would look well upon a three-toed sloth. There is not much that is human about the droop of those 4am eyelids and what there is recalls a man who has been either slugged or drugged into a sinister quiescence. If not the Incredible, Stallone is at least the Improbable Hulk.

RUSSELL DAVIES, 1977

BARBARA STANWYCK (born 1907)

■ . . . beloved by all directors, actors, crews, and extras. . . . Under her sullen shyness smouldered the emotional fires of a young Duse or a Bernhardt. Naive, unsophisticated, caring nothing about make-up, or hairdos, this chorus girl could grab your heart and tear it to pieces. She knew nothing about camera tricks. She just turned it on—and everything else on the stage stopped.

FRANK CAPRA

■ My father probably paid her his highest compliment when he said 'There's nothing phoney about her, either in life or on the screen.'

JANE FONDA, 1987

■ Here was an actress that never played just one side of a character. She always played the truth. I once asked Barbara Stanwyck the secret of acting, and she said, 'Just be truthful, and if you can fake that, you've got it made.'

WALTER MATTHAU

■ I was lucky enough to make four pictures with Barbara. In the first I turned her in, in the second I killed her, in the third I left her for another woman, and in the fourth I pushed her over a waterfall. The one thing all these pictures had in common was that I fell in love with Barbara Stanwyck, and I did, too.

FRED MACMURRAY

■ She's one of the greatest women and one of the grandest actresses I ever worked with.

WALTER HUSTON

■ I have never worked with an actress who was more cooperative, less temperamental, and a better workman, to use my term of highest compliment, than Barbara Stanwyck. When I count over those actresses of whom my memories are unmarred by any unpleasant recollection of friction on the set, or unwillingness to do whatever the role required, or squalls of temperament or temper, Barbara's is the first name that comes to mind.

CECIL B. DeMILLE

■ It [*My Reputation*] was fun, mostly because Barbara is a real pal, a real

192

trouper. You can pour water over her head or put a hot-foot on her and she takes it and laughs. The crew likes her, everybody likes her.

CURTIS BERNHARDT, 1969

■ Stanwyck can act the hell out of any part, and she can turn a chore into a challenge. She's fun, and I'm glad I had a chance to make three movies with her. *The Lady Eve* was the best ... She's a delicious woman.

HENRY FONDA

■ Barbara Stanwyck is a fantastic actress. When she makes a gesture as she speaks a line, she has a way of suspending that motion in mid-air for a split second on a certain word which gives an imperceptible emphasis to just that word.

MITCHELL LEISEN

■ ... nor did I find *her* sympathetic. Barbara Stanwyck, I mean. She was always so popular and everybody adored her, but I found her a cold person, and she was the only actress in my working experience who ever went home leaving me to do the close-ups ... with the script girl, which I thought was most unprofessional. I was quite surprised. There, that's the only unkind thing that's *ever* been said about Barbara Stanwyck.

MAUREEN O'SULLIVAN

■ Thirty-nine years ago this month, we were working in a film together called *Golden Boy*. It wasn't going so well, and I was going to be replaced. But, due to this lovely human being, and her encouragement, and above all her generosity, I'm here tonight.

WILLIAM HOLDEN

■ The best actress I ever worked with was Barbara Stanwyck ... She is great. She

never wants to quit acting; there is no becoming a housewife in her dreams. Barbara Stanwyck and Gary Cooper are both in the Cowboy Hall of Fame with me.

JOEL McCREA

■ I certainly agree with all those who find more sex appeal in Barbara Stanwyck and her ankle bracelet in *Double Indemnity* than in all these naked bodies rolling around on the screen today.

BETTE DAVIS

■ A professional's professional, a superb technician with a voice quality that immediately hooked you with its humanness.

KING VIDOR

■ Barbara Stanwyck, amenable and considerate, who could put more *real* meaning into one lifted eyebrow than Monroe into an entire script, got it all over within one take and zero tantrums.

KENNETH ANGER

MAUREEN STAPLETON (born 1925)

■ Mrs Carroll O'Connor came up to us and said, 'Isn't this a wonderful party?' And we all agreed. Then she said, 'But, you know, the one thing Carroll misses is his privacy.' And Maureen said, 'Well, don't worry. He'll get it back.'

ROY SCHEIDER

■ She is a genius.

TENNESSEE WILLIAMS

■ The greatest actress that ever lived.

PAUL ZINDEL

ROD STEIGER (born 1925)

■ But working with Steiger was, well, different. He was into himself a lot. He

193

was really W. C. Fields. I mean, *really*. And after the film was finished I just decided I didn't like the business anymore. I thought it wasn't fun and I don't believe in working if you don't enjoy it.

VALERIE PERRINE

■ I've never seen a man become a role [in *The Heat of the Night*] so much. Two weeks after we started the picture it was almost impossible to talk to Rod Steiger because he was in a Southern dialect night and day.

NORMAN JEWISON

GEORGE STEVENS (1904–1975)

■ George Stevens started as a cameraman with Laurel and Hardy, and he learned so many wonderful tricks, like having us walk forward while looking backward and then bumping into something. George was a darling man, so great with comedy. It's too bad he got serious.

JEAN ARTHUR, 1972

■ Stevens was a brilliant director and a fascinating guy. On some scenes he would run three cameras; he had a technique of taking his hat off and putting it over the lens of any of the cameras that would shoot something he didn't like. He wouldn't have it stop, but he'd see things he would know he didn't want and make an instant editorial decision.

RUSS MEYER

■ George photographs what goes on in the air between people.

SHELLEY WINTERS

■ His career is a slow dissolve from a master of comedy to a poet of sentiment.

NEIL SINYARD

ROBERT STEVENSON (born 1905)

■ I think Stevenson is an extraordinary technician. He probably knows more about film than almost anybody I can name. He's a lot more expert, in fact, than he's called upon to be in this kind of picture [*Bedknobs and Broomsticks*]. But his contribution to it is very large, because in fact he cuts the picture before it's shot. The shooting is done literally by the numbers. That's the Disney system—they always do it.

ANGELA LANSBURY, 1971

JAMES STEWART (born 1908)

■ Jimmy is everything the British audience wants an American to be but so rarely is.

ANTHONY QUAYLE

■ I adored working with Jimmy. He's such an endearing character, a perfectionist at his job, but with a droll sense of humour and a shy way of watching you to see if you react to that humour.

JOAN CRAWFORD

■ I sensed the character and rock-ribbed honesty of a Gary Cooper, plus the breeding and intelligence of an Ivy League idealist. One could believe that young Stewart could reject his father's patrimony—a kingdom on Wall Street.

FRANK CAPRA

■ James Stewart, the cynical chief reporter [in *Call Northside 777*], totally convinces . . . This in spite of Stewart using all the familiar stops in his range; head lowered and thrust forward in determination, open mouth, hands held low and stiff, with his voice deliberately flattened—a carefully established image of homespun simplicity and rugged worth.

KINGSLEY CANHAM

194

- Working with Jimmy Stewart in *It's a Wonderful Life* was very demanding. He's so natural, so realistic, that I never knew whether he was talking to me or doing the scene. He's the most demanding of all the actors I've ever worked with.

  DONNA REED

- If Bess and I had a son, we'd want him to be just like Jimmy Stewart.

  HARRY S. TRUMAN

- You personify for me part of this nation. You symbolise an America that is gentle, ironic, self-deprecating, tough and emotional.

  RICHARD DREYFUSS

MAURITZ STILLER (1883–1928)

- Stiller is the best human being I know. You never get angry or sad no matter how much he chastises you. He creates people and shapes them according to his will.

  GRETA GARBO

OLIVER STONE (born 1946)

- An artist whose vision transcends politics . . . And his passion isn't bogus—he doesn't play 'Imagine' at the end of the film *Platoon* to break people's hearts.

  JAMES WOODS

- *Platoon* is a visceral experience. It goes beyond politics. It makes you feel you've been through Vietnam, and never want to go back.

  STEVEN SPIELBERG

MERYL STREEP (born 1951)

- Oh God, she looks like a chicken.

  TRUMAN CAPOTE, 1986

- She's an ox when it comes to acting. She eats words for breakfast. Working with her is like playing tennis with Chris Evert—she keeps trying to hit the perfect ball.

  DUSTIN HOFFMAN

- Let's just say I found her a little distant. I hardly got to know her. We had dinner a couple of times, but she only spoke about work . . . I didn't find her easy to work with, but it's not her job to make it easy for me.

  CHARLES DANCE, 1987

- The world's best actress.

  CHER

- But oh, how she suffers. In this interview she was agonizing about having to meet the press. She was moaning that she didn't want a lot of people around. And I wanted to ask her, 'Then why the hell are you an actress?' They're so damned sincere these days.

  GEORGE CUKOR

- Before I saw *Sophie's Choice* the alleged magic of Meryl Streep eluded me totally. I didn't understand what the fuss was about. At best she seemed like a frozen, boring blonde, with ice water in her veins, from the Grace Kelly—Tippi Hedren School of Dramatic Art. I simply didn't get the message. Now I do. As Sophie . . . she is positively mesmerising.

  REX REED

BARBRA STREISAND (born 1942)

- I was trying to say that although we don't agree with each other on a lot of things, I respect Barbra and I think she respects me, and that's a terrific thing to preserve. Barbra and I care about each

195

other a great deal. She's very special to me. But at this point, both of us understand that marriage places you in a very difficult position.

ELLIOTT GOULD, 1970

■ I had no disagreement with Barbra Streisand. I was merely exasperated at her tendency to be a complete megalomaniac.

WALTER MATTHAU

■ She's got the balls of a Russian infantryman.

MARTIN RITT, 1976

■ Filming with Streisand is an experience which may have cured me of movies.

KRIS KRISTOFFERSON, 1981

■ The most extraordinary ... er ... uninteresting person I have ever met. I just found her a terrible bore ... She was doing something and asked the director if I wouldn't mind saying my lines in a certain way. I think I said something to her like 'I was acting before you were born, so please don't tell me how to act.' And she said, in her own inimitable way, 'Is this guy crazy or something?'.

WALTER MATTHAU, 1984

■ Barbra Streisand overwhelms her material with vocal pyrotechnics.

MICHAEL FEINSTEIN, 1986

■ She is unassuming, nervous perhaps, among her peers. 'I never have been a joiner,' she admits. 'I never even had fun at recess in grade school.'

JAMES WATTERS

■ Barbra Streisand, The Burt Lancaster Award that goes to the actor or actress whose performance most completely

196

depends upon hair styling. This award is to be shared by Miss Streisand's hair dresser for *The Way We Were*.

VINCENT CANBY

■ I'm Number 10 [at the box office]. Right under Barbra Streisand. Can you imagine being *under* Barbra Streisand? Get me a bag, I may throw up.

WALTER MATTHAU

■ Her speaking voice seems to have graduated with top honours from the Brooklyn Conservatory of Yentaism, and her acting consists entirely of fishily thrusting out her lips, sounding like a cabbie bellyaching at breakneck speed, and throwing her weight around ... Miss Streisand is to our histrionic aesthetics what the Vietnam war is to our politics.

JOHN SIMON

■ Barbra was real nice to work with. Fun. She and I said we'd like to someday do something like '*Macbeth*'. We were younger then ... Now I understand she wants to do classics, including Shakespeare, for television. I'm not lining up to do television, but if it's okay with Barbra ... I would be willing to work with her again—on a more equitable level.

JACK NICHOLSON

■ She's a real 'kvetch'—she's always moaning about something or other: a really hard-to-please lady. But I can handle that. When she's 'kvetching' I simply say: 'Shut up and give me a little kiss, will ya, huh?' or 'stick out your boobs, they're beautiful.' And after that she's fine for the next ten minutes.

PETER BOGDANOVICH

■ Not once did Prince Charming carry her off to the ball, or even to the corner candy store; and no one—not even her Mom—ever seems to listen to her. So the melancholy waif made a promise to herself: one day *everyone* would listen to her. They'd listen because she would be bright and amusing and beautiful and sexy and adorable and talented. Talented she was from the beginning.

GUY FLATLEY

■ Although I do not find her brimming over with warmth, I have always found her polite, honest and even today, somewhat shy.

BARBARA ELDER

■ I had some trepidation about working with her because she had a reputation for being difficult but I didn't find her so. I asked William Wyler and Vincente Minnelli if they had had any problems with her and they said they hadn't. I'd been told she had had some people fired but I couldn't find any proof of that either. She certainly is direct in her manner and her opinion but I prefer that.

GENE KELLY

■ I think Barbra Streisand is a genius, the creativity she has! And I am very impressed with her as a person. Some years ago when I was on the Academy Awards broadcast, she came up to me. I was standing in the wings and Barbra walked across the stage to greet me. Very polite, very nice. You don't find many young women who extend that kind of gracious courtesy to an older woman. Audrey Hepburn does. And Barbra. I've not forgotten how charming she was.

MYRNA LOY

■ It is difficult to quarrel with that kind of success, but if people only knew what she was capable of . . . After she schlepped through *Hello Dolly!* I wrote her a telegram with just three words: 'What a pity'. But I never sent it because it would not do her any good now.

BARRY DENNEN

■ All right, walk off! Just remember, Betty Hutton once thought she was indispensable.

WALTER MATTHAU

■ It [the song 'The Way We Were'] was one of Barbra's biggest hits, but I had to beg her to sing it. She never wanted to do it. . . . Everybody in the picture had to vote before she'd sing it. We all out-voted her. Now I'm afraid to go near her with a new song. She scares me to death.

MARVIN HAMLISCH

197

PRESTON STURGES (1898–1959)

■ The latest Preston Sturges film [*The Palm Beach Story*] surprises and delights as though nothing of the kind had been known before. Farce and tenderness are combined without a fault. It is funny, wildly funny, not only in visual disasters and off-hand jokes, but with a soaring fantasy that is the opposite of surrealism.

WILLIAM WHITEBAIT

■ He was too large for this smelly resort, and the big studios were scared to death of him. A man who was a triple threat, kept them awake nights, and I'm positive they were waiting for him to fall on his face so they could pounce and devour this terrible threat to their stingy talents. They pounced, and they got him good.

EARL FELTON

- I never could make a good film without a good writer—but neither could Preston Sturges. Only he had one with him all the time. He was a true auteur, the compleat creator of his own films.

    WILLIAM WYLER

- At the end of [this] shoot, he said 'It's been a pleasure working with you' and I said 'I wish I could say the same about you.' I don't like to be that way, but he was terrible, really cruel.

    FRED MacMURRAY, 1987

- Sturges was the only truly comic mind to emerge in American film in the late thirties and early forties, a deep-dyed eccentric who made some of the oddest, and (in their erratic way) funniest movies of the period.

    RICHARD SCHICKEL

198

MARGARET SULLAVAN (1911–1960)

- She had a pulsing and husky voice which could suddenly switch, in emotional moments, to a high choirboy soprano. Her beauty was not obvious or even standard. It showed as she tilted her head, as she walked, as she laughed, and she was breathtakingly beautiful as she ran. One of my girlfriends complained that I talked too much about Sullavan, and she was right. We were all in love with her.

    JOSHUA LOGAN

- She could do ... maybe a look, or a line or two, but they would hit like flashes or earthquakes.

    JAMES STEWART

- Do you know my favorite actress? ... She was very special in her appearance, her voice was exquisite and far away, almost like an echo. She was an excellent actress, completely unique ... This wonderful voice of hers—strange, fey, mysterious—like a voice singing in the snow.

    LOUISE BROOKS

- A special dream princess.

    HERMAN J. MANKIEWICZ

- With those enormous moonstone grey eyes, the enchanting, guileless smile, darkish blonde hair, and that voice murmuring in the lower register and then breaking crazily in the middle register, she projected a certain vitality from the screen, a rare ability to impart flesh to a role, a fascinating image. Star quality. You could place Maggie, who exuded a rare kind of sensuous innocence, in the category with Janet Gaynor, Jean Arthur, Olivia de Havilland, Grace Kelly.

    MAURICE ZOLOTOW

GLORIA SWANSON (1899–1983)

- She is a sullen, opaque creature, an unknowable, but as enkindled as a young lioness.

    ADELA ROGERS ST JOHNS

- There's a reincarnative force there. Gloria is special. I feel she is an old soul trying to remember its former lives. She makes all the Americans around her seem *young* by comparison.

    ELINOR GLYN

- Gloria, how you wear me out! Where do you get all this energy?

    GRETA GARBO

- She is courageous in a business where courage is as necessary as beauty and artistry. She has had to fight every inch of her way to her present high place in pictures. But there always seemed to be something pathetic about courageous, little five and a half inch Gloria.

JAMES R. QUIRK

■ Is there anyone who can flaunt a superb wardrobe with more dash than Gloria Swanson? To the smallest detail of ornament such as a buckle on a headdress, or a wrist trinket, this young woman has a knack of lending to her apparel a certain significance of modernity that makes you unconsciously think that whatever she happens to put on is, of course, the very latest thing.

MARSHALL NEILAN

■ Miss Swanson does more whole-souled and convincing acting than ever we have seen her do in all the years we have admired her [in *The Love of Sunya*]. Furthermore, we never had any idea that she was so beautiful . . . we decided the only way to describe her is to say that she is at least three Greta Garbos, and let it go at that.

HARRIETT UNDERHILL

■ Hollywood has called me in turn the Clothes Horse, the Old Grey Mare—and Death of a Saleswoman. Since my comeback [in *Sunset Boulevard*], I'm glad to say they've thought up a new title—Gloss.

HERSELF

ANDREI TARKOVSKY (born 1932)

■ But the pictorial stasis . . . appeared to harden, with the progress of Tarkovsky's career, into a series of stills; watching *Stalker* . . . was in fact like spending three hours on the Circle Line, and the

last two films seemed to me pretty nearly calcified. 'What *The Sacrifice* is after', we are told, [by Mark Le Fanu] 'is to capture pure poetic states of soul . . . I observed many people weeping at the end.' I observed even more people sleeping.

ANTHONY LANE

FRANK TASHLIN (1913–1972)

■ Tashlin indulges in a riot of poetic fancies where charm and comic invention alternate in a constant felicity of expression.

JEAN-LUC GODARD

LILYAN TASHMAN (1899–1934)

■ She was a great friend of mine and a very diverting creature. Before this, she'd played heavies. They never let her be as amusing on the screen as she was in real life. I was able to relax her, and that's why we got a good deal of her personality, outrageous and cheerful and good-hearted. Very dashing and gotten up, too!

GEORGE CUKOR

JACQUES TATI (1908–1982)

■ Perhaps he is simply another sketch talent hopelessly stretched out of shape by the relentless pull through time and space of the feature film.

ANDREW SARRIS

ELIZABETH TAYLOR (born 1932)

■ Mr Brown has also drawn some excellent performances from his cast, especially from little Elizabeth Taylor, who plays

199

the role of the horse-loving girl. Her face is alive with youthful spirit, her voice has the softness of sweet song and her whole manner in this picture is one of refreshing grace.

BOSLEY CROWTHER, 1944

■ She has a knack for choosing men who are bothersome and hurtful.

RICHARD BROOKS

■ Wobbling her enormous derriere across the screen [in *Hammersmith is Out*] in a manner so offensive it would bring litigation from any dignified, self-respecting performer, and saying lines like: 'I'm the biggest mother of them all,' inspires pity instead of laughs. She has been announcing plans to retire from the screen. Now is as good a time as any.

REX REED, 1972

200

■ ... forthcoming, frank, and completely natural. In a woman as celebrated for her beauty as she was, it surprised me to find hardly a trace of vanity. She would change her clothes several times a day; ... but that was not vanity. She just enjoyed it. It was fun. She wore her fame lightly, like a second skin. She never gave me the impression of having to live up to something, as I felt in Richard's case.

JOHN DAVID MORLEY, 1984

■ Elizabeth Taylor was a disaster [in *The Comedians*].

GRAHAM GREENE

■ I love her, not for her breasts, her buttocks or her knees but for her mind. It is inscrutable. She is like a poem.

RICHARD BURTON

■ She'll make life hell as a way of testing you—it's a common thing with all the indestructible Hollywood stars. They

want to find out your breaking point. Elizabeth was belligerent towards me at the start of *Boom* ... Unless she trusts her director completely, to film her is useless.

JOSEPH LOSEY, 1969

■ A pattern [for the Oscar ceremony] was set early in the evening, of the old people showing up the new people, and it followed all the way through to the end, when Elizabeth Taylor materialised in her new-found role as the Queen Mother, the crown jewels hanging down her throat and over a generous splash of bosom, and all in the service of Hollywood.

ANDREW SARRIS, 1970

■ Elizabeth Taylor was famous, at least in legend, for never reading an entire script, just her own lines. No one's had a more fabulous career; maybe she knew something the rest of us didn't.

WILLIAM GOLDMAN

■ The incredibly beautiful and curvaceous Liz Taylor, who disappointed me by having a rather squeaky voice, but you can't have everything, can you, and she had practically everything else in abundance.

STEWART GRANGER

■ I got so sick of starry-eyed close-ups of Elizabeth Taylor [in *A Place in the Sun*] that I could have gagged.

RAYMOND CHANDLER

■ When they try to bring out her regal, dignified qualities, nothing answers ... Her dignity is simply stiff and ladylike, a little girl on her best behaviour. As for her woman of smouldering sexuality in *The Comedians*, one can only cry, in memory of the old days, 'Get on a horse.' Her off-screen personality may have developed in all these directions and more. But her acting closed up shop long ago.

WILFRED SHEED

■ It's particularly sad that Elizabeth Taylor was unavailable to resume the role [in *International Velvet*]. Even at her latter-day worst, she's a far more compelling presence than Nanette Newman. Better still, she might have given Tatum more than a few pointers about how to grow up gracefully on the big screen.

FRANK RICH

■ *Ash Wednesday* is so bad that even Liz Taylor's performance becomes almost inconspicuous in it.

JOHN SIMON

■ Remember that there isn't anything more important than the sleep and rest of Elizabeth Taylor.

EDDIE FISHER

■ Basically she's a lazy girl, but a real professional in front of the camera. She brings to the role the kind of emotional intensity you can use. You have to dig for it, but it's there.

JOSEPH L. MANKIEWICZ

■ Liz is the only woman I have ever met who turns me on. She feels like the other half of me.

MONTGOMERY CLIFT

■ She's indestructible.

ROCK HUDSON

■ She is the single greatest press agent who ever lived. She knows how to turn adversity into prosperity.

ALEXANDER COHEN

ROBERT TAYLOR (1911–1969)

■ I had no trouble at all with him. He did everything I asked him to; he was wonderful . . . I have never gotten along with actors.

WILLIAM A. WELLMAN

SHIRLEY TEMPLE (born 1928)

■ During this depression, when the spirit of the people is lower than at any other time, it is a splendid thing that for just 15 cents an American can go to a movie and look at the smiling face of a baby and forget his troubles.

FRANKLIN D. ROOSEVELT, 1935

■ She knows all the tricks. She backs me out of the camera, blankets me, crabs my laughs—she's making a stooge out of me. Why, if she were forty years old and on stage all her life, she wouldn't have had time to learn all she knows about acting. Don't ask me how she does it. You've heard of chess champions at eight and violin virtuosos at ten. Well, she's Ethel Barrymore at six.

ADOLPHE MENJOU

■ She was a nice kid, with a really wonderful mother and father. We all liked her. But she was brilliant. She knew everyone's dialogue, and if you forgot a line, she gave it to you. We all *hated* her for that.

ALICE FAYE, 1987

■ . . . so amazing is the talent and persuasiveness of the most famous of baby actresses, that each time I am slowly won over by her remarkable expertness and filled with admiration. In her guileless baby fashion she is as much a technician of the drama as Elisabeth

201

Bergner, and every trick she manages is a miracle of persuasiveness.

RICHARD WATTS JR

■ After viewing the ingenuous performances of child actors in postwar French and Italian films, the art of Shirley Temple, in retrospect, at times appears mechanical and mannered. For her contemporaries, however, it was the content of her characterisation—the surfeit of sweetness and light—which sometimes met with criticism, seldom her execution, which was almost universally considered masterful.

NORMAN J. ZIEROLD

■ Shirley Temple was difficult. I used to have to go down to Palm Beach to coach her, and she'd get involved in a badminton game with me, and her father would call her and she'd say 'I'm not ready and *I'll* tell you when I'm ready. *I* earn all the money in this household.' Of course she's a different type of person now.

JULE STYNE

■ To claim Shirley Temple (seen winsomely patronising towards a coloured family) as an insult to the black race was a gross piece of arrogation: she was an insult to the entire race.

PHILIP PURSER

■ Shirley Temple was a sort of totem-figure in my childhood and I have longed to see her with an adult eye and without the mixture of envy, despair, fury and boiling admiration with which she once filled little girls. For she was everything one wasn't—poised, perfect, childish and at the same time unchildlike in her supreme self-confidence, and somehow

horrifically ageless, for while we grew she stayed the same.

ISABEL QUIGLEY

IRVING THALBERG (1899–1936)

■ Thalberg was intelligent enough. I remember very well he said to me one time, 'This picture [*Hallelujah*] may not make a dime but MGM can afford to make some experimental films.' He was that intelligent and it was true; they were making enough films and enough money that they could take a chance to open up some new fields.

KING VIDOR

GENE TIERNEY (born 1920)

■ It [*On the Riviera*] was all made in Hollywood. Gene Tierney was terribly photogenic. She had her problems, but she was a nice girl and is still a beautiful woman.

WALTER LANG

MIKE TODD (1907–1958)

■ I was hag-ridden by an indescribable megalomaniac named Mike Todd, a combination of Quasimodo and P. T. Barnum.

S. J. PERELMAN, 1956

GREGG TOLAND (1904–1948)

■ A great and happy influence on my work. Usually photography doesn't influence direction but Toland's deep-focus work did because we were able to let the audience do its own cutting . . . But if the photography allows you to see all four actors in one shot and in sharp focus, reacting to each other within the same shot, you've gained the opportunity to use a big close-up at the most important point. In this way Toland improved upon my direction.

WILLIAM WYLER

SPENCER TRACY (1900–1967)

■ I remember Spencer Tracy, who was one of the great film actors, telling me that when he was a young man in New York, he would wait outside a certain theatre at a certain time just to see Lionel Barrymore leave. He couldn't afford to see him act on the stage but at least he could watch and see him walk out of the theatre. I think this is terribly important.

ROBERT RYAN

■ Spence is the best we have, because you don't see the mechanism at work.

HUMPHREY BOGART

■ The guy's good. There's nobody in the business who can touch him, and you're a fool to try. And the bastard knows it, so don't fall for that humble stuff!

CLARK GABLE

■ I remember him working out this business of nut cracking, to be performed all during Gable's big scene [in *Test Pilot*], which he worked out very carefully all night long. Christ, he used up five pounds of nuts, and then he pretended on the set it had just occurred to him. It was perfectly timed so he would never crack a nut on Clark's line, but you would always have to cut to him.

JOSEPH L. MANKIEWICZ

■ I've learned more about acting from watching Tracy than in any other way.

LAURENCE OLIVIER, 1981

■ Spence was a master of phrasing. He could take a horrible line and phrase it so that it sounded very good. But all of a sudden he would give a reading which would give completely the wrong meaning . . . I would discuss it with him, but again not directly, because he was like Bogey. They were both men of pride, and you had to be very careful not to prick it, not to let them think they'd failed.

EDWARD DMYTRYK

■ Directing Mr Tracy amounts to telling him you're ready to start a scene. He hasn't let me down yet, and if he does, perhaps we'll get acquainted.

HAROLD S. BUCQUET

■ It was always Tracy and Hepburn. I chided him once about his insistence on first billing. 'Why not?' he asked. 'Well, after all,' I argued, 'she's the lady. You're the man. Ladies first?' He said, 'This is a movie, chowderhead, not a lifeboat.'

GARSON KANIN

■ The best film actor we ever had.

BURT REYNOLDS

■ As if [in *Guess Who's Coming to Dinner*, knowing it was his last film] he were saying over our heads to generations of actors not yet born, 'Here's how to seem to listen,' 'Here is how to dominate a scene by walking away from it.'

BRENDAN GILL

■ There was no barrier between Spence and the audience. In other words, he could just do it and he wasn't putting anything on at all. I think the secret of any artist is to have no barrier between the truth and themselves and the audience . . . But he was in a class almost

203

by himself. A consummate artist, his criticism was always brilliant.

KATHARINE HEPBURN

■ If I am to be remembered for anything I have done in this profession, I would like it to be for the four films in which I directed Spencer Tracy.

STANLEY KRAMER

■ What an actor should be is exemplified, for me, by him. I like the reality of his acting. It's so honest and seems so effortless, even though what Tracy does is the result of damn hard work and extreme concentration. Actually, the ultimate in any art is never to show the wheels grinding. The essence of bad acting, for example, is shouting. Tracy never shouts. He's the greatest movie actor there ever was.

RICHARD WIDMARK

■ Spencer does it, that's all. Feels it. Says it. Talks. Listens. He means what he says when he says it, and if you think that's easy, try it.

HUMPHREY BOGART

■ We were shooting a scene and I had nothing to do—just stand around. . . . I happened to be standing in the wrong place or something, and he looked and said, 'Who the fuck do you think is the star of this picture?' I said, 'Oh, Spence, come on.' Then he got embarrassed. That's the other side of Tracy. He could be very petty and egomaniacal.

RICHARD WIDMARK

■ I also liked Spencer Tracy . . . although think it a bit excessive to describe him as the greatest film actor. What he had was a deliberate, delicate mechanism

that could cogently envisage a vast area of experience.

PAUL SCOFIELD

■ The kind of actor I like to watch. The way he holds back—then darts in to make the point, darts back.

MARLON BRANDO

■ Spencer was a typical American product, he never gussied it up. He just did it, he let it ride along on its enormous simplicity. That's what was absolutely thrilling about Spencer's acting. . . . There was something unguarded . . . like an animal or child. It just got to me. That is the kind of actor I would like to be.

KATHARINE HEPBURN

■ It's not exactly true that Tracy was an actor without mannerisms (his superb nonchalance is the most elegant kind of mannerism) and there are films (notably *Without Love*) that might have been helped by an artificiality that didn't interest him.

VINCENT CANBY

■ Tracy as a man had many personal and emotional problems but that is not what came through on the screen. This is a paradox I won't attempt to explain here. Perhaps the answer is one of successful compensation. I do know that actors who have some sort of emotional problem going on underneath seem to give a more interesting performance on top.

KING VIDOR

■ One day there was Tracy walking right in front of me. He turned around and said, 'Who are you? Why are you always hanging around?' I said, 'I'm an actor.' And he looked at me and said. 'An actor,

204

huh?', and did that great wink. 'Just remember not to ever let anyone catch you at it.'

BURT REYNOLDS

■ *Judgement at Nuremberg* . . . gave me the joy of knowing Spencer Tracy. What a man! There was never anyone like him and there never will be. If he gave so much worth to his roles it's precisely because he was a man of true worth.

MARLENE DIETRICH

JOHN TRAVOLTA (born 1954)

■ He is the street Tyrone Power.

ALLAN CARR

■ Maybe the major thing is how sensual he is. And how sexy too. The sensitivity and the sexuality are very strong. It's as if he has every dichotomy—masculinity, femininity, refinement, crudity. You see him, you fall in love a little bit.

LILY TOMLIN

■ John is the perfect star for the 1970s. He has this strange androgynous quality, this all-pervasive sexuality. Men don't find him terribly threatening. And women, well . . .

LORNE MICHAELS

■ He's not a dancer. What he did in those dance scenes was very attractive but he is basically not a dancer. I was dancing like that years ago, you know. Disco is just jitterbug.

FRED ASTAIRE

■ John Travolta is an extraordinary young performer—part colt, part garage hand, half Achilles, half heel—a kind of centaur of the street-corners. His face and figure, indeed his name, seem to hold in balance the forces of attraction and repulsion. Like many swoon-idols, he looks not quite finished, as if waiting for that varnish of admiration only an audience can supply.

ALAN BRIEN

■ The closest we've had to me lately is John Travolta. Whether he'll want to work hard enough on his dancing I don't know. Travolta moves well, but the facts of dancing life mean that you have to work very hard to keep up the level you're already at.

GENE KELLY

JEAN-LOUIS TRINTIGNANT (born 1930)

■ I adore working with him. He's so generous, he doesn't play only for himself, but for his partner. He's also concerned with everyone on a set. That's why the technicians have great respect and tenderness for him.

CATHERINE DENEUVE

FRANÇOIS TRUFFAUT (1932–1984)

■ He's now making the sort of films he used to rail against when he was a critic.

CLAUDE CHABROL

■ I suppose he was the first director, the first film person, with whom I'd enjoyed having a conversation about film, or the hope of film. There weren't many about in those days.

NICHOLAS ROEG

■ I like Truffaut personally, but I don't think he's a good film-maker. *The Bride Wore Black*, his homage to Hitchcock, only proved he never learned anything from watching Hitchcock films.

JAMES POE

LANA TURNER (born 1920)

- Probably the very worst actress that ever made it to the top.

JOHN CROMWELL, 1969

- The real Lana Turner is the Lana Turner everyone knows about. She always wanted to be a Movie Star, and loved being one. Her personal life and her movie star life are one.

ADELA ROGERS ST JOHN

- . . . couldn't act her way out of her form-fitting cashmeres.

TENNESSEE WILLIAMS

206

TWIGGY (born 1949)

- She was only a tiny beam of pathos in a *Walpurgisnacht* of self-indulgence [*The Boyfriend*].

SANDY WILSON

LIV ULLMAN (born 1939)

- When you then add to this disturbing immediacy Liv's uncanny relationship with the movie camera, something else happens. Insidiously, she enters the audience's lives and becomes a centre for every floating fantasy. To the women, she is the woman they think they are or would be; to the men, she is all the women they have known or would like to know.

A. ALVAREZ, 1975

- I saw Liv on television being interviewed by Dick Cavett. I felt her power at once,

more than in any of her films. Her face had a ravishing sensuality. Those blue eyes were veiled. She was amiable, a bit coquettish, saying kittenish little words, but there was a panther underneath. She could have swallowed Cavett in one gulp.

SAMSON RAPHAELSON, 1977

- I'd seen Miss Ullman in Ingmar Bergman's films, so when Mike Frankovitch phoned and told me he had a picture with her as leading lady I said 'I'll do it.' 'Hey, wait a minute,' Mike said, 'You don't have the leading part. Hadn't you better read the script?' I said 'No, it doesn't matter. I'll do it.' I just wanted to work with her.

GENE KELLY

- She'll be doing a scene and then suddenly you'll see the most amazing things pass across her face. You can't believe they're happening. She has this diary which she writes in Norwegian, in long-hand, noting down everything she does, everything she feels. It's a very intense thing—I suppose she got it from Bergman.

ANTHONY HARVEY

- Liv Ullman, so fascinating in Bergman's films, registers with all of the impact of boiled ham on white bread in the Hollywood-made *Lost Horizon* and *40 Carats*. Is this her fault? Does it mean she's really a lousy actress? Probably not. Yet it makes us re-evaluate some of the things we've thought about her in the past.

VINCENT CANBY

- I've always wanted to make a film with Liv Ullman. She's such a marvellous actress and such a happy lady. She's always laughing and yet, like Ingrid Bergman she has these great Nordic shadows.

ANTHONY HARVEY

■ The older one gets in this profession, the more people there are with whom one would never work again.

HERSELF

PETER USTINOV (born 1921)

■ The basis of his acting palette is compassion. He doesn't have to work at it, it's just there, a part of his own nature. This is particularly true of his work in films; his characters are humane, and no matter how comical they are never grotesque.

KARL MALDEN

■ You can't hide your inner self from the camera for long. With Peter, the humanity in the man comes across and you feel bound to respond to it. There's a line in *The Merchant of Venice* to the effect that a man who has no music in himself is fit for treasons, stratagems and spoils. You could say the same about a man who has no warmth. Peter has enough for a lot of people.

SAM JAFFE

RUDOLF VALENTINO (1895–1926)

■ His acting is largely confined to protruding his large, almost occult eyes until the vast areas of white are visible, drawing back the lips of his wide, sensuous mouth to bare his gleaming teeth, and flaring his nostrils.

ADOLPH ZUKOR

■ He was essentially a highly respectable young man; his predicament touched me. Here was one who was catnip to women . . . he had youth and fame . . . and yet he was very unhappy.

H. L. MENCKEN

■ That Valentino was certainly a very splendid fellow. And his unique glamour was not entirely due to the fact that he was unhampered by banal dialogue. Modern dialogue is not always banal, and the screen hero who could match Valentino's posturing technique with an equally polished vocal technique has a perfectly fair chance of becoming his romantic peer. It was his magnetism and dignity that assured him a peak of magnificent isolation.

JAMES MASON

■ Nita Naldi's vamp [in *Blood and Sand*] was wild and rather marvellous—sheer ham, but played with an elan and an animal quality that made it work. But in trying to match his emotional peaks to hers, Valentino overacted badly, resorting to nostril-quivering and other facial contortions which suggested that he was in pain rather then ecstasy.

WILLIAM K. EVERSON

207

W. S. VAN DYKE II (1889–1943)

■ Woody was a great friend—a great director—he shot in a great hurry, a tall skinny guy who liked his booze.

WILLIAM A. WELLMAN

■ Woody Van Dyke used to get very spontaneous performances out of people because he would take it and he'd say, 'Okay. Print it.' If you said, 'Oh, please, can we do it again? I wish I had done it differently,' he'd say,'Well, you should have thought of it sooner.' . . . perhaps I was a better actress than I thought I was, or perhaps we all were, because the results were always very fresh and good.

MAUREEN O'SULLIVAN

JEAN VIGO (1905–1934)

■ The cinema's Rimbaud, not only because of his brief career but also because of his peculiarly personal mode of expression, the vividness of his imagery, his compelling lyricism, and the directness of his language.

GEORGES SADOUL, 1965

LUCHINO VISCONTI (1906–1976)

208

■ He has an aristocratic manner. If you go to dine at Visconti's, you have a footman to each chair, wearing white gloves with a crest on them. You also have the most fantastic meal. . . . he is utterly regal— yet he has this remarkable awareness of people's feelings, and who they are and what they are—like the fishermen in *La Terra Trema* and the two people in *Senso*. He knows the family in *Rocco*.

DIRK BOGARDE, 1973

■ Visconti is very difficult to work with, but at the same time he is a marvellous director. He's a bit of a tyrant, because he knows exactly what he wants—and that's it.

FARLEY GRANGER, 1974

■ I hate melodrama as in the films of a director like Visconti. Melodrama is the easiest thing in the world to do.

MICHELANGELO ANTONIONI, 1975

■ The film [*Senso*] bears the authentic Visconti stamp; like all his previous work it has brought to the screen something wholly original and new, whilst remaining true to the themes he has previously developed. The direction itself is masterly; the decors, costumes and colours are in faultless taste. The elaborate angles and composition of the images show not only an aesthetic but a dramatic concern.

ALAIN TANNER

JON VOIGHT (born 1939)

■ Jon agonises his way toward every decision; what his next movie should be; whether to go out to lunch. He's a good, tortured person.

JANE FONDA, 1982

■ Voight brings a sincerity and a winning naivete to the shambling, untidy young thinker [in *The Revolutionary*] who's not above going home for a bit of bourgeois comfort or doing a little social-climbing cum seduction; his charm is his uncertainty, his seriousness, his essential youngness.

JUDITH CRIST

■ To filmgoers who recall Valentino's Latin swank, Gable's derisive charm, or Bogart's fake-hard arrogance, Jon Voight must seem a remarkably ordinary Hollywood creation . . . His face, at first sight anyway, has the agreeable neutrality of a male model . . . But in Joe Buck, the inexpert Texan hustler [of *Midnight Cowboy*], he may even have created a classic figure of the cinema, ranking with the durable Captain Bligh, Rhett Butler, and *Streetcar's* Stanley Kowalski.

PETER EVANS

■ I think that Jon Voight is a brilliant actor, he's really a *star*. I didn't particularly like *Midnight Cowboy*, but his performance was remarkable. Jon has a problem in knowing what parts to choose, which we all have. It's 50% of the job.

MALCOLM McDOWELL

JOSEF VON STERNBERG (1894–1969)

■ It was apparent that von Sternberg and Marlene had a very close professional relationship ... But it was only, in my experience, professional, without any love element. ... I got along with von Sternberg reasonably well, as all his direction and his instructions were given to Marlene, and the rest of us were left more or less to do as well as we could. I cannot remember that he ever told me how to play a scene.

GARY COOPER

■ Exasperated, I ventured to suggest that Sternberg's choice of subject matter was not exactly distinguished; he was notorious for basing his movies on cheap melodrama.

LUIS BUÑUEL

■ But Josef was a strange guy. He made a couple of great films and became very hard to get along with.

WILLIAM CLOTHIER

ERICH VON STROHEIM (1885–1957)

■ In my opinion, there were only two directors in Hollywood who made films without regard to box-office success: Von Stroheim and myself.

FRITZ LANG, 1977

■ He was fascinating, *le grand seigneur* at all times, ... Of course he influenced me as a director: ... When I first saw him at the wardrobe tests for his role as Rommel [in *Five Graves to Cairo*], I clicked my heels and said 'Isn't it ridiculous, little me, directing you? You were always ten years ahead of your time.' And he replied 'Twenty'.

BILLY WILDER

■ A figure at once superb and pathetic: an artist with integrity, a supreme contempt for conventions and a disastrous inability to be practical; a man with courage, arrogance and, from the beginnings of his career, with grievances so overwhelming that recriminations became second nature to him.

CATHERINE DE LA ROCHE

209

■ The experience of working with him was unlike any I had had in more than 50 pictures. He was so painstaking and slow that I would lose all sense of time, hypnotised by the man's relentless perfectionism.

GLORIA SWANSON

■ I believe that he was a man profoundly wounded, profoundly abused, who stubbornly insisted on acting, to offer an image of himself, an image which producers could purchase and for which he had the greatest contempt ... In his personal life he was a megalomaniac.

CHARLES SPAAK

MAX VON SYDOW (born 1929)

■ He was the unqualified front runner— the most generous man I've ever met. And he had such a lovely light sense of humour. I consider it a privilege to have worked with him.

JULIE ANDREWS, 1967

ANTON WALBROOK (1900–1967)

■ Anton Walbrook, who was also in the play [*Design for Living*], was a gentle man with a rather heavy *Gotterdammerung* personality, not in my opinion God's gift to the comedy stage. . . . whenever I was off I played New Orleans jazz flat out in my dressing room. Anton, poor man, was next door, and I used to hear his groans over the uproar of my machine. If only I had liked Bach, or Beethoven . . .

REX HARRISON, 1974

210   JERRY WALD (1911–1962)

■ His greatest asset was his enthusiasm. He shot out ideas like bullets. . . . After a day at the studio he'd go home and watch a movie through dinner and then another. I was often at his home while he took notes after seeing a film. He had this tremendous wall of files in his study containing hundreds of possible film subjects all indexed and cross-referenced. Fantastic. He was an unusual man.

CURTIS BERNHARDT

■ He was a vulgar, nice man. He was what we used to think of as the typical Hollywood producer. Now that I look back, he's Jesus Christ by comparison to some of the people I see today at the studios. The barracudas have taken over. He was a saint. And he was a smart cookie, too.

RAY BRADBURY

RAOUL WALSH (1887–1980)

■ I've been very lucky in the men I've worked with. . . . Raoul Walsh—the heartiness and lustiness he gave to pictures I thought was tremendous.

JOHN WAYNE

JULIE WALTERS (born 1950)

■ It [*Educating Rita*] was wonderful, I did it with Julie Walters, the original girl. She is sensational, really fantastic, and she is a very nice person as well which is always a bonus.

MICHAEL CAINE

WALTER WANGER (1894–1968)

■ Walter Wanger was a man who always wanted to be European. He didn't know how to be European but he wanted to be European so this [*The Reckless Moment*] was rather the kind of film—I suppose, like *Brief Encounter*—that he was trying to make, but it wasn't very good.

JAMES MASON, 1970

■ He was a rarity among producers. He encouraged creativity. He wasn't only interested in protecting himself, which is what most producers do.

DON SIEGEL, 1973

■ The reports were true about what Walter Wanger said when I won the Academy Award. He said, 'Thank God, now we can all relax. Susie finally got what she's been chasing for twenty years.' I was glad I got the award for *I Want To Live!* because it was Walter's picture. I was devoted to that man.

SUSAN HAYWARD

JACK L. WARNER (1892–1978)

■ Once I had a terrible fight with Jack
Warner, who asked me what I thought
of a picture I had done with Humphrey
Bogart. I told him I didn't go to see it.
Mr Warner was furious. I said that I only
get paid for making pictures. If he wanted
me to see them, he'd have to pay me
extra.

PETER LORRE

JOHN WAYNE (1907–1979)

■ The problem is, he's a very set guy.
Stubborn as hell. . . . I told him, 'Look,
I'm a goddamn sight better director than
you are and you're a goddamn sight
better actor than I am. And you, coming
back here and doing my work is going
to be just as foolish as my going up and
doing your personality with that lousy
fairy walk that you've got. So behave
yourself and we'll make a picture.'

WILLIAM A. WELLMAN

■ We had it quite clear from the start that
I was producer and director. He was
delighted to surrender all managerial
rights and be just an actor in this film.
He was as happy as a twenty–year–old
and he called me 'Sir' right the way
through the shooting. Me! He's been a
star for more years than I've even been
alive.

MARK RYDELL, 1974

■ John has only one kind of theatrical
experience, the movies. He became an
outdoor movie star and remained one.
But he is a true artist and real wit. He is
not lacking in true talent. He is a most
sensitive creature.

KATHARINE HEPBURN

■ He is as tough as an old nut and as soft
as a yellow ribbon.

ELIZABETH TAYLOR, 1978

■ He wasn't as clever as Spence, but a
brilliant actor nonetheless, bigger than
life in his performance—and often when
he didn't have to be.

KATHARINE HEPBURN

■ Wayne was a stickler at work. He was
fine if he realised you knew what you
were doing. But if you weren't prepared,
or fluffed anything, and fortunately I
never did, well, then you could be in
trouble. He *was* tough, but then
so am I!

BURT KENNEDY

■ I certainly would have given anything to
have worked with John Wayne. He's the
most attractive man who ever walked the
earth, I think.

BETTE DAVIS, 1974

■ John Wayne was a star because he
always played John Wayne. Frankly, he
wasn't an excellent actor, but good
heavens, what a star! It wasn't John
Wayne who served the roles: the roles
served John Wayne.

KIRK DOUGLAS

■ A recent poll showed that more people
recognised John Wayne's name and face
than any other man in US history, except
Abraham Lincoln.

JIM BEAVER

■ I play John Wayne in every part
regardless of the character, and I've been
doing okay, haven't I?

HIMSELF

■ Wayne endures and is here to stay,
whether he is wanted or not; a dubious

211

American hero but undoubtedly a remarkable screen presence.

GRAHAM FULLER

■ How can I hate John Wayne upholding [politician Barry] Goldwater and yet love him tenderly when abruptly he takes Natalie Wood into his arms in the last reel of *The Searchers*?

JEAN-LUC GODARD

■ His performance [in *The Conqueror*] drunk or sober was the way other actors tend to perform if drunk.

OSCAR MILLAND

■ John Wayne has been the success he has been over the years because he does what he does better than anybody else can. A lot of people have said he doesn't really act. Just let them try to act like he does and they'll find they can't do it.

CLINT EASTWOOD

212

■ That's why John Wayne finally became a good actor in *True Grit*: he's got 150 of them [films] behind him. Now he's developed a saltiness and an earthiness and a humour and a subtlety that comes from mining that same vein over and over and over again.

GREGORY PECK

■ Way back on *Red River* he asked my theory about acting and I said, 'Duke, you do two or three good scenes in a picture and don't offend the audience the rest of the time ...' So even today he says, 'What's coming up?' and I say, 'This is one of the ones that you're liable to offend them. Get it over with as soon as you can. Don't do anything.'

HOWARD HAWKS

■ Duke hasn't any patience with anybody: his family, other actors, anybody. If

you've got a Big Name Star, he'll keep quiet; ... Howard Keel on *The War Wagon*, I remember. One day Duke started pushing him around, grabbing him, showing him how to play the scene. ... After the scene was over, ... [Keel said] 'if he puts his hands on me again, I'm gonna clobber that son of a bitch.'

WILLIAM CLOTHIER

■ Intellectually, John Wayne is rather barren. He has little liking for any of the classical arts. His home is filled with a hodgepodge of expensive nick-nacks ... In art, he has a few things, selected without knowledge of their quality. ... [he has a] habit of reading encyclopedic literature. Any other reading he does is entirely in the interest of his profession— making motion pictures.

JAMES HENAGHAN

■ He wasn't your friend in those days, but you knew exactly where he stood. He was out in the open. I don't care about his politics and I don't expect him to care about mine. ... But the point is he shows up on the goddamn set, knowing his lines and ready to work. He's the first to arrive and the last to leave. I have actively looked for a picture on which we could work together.

MARTIN RITT

SIGOURNEY WEAVER (born 1949)

■ I like her very much. She's just a natural. Not too exotic. Very hard-nosed, intelligent. And flawed too, in the sense that she is flawed by emotion. People root for her in *Alien* because she's so often coming up with the logical solution to some problem and then it just won't work.

JAMES CAMERON

JOHNNY WEISMULLER (1904–1979)

■ I could never feel much sympathy for Cheetah the Chimp—who was really rather queer, I'm afraid. Didn't like girls at all. But he adored Johnny Weismuller and was terribly jealous of me.

MAUREEN O'SULLIVAN

RAQUEL WELCH (1887–1980)

■ I have never met anyone so badly behaved.

JAMES MASON

■ She's silicone from the knees up.

GEORGE MASTERS

■ I still don't believe that Raquel Welch really exists. She has been manufactured by the media merely to preserve the sexless plasticity of sex objects for the masses.

ANDREW SARRIS

■ Raquel Welch is not the type of girl who is likely to be left as the only sex symbol on the set without literary involvement. At some point, Miss Welch and/or her advisers must have decided that she should be presented as not just a sex goddess but an intelligent sex goddess— not just shrewd but thoughtful and intellectual.

CALVIN TRILLIN

■ She isn't an actress of fathomless talent, but she is very professional and hard-working. It's just the strange way people are brought up in America, to promote themselves before the character.

PETER YATES

TUESDAY WELD (born 1943)

■ Tuesday was a dream to work with. She seemed to have an instinct for how to act a scene. I also noticed she seemed to be heading for serious trouble. ... it was apparent stardom was well within her grasp, but she conducted herself in a manner that made you think she was just another Hollywood joke—and I followed her career—it was as though she were some dizzy blonde who had no idea about what she was doing.

DANNY KAYE

■ She's a complicated lady and a gifted one ... she finally does emerge in this picture [*Play It As It Lays*]. She's really so good in this, so super, *and* as far as her behaviour is concerned, her comportment, she was just flawless—I mean just a perfect child. She was there every day, on time, and worked like a tremendous professional. All that talk about her being a terror—not a trace.

FRANK PERRY

ORSON WELLES (1915–1986)

■ You should cross yourself when you say his name.

MARLENE DIETRICH

■ It's like meeting God without dying.

DOROTHY PARKER

■ It never occurs to him that there is any solution other than his own. Despite yourself, you find yourself accepting this notion.

HERMAN J. MANKIEWICZ

■ You cannot battle an elephant. Orson was such a *big* man in every way that no one could stand up to him. On the first day ... at 4 o'clock, he strode in followed by his agent, a dwarf, his valet and a whole entourage. Approaching us, he proclaimed, 'All right, everybody turn

213

to page eight.' And we did it (though he was not the director).

JOAN FONTAINE

■ The oldest enfant terrible in the world.

PAUL HOLT

■ There, but for the grace of God, goes God.

HERMAN J. MANKIEWICZ

■ Every time I bring out a new movie, nobody bothers to review it . . . They don't review my work, they review me.

HIMSELF

■ During *Magnificent Ambersons*, Orson Welles, drunk on Joe Cotten's Machiavellian martinis, secretly sending his chauffeur home and pleading no transport, would I drive him? Gad, what a drive. I prayed for a policeman. Six feet four, 250 pounds, and what seemed like six hands in my shirt.

ANNE BAXTER

■ Awesome Orson, the self-styled genius.

LOUELLA PARSONS

■ An active loafer, a wise madman.

JEAN COCTEAU

■ A superb bravura director, a fair bravura producer, and a limited bravura writer; but an incomparable bravura personality.

KENNETH TYNAN

■ We were talking about Renoir one day on the set, and Orson said, very touchingly, that Renoir was a great man but that unfortunately, Renoir didn't like his pictures. And then he said 'Of course, if I were Renoir, I wouldn't like my pictures either.'

MIKE NICHOLS

■ Orson must have been about 22 then [making *Citizen Kane*], and I still think

he's one of the greatest directors in the world. I don't know why people regard him as a difficult man. He was the easiest, most inspiring man I've ever worked with. He was the only one who seemed to know what he was doing because we were all virgins on that picture.

JOSEPH COTTEN

■ I wanted him and he did it [*The Black Rose*] on the basis that he was preparing a picture and could he bring a couple of writers with him. But Jesus Christ! Before we knew it, he had a house and he had about ten people with him and it was murder to get him out of there to go to work—all he'd do was work on his own picture.

HENRY HATHAWAY, 1970

■ I had been crazy about Orson—in the Forties when he was married to Rita Hayworth and when we toured doing his magic act—I was crazy about him— we were great friends, you know, but nothing. . . . Because Orson doesn't like blond women. He only likes dark women. And suddenly when he saw me in this dark wig, he looked at me with new eyes.

MARLENE DIETRICH

■ [On why she divorced him:] I can't take his genius any more.

RITA HAYWORTH

■ He can be both wonderful and impossible, and often, being a born juggler, he will be both at the same moment, so that it seems natural, as one watches the wonders and the impossibilities spinning like mad through the air between his hands, that one should feel, as he doubtless intends one should, a little bewildered.

MICHEÁL MACHIAMMÓIR

■ By any *auteur* principle, *Kane* was Orson's picture. His stamp, his signature is on every frame of it. But he didn't write it. Herman Mankiewicz and I wrote it together. Orson claimed differently and that's where the trouble began.

JOHN HOUSEMAN

■ The man on the cinema's conscience.

PENELOPE HOUSTON

■ On the first night [of *Macbeth* in Paris] there was a fight in the cinema between the supporters and adversaries of the picture. Indifference would hurt me much more. After all, the film cannot be worthless if people like Jean Cocteau like it. On the other hand, I don't take it as a compliment that the picture is having terrific success in Germany, where people are probably attracted by the medieval savagery of the subject.

HIMSELF

■ Orson spent most of his money on women. That's why he didn't have the money to make films.

EARTHA KITT

■ He was not an extravagant director. I mean, Warren Beatty can spend $60 million making *Reds* half an hour too long and it crosses nobody's lips that that's too much money.

CHARLTON HESTON

■ Since Orson's death all these people have been going on television talking about how dear Orson was. Yet these same stars and whizz kid directors wouldn't help him get one of his movies made. Any one of these people could have made Orson's life so much happier these past 10 years just by nodding their heads. Last Saturday over lunch Orson said,

'When I die, watch them come out of the woodwork. Watch them praise me.'

HENRY JAGLOM

■ Orson Welles, a very funny man, once said to me. 'You know, the French ruin everything. The come up to you and say, "You are one of the three great directors of the cinema" ' Orson said. 'I nod, I nod. "There is D. W. Griffith. There is Orson Welles. And there is Nicholas Ray." ' He said. 'There is always that third name that crushes you.'

GORE VIDAL

WILLIAM A. WELLMAN (1896–1975)

■ I was working with a man, Bill Wellman, who was said to be very difficult. But, no, I found he was wonderful to work with, and we became great friends before the picture was over.

BEULAH BONDI

■ Wild Bill Wellman—a great guy.

WILLIAM CLOTHIER

MAE WEST (1892–1980)

■ She has vitality, style and the unsentimental wit born of total impertinence.

PETER JOHN DYER

■ Her ability to overpower any surroundings was incredible for I found her to be as tiny as I, who couldn't have dominated an anthill. But a corset that pinched her waist pushed a smallish bosom upward and outward until it gave Mae a facade that the most buxom belle might envy.

ANITA LOOS

- She's a tremendous personality. I want to see whether there's anything I can learn from her. It may come in handy sometime.

  INGRID BERGMAN

- Sex is for her an animated cartoon.

  JOHN MASON BROWN

- In a world of Garbos, Barrymores, Harlows, Valentinos and Clara Bows, Mae West is the only type with an ironic edge, a comic spark, that takes on a more cosmopolitan case of life's enjoyments.

  F. SCOTT FITZGERALD

- She is an earthquake, a tornado, an admirable scourge, a sky-rocket, a liberating explosion.

  ADO KYROU

216

- Only Charlie Chaplin and Mae West in Hollywood dare to directly attack with their mockery the greying morals and manners of a dreary world.

  HUGH WALPOLE

- I've learned everything from her. Well, not everything, but almost everything. She knows so much. Her insight is so true. Her timing so perfect, her grasp of a situation so right.

  CARY GRANT

- Actually, while her films reeked of the innuendo and of unspeakable things that had happened in the past—or off-screen—they were fairly decorous in what they actually presented *on* screen. One had to understand sex to begin with to know what Mae's kidding was about.

  WILLIAM K. EVERSON

- We went down to her house for rehearsals. ... And she was always in a sort of pale beige negligee with a train about twenty feet long. That's how we rehearsed every day. And when we'd stop for a breather, we'd sit and talk. She was just plain and simply a sweet old lady, who told me marvellous stories about her life.

  ROCK HUDSON

- 'And who would play Lil?' [in a revival of *Diamond Lil*]. There was an awkward silence, but Miss West was not at all disconcerted. 'Why, I would of course dear. I could do that. I still look like Mae West.' This unaffected recognition of 'Mae West' as a product, to be protected, developed, marketed, and functionally quite separate from her own private self, has carried her through a lot, and continues to do so.

  JOHN RUSSELL TAYLOR, 1977

- I told her that she was one of the three greatest talents ever to come out of the movies, the other two being W. C. Fields and Chaplin. She said, 'Umm, well, I don't know about Fields.'

  TENNESSEE WILLIAMS

- She is presented as a national institution, rather like having Dwight D. Eisenhower on the set [of *Myra Breckinridge*]. There is constant talk of how coolly she delivers her lines, how remarkably young she looks, and how she is the last of the Great Troupers. In fact, she appears somewhat nervous on the set, as if she might be more comfortable looking her age, or at least some specific age. She walks carefully as if coming down too hard on her right foot might cause her left ear to crack and tinkle to the floor.

  CALVIN TRILLIN

- My public expects certain things from me—and I'd never do anything the Mae

West character wouldn't do. I'd never play a mother. I always think of a mother as a wonderful person and I don't often play a wonderful person. You know, I used to be Snow White, but I drifted.

HERSELF

■ When I'm with Mae, life has a rose glow. She makes you feel good. I go and see her to forget about all the crap on this film [*Myra Breckinridge*].

ROBERT FRYER

DAME MAY WHITTY (1865–1948)

■ During the shooting of *Mrs Miniver*, Dame May Whitty had a 'two-shot' with young actor Richard Ney, . . . She asked the handsome new-to-Hollywood actor to react so that the next line would make more sense. Richard replied, 'Of course, Dame May. I shall do as you say, but I think my way is better.' The titled English actress looked down her nose, 'Young man, you haven't got a way!'

JOAN FONTAINE

RICHARD WIDMARK (born 1914)

■ The moment he came into the studio he set the tone.

RACHEL ROBERTS

BILLY WILDER (born 1906)

■ Wilder is the most exciting director of satire in the world. He made films in his early days which were an unequalled mixture of vulgarity and good taste.

ANTHONY HARVEY, 1969

■ Billy Wilder came up to me in a little restaurant and introduced himself and said 'Now, leesen, I got dis film here, and it's a period piece, 'bout a couple of museecians who vitness the St Valentine's Day Massacre, . . . and you're in drag for 85 per cent of the picture. You want to do it?' If Billy called me tomorrow with one line, I would do it because it's the good fortune of even just knowing him. He's one of the most stimulating things in my life. I don't know what it would be like to spend 60 seconds with him that were dull.

JACK LEMMON, 1971

■ It's become very difficult to make a picture. Where are those butchers and scrap iron dealers and illiterate giants that ran the industry now that we need them? Would you believe that one would suddenly wake up in the morning with nostalgia for Louis B. Mayer? Give me a strong man. Give me somebody, but not a committee sitting up there deciding your fate.

HIMSELF, 1978

■ I've had directors who were marvellous at breaking scenes down and handling people. But when you would string all the pearls together, they wouldn't make a beautiful necklace. But Billy is the kind of picture-maker who can make a beautiful string of pearls. He makes the kind of movies that are classics and last forever.

JACK LEMMON

■ Long before Billy Wilder was Billy Wilder, he thought he was Billy Wilder.

MRS BILLY WILDER

■ The wittiest man in Hollywood. And if you really want to know what's going on in Hollywood, see Wilder.

ANDRE PREVIN

217

■ Let's face it, Billy Wilder at work is two people—Mr Hyde and Mr Hyde.

HARRY KURNITZ

MICHAEL WILDING (1912–1979)

■ I'm afraid in those last few years I gave him rather a rough time. Sort of hen-pecked him, and probably wasn't mature enough for him. It wasn't that we had anything to fight over. We just weren't happy.

ELIZABETH TAYLOR, 1970

■ He steals the film [*An Ideal Husband*]. None can match him for his wit, charm and sheer dazzlement of personality.

KENNETH TYNAN

218 ESTHER WILLIAMS (born 1923)

■ Wet, she's a star. Dry, she ain't.

FANNY BRICE

■ She's a dear dame. The only person I know who didn't want a theatrical career—she got into the business by mistake.

CHARLES WALTERS

■ Her films all conspired to lull most viewers into the belief that they were being entertained.

TED SENNETT

ROBIN WILLIAMS (born 1952)

■ I tried to take advantage of Robin's amazing mind, and give him absolute freedom. We went after whatever he was doing. I used a longer lens than usual so the camera wasn't on top of him; it wasn't like those shots that are so handsomely composed that the actor can't step out of the lighting. I just let him work.

BARRY LEVINSON

■ They [the acting school] were trying to mold Robin into a standardised Juilliard product—Kevin Kline is the perfect example of it—but Robin was too special, too original, to be that.

CHRISTOPHER REEVE

DEBRA WINGER (born 1955)

■ Look, Debra is 21 years younger than I am. She has very different interests and different ways of looking at life. Just because you work intimately with someone for three or four months on a film doesn't mean there's any breeding ground for friendship. I don't think there was much of one. She loved to sit in her trailer in her combat boots and miniskirt, listening to real loud rock 'n' roll. Right there, I mean, what am I going to do that for?

SHIRLEY MACLAINE

■ When the chips were down, they were absolutely in each other's corners. [Shirley MacLaine and Debra Winger during the making of *Terms of Endearment*.]

JAMES L. BROOKS

■ Debra Winger now demonstrates [in *Legal Eagles*] that she is one of her generation's few first-rate screen comediennes. She's an original.

VINCENT CANBY

MICHAEL WINNER (born 1935)

■ To say that Michael Winner is his own worst enemy is to provoke a ragged chorus from odd corners of the film industry of 'Not while I'm alive'.

BARRY NORMAN

NORMAN WISDOM (born 1920)

■ Norman Wisdom once said to me: 'And that's where I put the pathos in.' Just like that, as if it were sugar or flour or something.

TONY HANCOCK

GOOGIE WITHERS (born 1917)

■ It [*Back Room Boy*] was, frankly, a good old flat-footed British comedy and nobody paid much attention to it. But Googie was what she has always been— a really fine actress and a good professional. In fact, I've always thought that she was really a cut above the film she made with me.

ARTHUR ASKEY

NATALIE WOOD (1938–1981)

■ The quality I remember about her was a kind of sweetness. When her persona fitted the role you couldn't do better. She was it.

ELIA KAZAN, 1987

JOANNE WOODWARD (born 1930)

■ Joanne, I'd say, is the best of the Actors Studio type of person. She makes the character a part of herself. She draws on her own resources. She deals with her own emotions. She doesn't impose something from the outside on what she's doing. She finds the solutions on the inside, and discovers a way of

materialising it. She's a great great actress who still hasn't reached the limit of her scale.

IRVING KERSHNER, 1969

■ She's a wonderful lady. She has so much strength and love and warmth that you instantly fall into. There isn't any actor ego where she's fighting for a scene. None of that wierd stuff. With Joanne, it's 'How can we make this scene better?' She was just lost in the work, like me.

SALLY FIELD

■ Joanne Woodward, already a proved actress of remarkable range, has never been better [than in *Rachel, Rachel*]. In one red-rimmed close-up, tears seem to happen to her remorselessly, like rain down a windscreen. She mugs, made plain by happiness elsewhere, joyously sucking in her lips to offer a clown's face.

JOHN COLEMAN

■ I have a steak at home, why should I go out for a hamburger?

PAUL NEWMAN

■ Joan Woodward is infallible.

DILYS POWELL

■ Joanne always made it her business to hold back her career while Paul was on the up and up. And that girl is one helluva talented actress. But she knew what side her bread was buttered on and let Paul become the superstar of the family. The result? They're still happily married today.

SHELLEY WINTERS

FAY WRAY (born 1907)

■ When Fay Wray, the greatest screamer in movie history, heard that she was the lucky ingenue that Colonel Merian C.

219

Cooper wanted to cast opposite 'the tallest, darkest leading man in Hollywood,' she naturally conjured up romantic visions of Clark Gable or Gary Cooper.

JAMES WATTERS

WILLIAM WYLER (1902–1981)

■ After 28 takes for a scene in *Jezebel* I said: 'Willy, for the sake of my sanity show me the first take, one in the middle and the one you're using.' I couldn't believe my eyes when I saw myself getting better in each one. After that Willy yelled 'Marrrrvellous!' no matter what I did till I told him to shut up and go back the way it was.

BETTE DAVIS

220

■ I made them [the films]—Willy only directed then.

SAM GOLDWYN

■ I wanted to do a scene over [on *The Big Country*: they were co-producers] because I had delivered my lines badly. Wyler refused to have a retake, so I walked off the set. When I returned he wanted me to apologise in front of the crew, but I wouldn't. We finished the film without saying a single word to each other. We kept the feud going even though our wives tried to patch it up. Finally the opportunity came for a reconciliation when he won the Oscar in 1960 for *Ben-Hur* and I was Academy president. As Wyler walked off stage with his Oscar, I stuck out my hand and said, 'Congratulations, you really deserved it.' He replied, 'Thanks, but I still won't re-shoot that scene.'

GREGORY PECK

JANE WYMAN (born 1914)

■ Miss Wyman is a fine actress, tenderness and restraint being her trump cards, and here [in *So Big*], whether battling singlehanded with a recalcitrant cabbage farm or mourning that her son, a potential emerald, has denied his artistic talents by becoming a successful salesman, she emits a steady effulgence, a glow which warms even the largest screen.

VIRGINIA GRAHAME

MICHAEL YORK (born 1942)

■ Somehow I am now being offered all the parts they used to offer to Michael York— and *I'm* turning them down. They're all right for Michael, I suppose, he hasn't a very large range, after all.

ROBERT POWELL, 1977

SUSANNAH YORK (born 1941)

■ Susannah was the personification of uninformed arrogance of youth.

JOHN HUSTON

GIG YOUNG (1913–1978)

■ Look at Gig Young. I loved him. Not a sweeter man would you ever want to meet in this world. Blew his fucking wife's brains out and his brains out.

GEORGE C. SCOTT

LORETTA YOUNG (born 1913)

■ If you want a place in the sun you have to expect a few blisters.

HERSELF

■ She worked with a full-length mirror beside the camera. I didn't know which Loretta to play to—the one in the mirror or the one that was with me.

ROBERT PRESTON

■ She was and is the only actress I really dislike. She was sickeningly sweet, a pure phoney. Her two faces sent me home angry and crying several times.

VIRGINIA FIELD

DARRYL F. ZANUCK (1902–1979)

■ Darryl was a little nervous of me. He had two categories of women—broads and librarians. I was neither. He was never sure *where* I fitted in. I guess I was lucky because he put me into all kinds of different movies.

ANNE BAXTER

■ He couldn't stand stubbornness in anybody but himself.

MEL GUSSOW

■ Goodbye, Mr Zanuck: it certainly has been a pleasure working at 16th Century Fox.

JEAN RENOIR

■ He has so many yes-men following him around the studio, he ought to put out his hand when he makes a sharp turn.

FRED ALLEN

■ Why doesn't that son of a bitch Darryl Zanuck get himself a striped silk shirt and learn how to play the piano? Then he could work in any room in the house. As much as I couldn't stand some of the old-time moguls—especially Harry Cohn—those men took an interest in the future of their business. They had integrity.

JOHN WAYNE

■ Nobody liked working for Zanuck, the little goddamn Napoleon, always walking round with his polo mallet. Nobody had any respect for him except as an executive. And he was a good editor at one time, but he fancied himself a writer, and he was not a good writer.

JOHN CARRADINE

CESARE ZAVATTINI (born 1902)

■ Reality is not observed for the social facts it may reveal, but for its own sake—for, in Zavattini's phrase, 'the love of reality', the joy and pain of observing human beings as they are. Zavattini's neo-realist technique imposes on the director a severe discipline, most notably in the demand to use non-professional actors. The players are asked not to 'act' but to 'be': the player must become inseparable from the part.

KAREL REISZ

FRANCO ZEFFIRELLI (born 1923)

■ Zeffirelli is a man of great vision and medium talent who's made one or two watchable films and I have a great affection for him now—if I met him today I'd be the first to open a bottle and give him a glass—but I didn't then because he was fucking vicious.

BRUCE ROBINSON

FRED ZINNEMANN (born 1907)

■ He really brings out of me—in a completely different way—an awful lot that perhaps I'd never have the courage to lay bare, to open up. He just knows

221

how to get you to do it, to bring out some inner quality.

DEBORAH KERR, 1972

■ I don't think I've ever seen anyone quite so respected on a set. You don't hear one word against him. He's only small, and very quiet, but when he blows—he blows! In good Austrian fashion. Very rarely, and there has to be a good reason. Normally, you hardly hear him. But when he walks on the set, you know who the guv'nor is.

JOHN HURT

■ Zinnemann managed to dramatise post-war 'problem' situations without glibness or sentimentality. He became an acute and accurate reporter, whose films, made in a mood of rueful urgency, seemed to demand sympathy and understanding of their heroes' problems. Without conventional happy endings these films closed on a hopeful note and implied—without the glibness that a bald statement of their intentions might suggest—that the problems they raised could be met by personal courage and good will.

KAREL REISZ

GEORGE ZUCCO (1886–1960)

■ Good old George Zucco, he of the Satanic smile and eyes that light up like neons every time he conceives of something especially nasty.

WILLIAM K. EVERSON

222

Bibliography

It is partly due to the way the material was collected that the quotations are mainly undated; I did not and do not think—for the most part—that dates are needed.

Grateful acknowledgement is made to the many writers and interviewers who are quoted in this book and to their publishers. The newspapers and magazines concerned are Action, After Dark, American Film, Cahiers du Cinema, Cavalier, Cinéma, Ciné-Revue, Daily Express, The Daily Mail, Daily Mirror, The Daily Telegraph, Esquire, Evening News, Evening Standard, L'Express, Film Comment, Film Dope, Film Fan Monthly, Film Quarterly, Film Review, Films and Filming, Films Illustrated, Films in Review, Financial Times, Focus on Film, Gay Times, The Guardian, Illustrated London News, In Cinema, Independent, Interview, Life, The Listener, Moma Notes, Monthly Film Bulletin, Montreal Star, Movie, The Movie, Moviegoer, The Nation, NFT programmes, News Chronicle, News of the World, New Statesman, Newsweek, New York Daily News, New York Herald Tribune, New York Magazine, New York Post, New York Review of Books, The New York Times, Le Nouvel Observateur, The Observer, Oui, Paris Match, Paris-Metro, People, Picturegoer, Photoplay, Playbill, Playboy, Playgirl, Premiere, Radio Times, Readers Digest, Rolling Stone, Saturday Review, Screen Facts, 7e Art, Sequence, Show, Show Business Illustrated, Sight and Sound, The Silent Picture, The Spectator, The Stage, The Sunday Express, Sunday Telegraph, Sunday Times, Take One, That Certain Age, Theatre Arts Magazine, Time, Time and Tide, Time Out, The Times, Town, TV Guide, Vanity Fair, Variety, The Velvet Light-Trap, Village Voice, You Magazine.

Grateful acknowledgement is also made to:

Ackland, Rodney and Grant, Elspeth *The Celluloid Mistress,* London: Wingate, 1954

Agate, James *Around Cinemas,* London: Home & Van Thal, 1946; *Around Cinemas Second Series,* London: Home & Van Thal, 1948

Agee, James *Agee on Film,* New York: McDowell, Obolensky, 1958; Grosset & Dunlap, 1969

Aherne, Brian *A Proper Job,* Boston: Houghton Mifflin, 1969

Anger, Kenneth *Hollywood Babylon,* San Francisco: Straight Arrow Books, 1975

Arce, Hector *Gary Cooper, An Intimate Biography,* New York: William Morrow, 1979

Arnold, Eve *Marilyn Monroe An Appreciation,* London: Hamish Hamilton, 1987

Astaire, Fred *Steps in Time,* New York: Harper & Bros. 1959

Astor, Mary *A Life on Film,* New York: Delacorte Press, 1967

Bacall, Lauren *By Myself,* London: Jonathan Cape, 1979

Bach, Stephen *Final Cut,* London: Jonathan Cape, 1985

Bacon, James *Hollywood is a Four Letter Town,* New York: Henry Regnery Co, 1976

Bailey, Margaret *Those Glorious Glamour Years,* Secaucus: Citadel Press, 1982

Balcon, Michael *Michael Balcon Presents ... A Life of Films,* London: Hutchinson, 1969

Beaton, Cecil *The Face of the World,* London: Weidenfeld & Nicolson, 1957

Behlmer, Rudy *Memo from David O. Selznick,* New York: Viking, 1972

Bergman, Ingmar *Bergman on Bergman,* Stockholm: Norstadt, 1970

Billquist, Fritiof *Garbo,* New York: G. P. Putnam's Sons, 1960

Blesh, Rudi *Keaton,* New York: Macmillan, 1966

Bogarde, Dirk *An Orderly Man,* London: Chatto & Windus, 1983

Bogdanovich, Peter and Dwan, Allan *The Last Pioneer,* London: Studio Vista, 1971; *Picture Shows,* London: Allen & Unwin, 1975

Boorman, John *Money Into Light, The Emerald Forest,* London: Faber & Faber, 1985

Brodsky, Jack and Weiss, Nathan *The Cleopatra Papers,* New York: Simon & Schuster, 1963

Brooks, Louise *Lulu in Hollywood,* London: Hamish Hamilton, 1982

Brown, David *Star Billing,* London: Weidenfeld & Nicolson, 1985

Brown, Peter Harry and Brown, Pamela Ann *The MGM Girls,* New York: St Martin's Press, 1983

Brownlow, Kevin *The Parade's Gone By ...,* London: Secker & Warburg, 1968

Buñuel, Luis *My Last Breath,* New York: Alfred A. Knopf, 1983

Burke, Billie *With a Feather in My Hat,* New York: Appleton-Century-Crofts, 1949

Cagney, James *Cagney by Cagney,* New York: Doubleday, 1976

Cahn, William *Harold Lloyd's Funny Side of Life,* New York: Duell, Sloan & Pearce, 1964

Canham, Kingsley *The Hollywood Professionals Vol. 1,* London: Tantivy, 1973

Capote, Truman *The Dogs Bark,* London: Weidenfeld & Nicolson, 1974

Capra, Frank *The Name Above the Title,* London: W. H. Allen, 1972

Carey, Gary *All the Stars in Heaven,* London: Robson Books, 1982

Carné, Marcel *La vie a belles dents,* Paris: Jean Vuarnet, 1979

Castanza, Philip *The Films of Jeanette Macdonald and Nelson Eddy,* Secaucus: Citadel Press, 1978

Castle, Charles *Joan Crawford, The Raging Star,* London: New English Library, 1977

Chandler, Raymond *Raymond Chandler Speaking,* New York: Houghton Mifflin, 1962

Chaplin, Charles *My Autobiography,* London: The Bodley Head, 1964; New York: Simon & Schuster, 1964

Chevalier, Maurice *With Love,* Boston: Little Brown & Co, 1960

Chierichetti, David *Hollywood Director: Mitchell Leisen,* New York: Curtis Books, 1973

Clarens, Carlos *George Cukor,* London: Secker & Warburg/BFI, 1976

Clooney, Rosemary *This for Remembrance,* London: Robson Books, 1978

Collins, Joan *Past Imperfect,* London: Michael Joseph, (updated) 1984

Connell, Brian *Knight Errant A Biography of Douglas Fairbanks Jnr,* London: Hodder & Stoughton, 1955

Cooke, Alistair *Douglas Fairbanks,* New York: Museum of Modern Art, 1940

Cooke, Alistair (Ed) *Garbo and the Night Watchman,* London: Jonathan Cape, 1937

Corliss, Richard *Garbo,* New York: Pyramid, 1974

Corliss, Richard (Ed) *The Hollywood Screenwriters,* New York: Avon, 1972

Coward, Noël *Diaries,* London: Weidenfeld & Nicolson, 1983

Crawford, Joan with Kesner Ardmore, Jane *Portrait of Joan,* New York: Doubleday, 1962

Crist, Judith *Take 22 Moviemakers on Moviemaking,* New York: Viking, 1984

Crosby, Bing *Call me Lucky,* New York: Simon & Schuster, 1953; London: Muller, 1953

Culver, Roland *Not Quite a Gentleman,* London: William Kimber, 1979

Davidson, Bill *The Real and the Unreal,* New York: Harper & Bros, 1961

Davidson, Sara *Rock Hudson, His Story,* London: Weidenfeld & Nicolson, 1986

Davis, Bette *The Lonely Life,* New York: G. P. Putnam's Sons, 1962

De Mille, Cecil B. *Autobiography,* New York: Prentice-Hall, 1959

Dickens, Norman *Jack Nicholson, The Search for a Superstar,* New York: New American Library, 1975

Dietrich, Marlene *Marlene Dietrich's ABC,* New York: Doubleday, 1962

Downing, David *Marlon Brando,* London: W. H. Allen, 1984

Dunne, John Gregory *The Studio,* New York: Farrar, Straus & Giroux, 1968

Evans, Peter *Peter Sellers, The Mask Behind the Mask,* London: New English Library, (revised edition, 1980)

Fadiman, Clifton *Party of One,* New York: World, 1955

Fadiman, William *Hollywood Now,* New York: Liveright, 1972

Ferguson, Otis *The Film Criticism of Otis Ferguson,* Philadelphia: Temple University Press, 1971

Finch, Christopher and Rosenkrantz, Linda *Gone Hollywood,* New York: Doubleday, 1979

Flynn, Errol *My Wicked, Wicked Ways,* London: Heinemann, 1960

Fontaine, Joan *No Bed of Roses,* New York: William Morrow, 1978

Fordin, Hugh *The World of Entertainment, Hollywood's Greatest Musicals,* New York: Doubleday, 1975

Freedland, Michael *So Let's Hear the Applause,* New York: Vallentine Mitchell, 1984

Frischauer, Willi *Bardot,* London: Michael Joseph, 1978

Garnett, Tay *Light Your Torches and Pull Up Your Tights,* New York: Arlington Press, 1973

Geist, Kenneth L. *Pictures Will Talk, The Life and Films of Joseph L. Mankiewicz,* New York: Scribner's, 1978

Gielgud, John *An Actor and his Time,* London: Sidgwick & Jackson, 1979

Gifford, Denis *A Pictorial History of Horror Movies,* London: Hamlyn, 1973

Gilbert Fountain, Leatrice (with Maxim, John R.) *Dark Star, The Meteoric Rise and Eclipse of John Gilbert,* New York: St Martin's Press, 1985

Gish, Lillian with Pinchot, Ann *The Movies: Mr Griffith and Me,* Englewood Cliffs; Prentice-Hall, 1969. London: W. H. Allen, 1969.

Godfrey, Lionel *Paul Newman Superstar,* London: Robson Books, 1981.

Goldman, Albert *Elvis,* New York: McGraw Hill, 1981.

Goldman, William *The Season,* New York: Harcourt Brace Jovanovich, 1969; *Adventures in the Screen Trade,* New York: Warner Books, 1983

Goodman, Ezra *The Fifty Year Decline and Fall of Hollywood,* New York: Simon & Schuster, 1961

Graham, Sheilah *Scratch an Actor,* London: W. H. Allen, 1969; *My Hollywood,* New York: St Martin's Press, 1985

Granger, Stewart *Sparks Fly Upwards,* London: Granada Publishing, 1981

Greene, Graham *The Pleasure-Dome,* London: Secker & Warburg, 1972

Guinness, Alec *Blessings in Disguise*, London: Hamish Hamilton, 1985

225

Hall, William *Raising Caine,* London: Sidgwick & Jackson, 1987

Halliwell, Leslie *The Filmgoer's Book of Quotes,* London: Hart Davies MacGibbon, 1973; *Double Take and Fade Away,* London: Grafton Books, 1987

Hampton, Benjamin B. *A History of the Movies,* New York: Covici, Friede, 1931

Hanna, David *Hollywood Confidential,* New York: Norden Publications, 1976

Hardwicke, Sir Cedric *A Victorian in Orbit,* London: Methuen, 1961

Harrison, Rex *Rex An Autobiography,* London: Macmillan, 1974

Harvey, James *Romantic Comedy in Hollywood,* New York: Alfred A. Knopf, 1987

Harwell, Richard (Ed) *Margaret Mitchell's Gone with the Wind Letters 1936–49,* New York: Macmillan, 1976

Heston, Charlton *The Actor's Life, Journals,* New York: E. P. Dutton, 1978

Higham, Charles *Hollywood Cameramen,* London: Thames & Hudson, 1970

Higham, Charles and Greenberg, Joel *The Celluloid Muse: Hollywood Directors Speak,* London: Angus & Robertson, 1969

Hirschhorn, Clive *The Films of James Mason,* London: LSP Books, 1975; *Gene Kelly,* London: W. H. Allen, (revised edition 1984); *The Hollywood Musical,* New York: Crown, 1981

Hopper, Hedda and Brough, James *The Whole Truth and Nothing But,* New York: Doubleday, 1963

Hotchner, A. E. *Doris Day, Her Own Story,* New York: William Morrow, 1975.

Howerd, Frankie *On the Way I Lost It,* London: W. H. Allen, 1975

Hunter, Allan *Walter Matthau,* London: W. H. Allen, 1984

Huston, John *An Open Book,* New York: Alfred A. Knopf, 1980

Hyams, Joe *Mislaid in Hollywood,* London: W. H. Allen, 1973

Hyman, B. D. *My Mother's Keeper,* London: Michael Joseph, 1985

Jacobs, Jack and Braum, Myron *The Films of Norma Shearer,* Cranbury, New Jersey: A. S. Barnes, 1960

Jordan, René *Barbra Streisand,* London: W. H. Allen, 1976

Kanin, Garson *Great Hollywood Teams,* New York: Doubleday, 1981; *Tracy and Hepburn,* New York: Viking, 1971

Karney, Robyn (Ed) *The Movie Stars Story,* London: Octopus Books, 1984

Keaton, Buster with Samuels, Charles *My Wonderful World of Slapstick,* New York: Doubleday, 1960

Kerr, Walter *The Silent Clowns,* New York: Alfred A. Knopf, 1975

Keyes, Evelyn *Scarlett O'Hara's Younger Sister,* Secaucus: Lyle Stuart, 1977

Knef, Hildegard *The Gift Horse,* London: André Deutsch, 1971

Knight, Arthur *The Liveliest Art,* New York: Macmillan, 1957

Kobal, John *Gotta Sing Gotta Dance,* London: Hamlyn Publishing, (revised edition 1983)

Koch, Howard *As Time Goes By,* New York: Harcourt Brace Jovanovich, 1979

Kyron, Ado *Buñuel,* Paris: Editions Seghers, 1962

Lake, Veronica and Bain, Donald *Veronica,* London: W. H. Allen, 1969

Lambert, Gavin *On Cukor,* London: W. H. Allen, 1973

Lanchester, Elsa *Elsa Lanchester Herself,* New York: St Martin's Press, 1983

Lax, Eric *On Being Funny—Woody Allen and Comedy,* New York: Charterhouse, 1975

Lamour, Dorothy *My Side of the Road,* New York: Doubleday, 1980

Leamer, Laurence *As Time Goes By, The Life of Ingrid Bergman,* London: Hamish Hamilton, 1986

Lejeune, C. A. *Chestnuts in Her Lap,* London: Phoenix House, 1949 (second edition)

226

Levant, Oscar *The Memoirs of an Amnesiac,* New York: G. P. Putnam's Sons, 1965

Logan, Joshua *Josh,* New York: Delacorte Press, 1976

Loos, Anita *A Girl Like I,* New York: Viking, 1966; *Kiss Hollywood Goodbye,* New York: Viking, 1974

Losey, Joseph (with Ciment, Michel) *Conversations with Losey,* London: Methuen, 1985

Loy, Myrna (with Kotsibilas-Davis, James) *Being and Becoming,* New York: Alfred A. Knopf, 1987

Macdonald, Dwight *On Movies,* New York: Da Capo Press, 1981

Mankiewicz, Joseph L. *More About All About Eve,* New York: Random House, 1972

Marion, Frances *Off With Their Heads,* New York: Macmillan, 1972

Marx, Arthur *Life with Groucho,* New York: Simon & Schuster, 1954

Marx, Groucho, *The Groucho Letters,* New York: Simon & Schuster, 1967; (with Anobile, Richard J.) *The Marx Brothers Scrapbook,* New York: Darien House, 1973

Maugham, W. Somerset *A Writer's Notebook,* London: Heinemann, 1950; New York: Doubleday, 1949

McBride, Joseph *Hawks on Hawks,* Los Angeles and Berkely: University of California Press, 1982

McClelland, Doug *Starspeak,* Winchester: Faber & Faber, 1987

McDowell, Roddy *Double Exposure,* New York: Delacorte Press, 1966

Meryman, Richard *Mank, The Wit, World, and Life of Herman Mankiewicz,* New York: William Morrow, 1978

Miller, Arthur *Timebends,* London: Methuen, 1987

Mills, John *Up in the Clouds, Gentleman Please,* London: Weidenfeld & Nicolson, 1980

Minnelli, Vincente (with Arce, Hector) *I Remember It Well,* New York: Doubleday, 1974

More, Kenneth *More or Less,* London: Hodder & Stoughton, 1978

Moseley, Roy (with Macheter, Philip and Martin) *Rex Harrison, the First Biography,* London: Hodder & Stoughton, 1987

Moshier, W. Franklyn *The Alice Faye Movie Book,* Harrisburg: Stackpole Books, 1974

Newquist, Roy *Showcase,* New York: William Morrow, 1966; *A Special Kind of Magic,* New York: Rand McNally, 1967

Niven, David *The Moon's a Balloon,* London: Hamish Hamilton, 1971

Nogueira, Rui *Melville on Melville,* London: Secker & Warburg/BFI, 1971

Norman, Barry *The Movie Greats,* London: Hodder & Stoughton, 1981; *Film Greats,* London: W. H. Smith, 1986

Olivier, Laurence *Confessions of an Actor,* London: Weidenfeld & Nicolson, 1982

Paine, Albert Bigelow *Life and Lillian Gish,* 1932

Parish, James Robert *The RKO Gals,* London: Ian Allan Ltd, 1974

Peary, Danny *Cult Movies 2,* New York: Dell, 1983

Peary, Danny (Ed) *Close-Ups, The Movie Star Book,* New York: Workman Publishing Co Inc, 1978

Perelman, S. J. *Don't Tread on Me: Selected Letters*, London: Viking, 1987

Perkins, V. F. *Film as Film,* London: Penguin 1972

227

Pickford, Mary *Sunshine and Shadow,* New York: Doubleday, 1955; London: Heinemann, 1956

Pratley, Gerald *The Cinema of Otto Preminger,* New York: A. S. Barnes, 1977

Quirk, Lawrence J. *The Films of Gloria Swanson,* Secaucus: Citadel Press, 1984

Reed, Rex *Travolta to Keaton,* New York: William Morrow, 1979

Renoir, Jean *My Life and My Films,* New York: Atheneum, 1974

Ringgold, Gene and De Witt, Bodeen *The Films of Maurice Chevalier,* Secaucus: Citadel Press, 1973

Robbins, Jhan *Everybody's Man a Biography of James Stewart,* New York: G. P. Putnam's Sons, 1985

Robinson, Edward G. (with Spigelglass, Leonard) *All My Yesterdays,* New York: Hawthorn Press, 1973

Robinson, W. R. (Ed) *Man and the Movies,* Baton Rouge: Louisiana State University Press, 1967

Ross, Lillian *Picture,* New York: Rinehart, 1952

Ross, Lillian and Ross, Helen *The Player,* New York: Simon & Schuster, 1962

Roud, Richard (Ed) *Cinema a Critical Dictionary,* New York: Viking, 1978

Russell, Jane *An Autobiography,* London: Sidgwick & Jackson, 1986

Sadoul, Georges *Dictionnaire des Cineastes,* Paris: Le Seuil, 1982

Sanders, George *Memoirs of a Professional Cad,* New York: G. P. Putnam's Sons, 1960

Satchell, Timothy *Fred Astaire,* London: Century Hutchinson, 1987

Schickel, Richard *The Stars,* New York: Dial Press, 1962; *Harold Lloyd The Shape of Laughter,* Boston: New York Graphic Society, 1974

Schulberg, Budd *Moving Pictures,* New York: Stein & Day, 1981

Sennett, Ted *Hollywood Musicals,* New York: Abrams 1981

Shepherd, Don and Slatzer *Bing Crosby, The Hollow Man,* London: W. H. Allen, 1982

Shipman, David *The Great Movie Stars* (two volumes), New York: Hill & Wang, (revised editions 1981); *The Story of Cinema,* New York: St Martin's Press, 1984; *Brando,* New York: Doubleday, 1974

Simon, John *Private Screenings,* New York: Macmillan, 1967; *Movies into Film,* New York: The Dial Press, 1971; *Reverse Angle,* New York: Clarkson Potter, 1982; *Something to Declare,* New York: Clarkson Potter, 1983

Sinyard, Neil *The Films of Woody Allen,* London: Bison, 1983; *Directors: The All Time Greats,* New York: The Galley Press, 1985

Spada, James *Judy and Liza,* New York: Doubleday, 1983

Springer, John *The Fondas,* New York: Citadel Press, 1970

Stallings, Penny *Flesh and Fantasy,* London: Macdonald and Jane's, 1978

Steele, Joseph Henry *Ingrid Bergman An Intimate Portrait,* New York: David McKay, 1959

Steen, Mike *Hollywood Speaks,* New York: G.P. Putnam's Sons, 1974

Stine, Whitney (with Davis, Bette) *Mother Goddam,* New York: Hawthorn, 1974

Swanson, Gloria *Swanson on Swanson,* New York: Random House, 1980

Swindell, Larry *Charles Boyer The Reluctant Lover,* London: Weidenfeld & Nicolson. 1983

Taylor, Robert Lewis *W. C. Fields His Follies and Fortunes,* New York: Doubleday, 1949

Teichman, Howard *Fonda, My Life as told to ...,* New York: New American Library, 1981

Thomas, Bob *King Cohn,* New York: G. P. Putnam's Sons, 1967

228

Thomas, Tony *Ustinov in Focus,* New York: A. S. Barnes, 1971

Thompson, Charles *Bing,* London: W. H. Allen, 1975

Thomson, David *A Biographical Dictionary of the Cinema,* London: 1975

Truffaut, François *Hitchcock,* New York: Simon & Schuster, 1969

Turner, Lana *Lana, the Lady, the Legend, the Truth,* New York: E. P. Dutton, 1982

Tynan, Kathleen *The Life of Kenneth Tynan,* London: Weidenfeld & Nicolson, 1987

Tynan, Kenneth *Persona Grata,* Wingate, 1953; *Curtains,* London: Longmans, 1963; New York: Atheneum, 1961; *Tynan Right and Left,* London: Longmans, 1967; New York: Atheneum, 1967

Vidor, King *King Vidor on Film Making,* London: W. H. Allen, 1973

Von Sternberg, Joseph *Fun in a Chinese Laundry,* New York: Macmillan, 1965

Wallis, Hal with Higham, Charles *Starmaker,* New York: Macmillan, 1980

Watters, James and Horst *Return Engagement,* New York: Clarkson Potter, 1984

Wayne, Jane Ellen *The Life of Robert Taylor,* New York: Warner, 1973

Weatherbury, W. J. *Conversations with Marilyn,* London: Robson, 1976

Wilcox, Herbert *Twenty–Five Thousand Sunsets,* London: The Bodley Head, 1967

Wilding, Michael *Apple Sauce,* London: Allen & Unwin, 1982

Wilk, Max *The Wit and Wisdom of Hollywood,* New York: Atheneum, 1971

Willson, Meredith *But He Doesn't Know the Territory,* New York: G. P. Putnam's Sons, 1959

Wilson, Earl *The Show Business Nobody Knows,* New York: Cowles, 1971

Wilson, Sandy *I Could Be Happy,* London: Michael Joseph, 1975

Winderler, Robert *Burt Lancaster,* London: W. H. Allen, 1984

Winnington, Richard *Drawn and Quartered,* London: Saturn Press, 1948

Wlaschin, Ken *The World's Great Movie Stars and Their Films,* London: Peerage Books, (revised edition 1984)

Wood, Robin *Howard Hawks,* London: Secker & Warburg, 1968

Zec, Donald *Some Enchanted Egos,* New York: St Martin's Press, 1973; *Marvin,* London: New English Library, 1979

Zierold, Norman J. *The Child Stars,* New York: Coward McCann, 1965

Index

233

234

235

236

242

243

244